W9-BUD-916

Exceeding Expectations

Successful Adults with Learning Disabilities

Henry B. Reiff

Paul J. Gerber

Rick Ginsberg

pro·ed

8700 Shoal Creek Boulevard
Austin, Texas 78757-6897

pro·ed

© 1997 by PRO-ED, Inc.
8700 Shoal Creek Boulevard
Austin, Texas 78757-6897

Library of Congress Cataloging-in-Publication Data

Reiff, Henry B., 1953–
    Exceeding expectations : successful adults with learning
disabilities / Henry B. Reiff, Paul J. Gerber, Rick Ginsberg.
       p.   cm.
    Includes bibliographical references and index.
    ISBN 0-89079-705-6 (softcover : alk. paper)
    1. Learning disabled—United States—Interviews. 2. Learning
disabled—United States—Conduct of life—Case studies. 3. Success-
-United States—Case studies. 4. Learning disabilities—United
States—Case studies. I. Gerber, Paul Jay. II. Ginsberg, Rick,
1952– . III. Title.
LC4818.5.R45   1997
371.9—dc20
                        96-34106
                           CIP

This book is designed in Avant Garde and Goudy.

Production Manager: Alan Grimes
Production Coordinator: Karen Swain
Managing Editor: Tracy Sergo
Art Director: Thomas Barkley
Reprints Buyer: Alicia Woods
Editor: Lorretta Palagi
Editorial Assistant: Claudette Landry
Editorial Assistant: Suzi Hunn

Printed in the United States of America

1 2 3 4 5 6 7 8 9 10   01 00 99 98 97

*We dedicate this book to members of our families
who have exceeded expectations in the love
and joy they have brought to our lives:*

*Benjamin Alvin Reiff
Ariel and Rebecca Gerber
In memory of Al Ginsberg*

Contents

Foreword

My first attempt to write about learning disabilities in adulthood occurred in 1977. It was an assignment for a doctoral seminar on learning disabilities taught by Dr. Gerry Wallace at the University of Virginia. Gerry was extremely supportive of my paper on this topic, even though it navigated virgin territory. This particular paper was a feeble effort at organizing my thoughts on this topic, written during a time when few resources on learning disabilities existed. Nevertheless, this writing project propelled me into an area in which I have maintained a great interest ever since.

I am delighted that I have been asked to contribute to this project by writing the foreword. I feel that it is important to clarify the roles I play related to this project. First and foremost, in my role as professional in the field of learning disabilities, I consider Henry, Paul, and Rick to be colleagues in this area. We all share a special interest in the issues of adults with learning disabilities. My second role, that of editor for this book, affords me a closeness with the manuscript that most writers of forewords do not have. I have been fortunate to be involved with this project since the first stages of the publication process. It is safe to say that my comments in this foreword have emerged from the activities associated with both roles described above.

A number of events have underscored my interest in this topic since the early days. I was extremely fascinated by the first published article I read on adults with learning disabilities, written by Robert Gray and published in 1981 in *Learning Disabilities Quarterly*. A subsequent invitation to contribute an article on "learning disabilities in the adult years" for a special series helped me gain a better sense of what the field knew about this disability beyond the school years. I also was affected by working with adults who had learning disabilities when I worked at the University of Hawaii. The Learning Disabilities Association of Hawaii (then called the Hawaii Association for Children and Adults with Learning Disabilities) provided me with opportunities for understanding the family perspective that is always needed. Working with individuals at Honolulu Community College, Kapiolani

Community College, and Leeward Community College expanded my focus to a host of other challenges facing young adults with learning disabilities.

All of this is background to lead me to the major point I want to make. The realization that colleagues of mine have also become interested in this area has provided me with encouragement. I have witnessed the emergence of wonderful work done by individuals who have been able to spend more time and energy researching various aspects of learning disabilities in adulthood than I have been able to do. This book is a perfect example of such work.

There is no question that the topic of adulthood and learning disabilities has received more attention in recent years. Reflections of this change have become apparent in the number of journal articles written, books published, and presentations given on a range of issues related to this area. This increased interest in adulthood issues can be explained by a number of factors. However, the simplest explanation is that many professionals have become aware that learning disabilities are a lifelong circumstance.

Far too much of what we have studied related to learning disabilities focuses on the problems, difficulties, and setbacks associated with the condition. This is what we in special education have been trained to do. The extensive work of Henry, Paul, and Rick helps us move beyond the deficit orientation that dominates the disability fields. Their research has assisted the field in looking at the strengths and successes of individuals who have faced challenges associated with their learning disabilities but who also have enjoyed the pleasures of success.

This book provides a way of understanding the complexities of being an adult while having to face a learning disability. It goes further, though, by suggesting how these same adults can achieve success. The authors have done a masterful job of blending the findings of their research with a personal feel. The personal reactions to the model of employment success by adults who are learning disabled (Elizabeth Wiig, Stanley Antonoff, Coller Ochsner, and Paul Grossman) offer a unique real-world validation of what the authors identified through their research.

The model of employment success discussed in this book acts as a useful referent for professionals who work with adults who are learning disabled. More importantly, this book serves as a needed resource not only for adults with learning disabilities but also for all of us who work, play, and live with relatives, friends, and colleagues who are learning disabled and who must deal every day with the challenges of adulthood.

This book has great potential for changing professional thinking about adults with learning disabilities. The research described in this work is one of the most unquestionably innovative lines of inquiry that has evolved from the field of learning disabilities.

James R. Patton

Preface

Awareness of adults with learning disabilities is on the rise. However, few works have specifically addressed successful outcomes of adults with learning disabilities, particularly from the vantage point of a large-scale empirical study. On the other hand, a recent wave of business-related books has focused on success in the workplace. The popularity of this literature attests to a growing interest in understanding the process of success. The confluence of these two issues, successful outcomes of adults with learning disabilities and a pragmatic analysis of the process leading to those outcomes, is a current running through *Exceeding Expectations: Successful Adults with Learning Disabilities*. Highlighting abilities rather than deficits of persons with learning disabilities, this book's holistic approach provides a radical departure from traditional approaches to understanding learning disabilities.

To answer questions about success and learning disabilities, the authors interviewed 71 successful adults with learning disabilities. The open-ended interviews allowed these individuals to speak for themselves, to share their perspectives, to tell their stories. Relying heavily on these firsthand accounts, *Exceeding Expectations* gives the reader the opportunity to see the world through the eyes of adults who have triumphed in their struggles with learning disabilities.

Part I of the book, "A Lifetime of Being Learning Disabled," looks at persons with learning disabilities from a developmental perspective: An adult with learning disabilities is the sum of all of his or her previous experiences. Chapter 1, "Finding the Road to Success When You Can't Read the Directions," describes how we developed and carried out a study of 71 successful adults with learning disabilities. Our interest is rooted in personal, professional, and theoretical curiosity.

The 71 adults who were interviewed are the subject of Chapter 2, "Who Are Successful Adults with Learning Disabilities? A Closer Look." The first part of the chapter focuses on how we developed the study and found and selected the successful adults with learning disabilities. In the second part, individual vignettes of several representative members give the reader a more personal relationship with the adults in the study.

Chapter 3, "How It Feels To Grow Up with Learning Disabilities," delves into the childhood of these successful adults. Most of them came from supportive families, which they believe has been a factor in their success. The chapter contains recollections of family life and reflections on family dynamics. The majority of the participants did encounter tremendous difficulty in school; their own words present those problems in a very human dimension. As students, some triumphed, but most floundered, at least until the latter part of their education. Whether good or bad, their education left indelible impressions. Growing up with learning disabilities directly and indirectly shaped many of the attitudes and behaviors of adulthood.

Part II, "Creating a Context," creates a broader context for understanding issues related to successful employment outcomes of adults with learning disabilities. Chapter 4, "What It Means To Have Learning Disabilities: The Insider's Perspective," discusses a fundamental question: "What are learning disabilities?" Medical models have influenced traditional definitions, which may not fully encompass the experiences of successful persons with learning disabilities. Moreover, a number of definitions exist, indicating a lack of professional consensus and further clouding a comprehensive understanding. Chapter 4 explores the controversy and confusion surrounding definitions. In keeping with the philosophy that persons with learning disabilities are in an advantageous position to offer direct insights, the views of successful adults provide a framework within which we can assess the components of commonly used definitions. These perspectives form the basis for a new definition that describes learning disabilities in adulthood in a holistic context.

Chapter 5 examines what we know about outcomes on employment. After addressing general economic and demographic trends in the workplace as well as studies of employment outcomes for individuals with learning disabilities, the chapter reviews cases of remarkable accomplishments. The reader should begin to develop a context of what works for persons with learning disabilities, why it works, and how this knowledge may have direct and practical import for adults who are currently taking their rightful places in the workplace.

The third part of the book, "A Conceptual Framework of Employment Success," centers on the model for employment success for adults with learning disabilities that resulted from the study. In any discussion about success, the development of a definition is important. Success is a subjective construct that reflects individual attitudes and orientations. Chapter 6, "What Is Success? Perspectives of Adults with Learning Disabilities," reviews current notions and constructs of success, particularly in the workplace. In addition, each participant was asked for a personal definition of success at the outset of the interview. Their responses offer a yardstick for comparison and reiterate the personal nature of the concept. For a number of these adults, their notion of success is linked as much to who they are as what they have done.

Chapter 7, "A Model of Success," represents the heart of the book in many ways. The success of these adults resulted largely from their ability to gain or regain control in their lives. They accomplished this process through a set of internal decisions: desire, goal orientation, and a reframing of the learning disabilities experience. They turned these decisions into actions, or external manifestations, of perseverance and determination, goodness-of-fit, learned creativity, and favorable social ecologies.

Chapter 8, "Personal Perspectives on the Model," contains four reactions to the "model of success," each written by a successful adult with learning disabilities who was a participant in the study. These perspectives not only increase the reader's understanding of the success model, they also supply a uniquely personal and human tone. The chapter concludes with a synthesis and discussion of these perspectives.

The theme of critical incidents receives attention in Chapter 9, "Critical Incidents: Stops, Starts, and Turning Points." Critical incidents are those significant events that have a profound effect on thoughts about self, decisions about behaviors, and pathways chosen. In a sense, they may appear as signposts along the road to success. Specific examples from interviews demonstrate that in addition to predictable experiences, a set of often uncontrollable events provides part of the foundation for successful outcomes.

In the last part, "Implications for Practice," the information provided by these adults becomes the basis for practical suggestions to improve the quality of life for other persons with learning disabilities. The components of the model of success represent processes and skills that can be taught and learned. Chapter 10, "Turning the Model into a Teaching Tool," discusses specific classroom strategies derived from each component of the model. Practitioners can use these strategies to help students with learning disabilities inculcate behaviors that will facilitate successful adult adjustment. Teaching approaches that integrate this resource will embrace a success rather than a deficit model, a focus on strengths rather than a preoccupation with weaknesses.

Self-advocacy is a theme that pervades the success model. The successful adults found ways to stand up for themselves, sought out necessary accommodations and adjustments, and surrounded themselves with supportive and helpful people. Chapter 11, "Self-Advocacy in the Era of the Americans with Disabilities Act," explores self-advocacy within the current sociopolitical context. Persons with learning disabilities have much to gain from the ADA, but they will have to advocate for themselves if they are to reap its benefits.

The final chapter, "Thoughts and Advice from Adults with Learning Disabilities," uses the words of adults with learning disabilities to develop implications for best practices. In the course of our interviews, we solicited advice and suggestions about parenting, teaching, and employment practices. We offer these thoughts and advice as data from firsthand experience. The book ends in the same spirit that underscored the whole research project. We have much to gain simply by listening to the voices of successful adults with learning disabilities.

In *Exceeding Expectations*, the reader will encounter perspectives that focus on success rather than failure, on what people can do rather than what they cannot, on ability rather than disability. In this book, we have attempted to explain how and why some adults with learning disabilities are able to beat the odds and exceed expectations. We hope the reader will develop an increased appreciation for the potential that all persons have to succeed.

Acknowledgments

We gratefully acknowledge the following individuals who have made invaluable contributions to this book: Pat Popp and Dr. Chris Schneiders, the project directors of the investigation of successful adults with learning disabilities. Their unflagging determination and organizational ability kept the project (and the authors) moving ahead. We also acknowledge the 71 successful adults with learning disabilities, the participants in our investigation. Their stories provide the foundation for this book. Their gracious willingness to share their experiences with virtual strangers was bred by a desire to help others. We believe they have helped others; we know they have inspired us.

Part I

A Lifetime of Being Learning Disabled

Finding the Road to Success When You Can't Read the Directions

Chapter 1

This book tells the story of 71 successful adults who just happen to have learning disabilities. To some ways of thinking, the combination of success and disability would seem contradictory. By definition, a disability connotes a disadvantage or restriction, something that makes achievement, much less high levels of achievement, unusually difficult. When such limitations occur in the sphere of learning, the possibility of competing in the American workplace may seem remote indeed.

Yet the adults in this story proved themselves capable of learning, albeit in their own way. Almost all experienced significant difficulty with the learning process when they attended school. As things turned out, what they learned or did not learn in school may not have been that important. "Book learning" did not always give them the types of skills and knowledge that were useful for success in their careers. Instead, they acquired knowledge and understanding largely through their own resourcefulness. Although they did not learn in the same ways as their peers, they found out by trial and error what they needed to know, and, most of all, they applied what they had learned in their own way. Many never did learn to read, write, spell, or compute particularly well. They may not have inspired confidence in those around them initially, but ultimately they accomplished more than their teachers, and sometimes even their parents, thought possible. They exceeded all expectations. They may not have been able to read the directions, but they found the road to success.

The authors' research of successful adults with learning disabilities evolved from a natural chain of events marked by both professional and personal interests. Two of us, Gerber and Reiff, began our careers teaching young students with learning disabilities. As time passed, the children we taught grew up and became young adults. We faced a humbling experience (related to our own mortality) and, perhaps more importantly, a major awakening in our teaching careers. We became increasingly curious about the transition into adulthood that our former students were making. Had they simply outgrown learning disabilities and put that phase of their lives behind them? Or did learning disabilities continue to affect them in adulthood, and, if so, in what ways?

At the beginning of the 1980s professionals and parents began to acknowledge that individuals with learning disabilities do grow up. A national conference of the Association of Children with Learning Disabilities (now the Learning Disabilities Association of America) sounded the call with their theme, "Coming of Age." Adults had made it to the learning disabilities agenda, but it was still unclear in what direction or directions the agenda would head. In 1981, Madeleine Will, then assistant secretary of the Office of Special Education and Rehabilitative Services (OSERS) and a parent of an adolescent with severe disabilities, offered her initiative of transition from school to work to the field. At about the same time, the Rehabilitation Services Administration (RSA), the federal agency that administers the vocational rehabilitation program, began serving individuals with learning disabilities. All this activity prompted the National Institute for Handicapped Research (now the National Institute for Disability Rehabilitation Research) to hold a state-of-the-art conference on adults with learning disabilities. It became increasingly clear that individuals with learning disabilities were dealing with a multiplicity of issues in adulthood, particularly employment and vocational adjustment. The decade ended with the passage of the Americans with Disabilities Act (ADA), which provided persons with disabilities equal access to all areas of employment in our country. In response to this landmark legislation, the President's Committee for the Employment of People with Disabilities held a consensus conference on the employment of individuals with learning disabilities. It generated a blueprint for action in the area of employment in the 1990s. The issue of employment had taken its rightful place in the field of learning disabilities. Adult issues were finally beginning to share equal billing with school-age issues.

Despite this flurry of activity, the attention that adults with learning disabilities received was restricted to a relatively small professional community. The existing research on adults with learning disabilities was still relatively sparse. Throughout the 1980s, much of the literature continued to reflect a school-based orientation and perhaps a tacit assumption that what happened in adulthood was not particularly significant. The small research base posed a problem because services for adults with learning disabilities were being developed without the knowledge derived from basic research. In addition, much of the thinking about learning disabilities in adulthood was an extension of what was known about learning disabilities in children.

At the same time, the small research base may have been a blessing in disguise for us. In most educational research, a theoretical framework tends to guide a study and creates an agenda that determines what one expects to discover. The existing theory indicates that certain variables are likely to play a significant role. These variables may focus the research but inherently limit it.

We did not feel that we had sufficient information to develop a sound theoretical framework. We could not rely on the collective wisdom of the professional community. We did not want to presuppose what we thought would be important. However, the pioneering work of Drs. Laura Lehtinen-Rogan and Laura Hartman did intrigue us. Their longitudinal and follow-up studies of students from the well-known Cove School (Rogan & Hartman, 1976, 1990) depicted a wide array of outcomes for adults with learning disabilities, even within a demographically homogeneous population.

The Cove School studies highlighted a diversity of employment outcomes for these adults with learning disabilities. Some former students had advanced degrees in medicine, law, and business. Others were semiskilled, unemployed, and unemployable. The continuum ran the full gamut from independence to marginal adjustment. These findings begged the question, "Why did some of the Cove School students become so successful while others failed miserably?" In other words, how do children and youths with learning disabilities become successful in their adult lives?

To our surprise, we found very little research on how people with learning disabilities became vocationally successful. A study by Baker (1972) examined famous people with physical and sensory disabilities in history. Another study by Maker (1978) investigated the successes of eminent scientists with similar disabilities. Yet the Baker and Maker studies did not include any individuals with learning disabilities. Adelman and Adelman (1987) had warned against identifying famous people in history with learning disabilities based on a posthumous diagnosis. Thus, we had few clues about how individuals made it in spite of their learning disabilities. It almost seemed that the notion of success was incompatible with any kind of learning disability. Despite a rhetoric of strengths as well as weaknesses in the learning disability literature, a deficit model continued to dominate thinking in the field. Could we look at learning disabilities, particularly in adulthood, in a different way?

We reasoned that the best way to find out about learning disabilities in adulthood would be to talk with adults with learning disabilities. We could use a combination of our naïveté and intuition to advantage by posing open-ended questions that would help us see through the eyes of the persons we interviewed. This method would allow us to enter their world, to ascertain what anthropologists term the *native perspective* (Spradley, 1979). We recognized the utility of listening, of allowing and encouraging adults with learning disabilities to speak for themselves rather than having professionals and experts do the speaking for them.

Consequently, we set out to interview nine adults with learning disabilities in our local area. This project resulted in the book *Speaking for Themselves: Ethnographic Interviews with Adults with Learning Disabilities* (Gerber & Reiff,

1991). We collected information by spending 3 to 4 hours in an open-ended interview with each of these persons. The nine adults, who ranged in age from 22 to 56, fell into three clearly differentiated groups based on educational and vocational achievement: high adjustment to adulthood, moderate adjustment, and low (marginal) adjustment. The members of the high-adjustment group had all received advanced educational degrees and had established successful professional careers. The moderate group tended to be younger, less educated, and less established, yet were progressing successfully through the initial stages of adulthood, with many possibilities for further educational and career advancement. The marginally adjusted participants had not graduated from high school and were all unemployed at the time of the interviews. Equally significant was the wide variety of functioning within each group. In spite of a degree of categorization, the interviews revealed nine individual adults. At the same time, we were curious as to why some of these adults were either quite successful (high) or possibly on the road to success (moderate), while three adults in the low group were leading lives of dependency and despondency.

The adults with the most severe learning disabilities were having the most difficulty in terms of overall adjustment. They had no systematic short- or long-range plans for further training or employment. School had generally been a disastrous and demeaning experience with psychological repercussions that continued to plague them in adulthood. They had not effectively made sense of what had gone wrong in their lives, had not figured out efficient ways of coping with their learning disabilities, and seemed largely confused as to why their lives were less than satisfactory. Whereas the focus of their learning disabilities in school had largely been in academic areas, adulthood demonstrated the global nature of their disabilities. Their difficulties in areas such as comprehension, attention, self-concept, self-esteem, and social skills affected not only their education, but their vocation, daily living, interpersonal relationships, and social and emotional functioning. To suggest that an appropriate educational experience alone would have resulted in significantly different outcomes would be simplistic, but a different alignment or confluence of alterable factors might have led to more satisfying adult adjustment. We believed that each of the marginally adjusted adults could have done better.

Although the marginally adjusted group evidenced the most severe learning disabilities, the other participants certainly dealt with significant and, in some cases, severe disabilities. Their ability to cope and compensate—to exceed expectations—accounted more for the differences in outcomes than the degree of disability per se. The successful adults did a better job comprehending their learning disabilities and figuring out what to do about them. They came to understand their individual strengths and weaknesses and applied this knowledge in many different areas of functioning. They devised specific strategies for specific situations. They learned new ways to use their own abilities to accomplish some tasks; they learned ways to bypass their areas of disability for other tasks. They planned, set attainable yet demanding goals, and prepared themselves to meet those challenges.

Success was not without a cost. To a large extent, the road to success was paved by an absolute determination to achieve. The adults in the highly adjusted group had worked harder than other classmates or coworkers. They often sacrificed time for family, friends, and themselves. One participant recounted that he had never developed a sense of social ease because his all-consuming studiousness in school caused him to miss out on normal adolescent social development and activities.

In spite of the differences between the groups, the effects of learning disabilities in adulthood resulted in striking similarities. Our interviews provided compelling evidence that not only do learning disabilities persist into adulthood, they continue to affect the whole range of adult functioning. Problems in areas as diverse as shopping, dating, work habits, and decision making pervaded the marginally adjusted group, but the other groups faced equally significant challenges in day-to-day life. Although they coped more successfully in some cases, they nevertheless had to make conscious and determined adjustments. And they were not necessarily successful in all areas of their lives. For all the participants, learning disabilities presented significant challenges on a daily basis. Equally debilitating, all these adults carried some degree of psychological baggage from childhood and school. Again, some had resolved these issues more successfully than others, but in all cases, learning disabilities presented issues that were persistent and unique.

An emerging theoretical base in the field of psychology has come to characterize adulthood as a period of ongoing development. Transitioning and progressing from one developmental period to another necessarily involves degrees of disequilibrium, accommodation, and adaptation. In other words, adulthood is not the stable state of enlightenment, contentment, and competence that many of us may have imagined in childhood or adolescence! Rather, it is accompanied by ongoing demands and challenges to change and evolve. With the superimposition of learning disabilities, the adult experience becomes even more complex.

The experience of entering the lives of these nine adults profoundly altered both our understanding of learning disabilities in adulthood and our perceptions of ourselves. Despite laying claim to being academic professionals or experts, we found that our interviewees were the teachers and the experts; we were the students. The project was a chance to learn about differences in the learning disability experience, to be sure, but also about essential similarities that we all share. Even the condition of learning disabilities may have a universal quality, that is, a sense of vulnerability, surely an ingredient in anyone's life. The adults we interviewed were vulnerable simply because they learned in different ways from the majority. Yet they were able to learn.

The ability of at least some of these adults to cope, compensate, overcome, and achieve challenged the very core of our training as professionals. Our training had been based primarily on a medical model that conceptualized learning disabilities as a kind of pathology. The focus of interventions tended to be on ways of curing or healing. Yet the adults in our study were not sick. They dealt with a condition, a serious and significant one, but one that ultimately drew out strengths rather than just weaknesses. From a different perspective, this condition is a demand for adaptation, which some persons do better than others. It is persistent and does not seem to go away. At the same time, it is neither fixed nor intransigent.

This project led us in a full circle. Contemplating our results reinforced the notion that we were only at the beginning. We wanted to explore this different conceptualization of learning disabilities further. In particular, we felt it was important to examine the process by which some persons with disabilities are able to succeed in adulthood. In this book, we present a perspective that emphasizes the possibilities for success rather than failure, ability rather than disability. Our suggestions for facilitating achievement of success come not from the opinions of professionals and experts based on what is thought to be important. Rather, they are the result of an attempt to present hard data culled from ethnographic interviews detailing how 71 adults with learning disabilities became successful.

Welcome to the world of these adults. Along with presenting the results and findings of our study, we also hope this book will allow readers to get to know the people we interviewed. They are an impressive lot. Most of them spent considerable time being told that they would not be successful. Yet they found the road to success, even if they could not read the directions. They beat the odds; they confounded the experts; they exceeded the expectations. Their journey was not an easy one, but maybe that is why they reached such an unlikely destination.

"Ad astra per aspera"—Through adversity we reach the stars.

Who Are Successful Adults with Learning Disabilities? A Closer Look

Chapter 2

> *If you would particularly gain the affection and friendship of particular people, whether men or women, endeavor to find out their predominant excellency, if they have one, and their prevailing weakness, which everyone has; and do justice to the one, and something more than justice to the other. Men have various objects in which they may excel, or at least would be thought to excel; and, though they love to hear justice done to them, where they know that they excel, yet they are most and best flattered upon those points where they wish to excel, and yet are doubtful whether they do or not.*

> —Lord Chesterfield, *Letter to His Son*, London, October 16, 1747

Can We Talk?

As we began our research project we faced a basic question: How would we find successful adults with learning disabilities? We also realized we would have to decide what to ask and how to ask it. Given that many persons with learning disabilities have difficulty with reading and writing, using a written questionnaire mailed to prospective participants would not make a great deal of sense. Moreover, we wanted to use a more open approach in which respondents would have the freedom to explore, expand, and elucidate issues they felt were important. We wanted to see the world through their eyes. Consequently, we decided to utilize a more qualitative approach. We knew that gathering in-depth information directly from those successful adults we could identify would best serve the purposes of our inquiry. In their text on doing qualitative research, Glesne and Peshkin (1992) succinctly explain, "Qualitative researchers seek to make sense of personal stories and the ways in which they intersect" (p. 1). It is through such personal stories that we hoped to gain an understanding of the success patterns of adults with learning disabilities, an area heretofore largely ignored by researchers in education, special education, and psychology.

Consequently, we thought that simply talking with some highly successful and moderately successful adults with learning disabilities could provide the kind of personal stories we were seeking. We specifically chose to rely on retrospective interviews as the main source of information. Interviews permit researchers to learn about individuals and events when behavior cannot be observed. As Patton (1980) very clearly explains:

> The fact of the matter is that we cannot observe everything. We cannot observe feelings, thoughts and intentions. We cannot observe behaviors that took place at some previous point in time. We cannot observe situations that preclude the presence of an observer. We cannot observe how people have organized the world and the meanings they attach to what goes on in the world—we have to ask people questions about those things. The purpose of interviewing, then, is to allow us to enter into the other person's perspective. (p. 196)

Interviews can be of several types, ranging from highly structured questionnaire-style to open-ended, very conversation-like ethnographic interviews (Merriam, 1988). For our research, we used elements of both structured and unstructured formats. Because our purpose was to learn about patterns of success from the adults with learning disabilities, we provided many opportunities for those in our sample to discuss their personal experiences. At the same time, we made certain that every adult with learning disabilities we interviewed was asked the same set of questions.

We hoped these interviews would help us (a) broaden our understanding of the issues of learning disabilities in adulthood, (b) uncover patterns of success for adults with learning disabilities, and (c) develop a "model" of success. The richness and detail of the interview process would help us understand the meaning these individuals place on events, processes, and other aspects of their lives. In the remainder of this chapter we explain our research design: how we chose participants and developed our questions, how we did the interviews, and how we analyzed the data. We also describe the participants in some detail, then present small vignettes describing five of the people we interviewed.

The Design of the Project

As we were planning the interviews, we knew we wanted to examine the reasons why some adults with learning disabilities are successful, and why others are not. We decided not to compare highly successful individuals with clearly unsuccessful ones; the differences seemed so distinguishable and obvious.

Instead, we chose to focus on highly successful and moderately successful adults with learning disabilities as the best means of depicting those factors that differentiate high degrees of success.

We proceeded to develop a research design to determine how and why highly successful adults with learning disabilities differ from moderately successful ones. (See Gay, 1981, for a discussion of causal comparative or ex post facto research designs.) Comparing two predetermined groups of people has limitations; it is possible to confuse a cause-and-effect relation with coincidence. Nevertheless, by carefully controlling the sample selection and group assignment processes, we felt that a comparison of highly successful adults with learning disabilities with moderately successful ones could isolate factors related to the employment success of adults with learning disabilities. The ultimate goal was to identify a model of success for adults with learning disabilities composed of alterable factors or variables that others could emulate. (See Bloom, 1980, for a discussion of alterable variables.)

How We Found 71 Successful Adults with Learning Disabilities

This type of research project involves several stages. First, we had to find, screen, select, and place participants into the high success or moderate success group. To carry out our study properly, we needed to identify the appropriate population and pull a representative sample from that larger group. The target population, vocationally successful adults with learning disabilities, was identified through a nomination process encompassing all of North America. Nominations of names of vocationally successful adults with learning disabilities were sought from the National Network of Learning Disabled Adults, presidents of state chapters of the Orton Dyslexia Society, the Association for Children with Learning Disabilities (now the Learning Disabilities Association of America, LDA), the National Institute for Dyslexia (now defunct), the professional advisory board of the Foundation for Learning Disabilities (now the National Center for Learning Disabilities), the leaders of the Vocational Services Committee of LDA, the special interest groups involved with students with learning disabilities in the Association on Handicapped Student Service Programs in Postsecondary Education (AHSSPPE, now the Association for Higher Education and Disabilities, AHEAD), a number of other related organizations, schools of education, and institutions and individuals with knowledge of and experience working with persons with learning disabilities. In addition, nominations were solicited at selected special education national conferences. We purposely did not define what we meant by "success" at this point so as not to limit the potential pool, hoping to gather a large number of possible participants for the study. In all, more than 240 persons were nominated for the research, with 181 actually eligible for screening into the participant pool (persons were eliminated because they were not learning disabled or information was incomplete, or because the person was inaccessible, or identified as having additional disabilities beyond the learning disability).

We screened candidates for the study through a lengthy telephone interview, averaging about 20 minutes. The interview included gathering demographic data on age, race, gender, income, and education and information concerning current occupation, recognition attained in the field, and parents' occupation levels. Another set of questions gathered information on levels of job satisfaction, derived from the *Minnesota Satisfaction Questionnaire–Short Form* (Weiss, Davis, England, & Lofquist, 1967). We included this variable given our belief that high financial or other rewards or accomplishments without some degree of job satisfaction do not equate to complete vocational success. In addition, we designed a screening inventory to verify the existence of a learning disability and to provide information about its specific characteristics. (See Gerber et al., 1990, for a discussion of this instrument and its use.)

We still had to determine how we would distinguish a high success group from a moderate success group. Recognizing that success is a subjective and multidimensional construct, we decided to define it across five variables: income level, education level, prominence in one's field, job satisfaction, and job classification (derived from the *Duncan Socioeconomic Index* [Reiss, 1961] most popularly used as part of the System of Multicultural Pluralistic Assessment [Mercer, 1973]). A panel of five experts rated each candidate for each of the five criteria. Interrater agreement was greater than 90%, and panel members discussed any disparities until they reached consensus on the appropriate rating. To be placed in the high success group, candidates needed a rating of high on four of the criteria and no ratings of low. To be placed in the moderate success group, candidates needed to have a majority of moderate ratings and no more than one rating of low. In this way, we distinguished two clearly identifiable groups.

We selected the participants in the study from the pool of candidates in the two groups. We attempted to control for possible confounding variables by using a matching process across several variables in the final selection of participants. These included age (within 5 years), gender, race, level of disability (determined by our screening form and rated as either severe, moderate, or low by the panel), specific learning disability problem, mother's and father's occupation, and parent socioeconomic status. We tried to match two highly successful participants with one moderately successful participant across these variables. We purposely, therefore, oversampled the highly successful participants due to the project's main interest in identifying key factors related to high levels of success. Thus, although the final sample included a larger number of highly successful individuals to be interviewed, we still included sufficient numbers of moderately successful adults with learning disabilities to permit meaningful comparisons. The ratio was about two highly successful subjects to one moderately successful subject. In several instances, however, we were only able to match one highly successful with one moderately successful subject. Those who could not be matched across these variables were excluded from the study.

The final sample included 46 highly successful and 25 moderately successful adults with learning disabilities, for a total of 71 interviewees. Tables 2.1 through 2.5 present the count of participants by their location (Table 2.1), their average age and gender (Table 2.2), their income distribution (Table 2.3), their education level (Table 2.4), and their occupations (Table 2.5).

How We Decided What To Ask

We needed to develop several instruments for this study. To prepare a retrospective interview form, we first reviewed the interview protocol we had used in *Speaking for Themselves: Ethnographic Interviews with Adults with Learning Disabilities* (Gerber & Reiff, 1991) as a possible prototype for this project. An exhaustive review of literature was conducted on vocational success in general and vocational success for persons with learning disabilities. We also held discussions with educators of individuals with learning disabilities and experts in the field to identify other factors that might be associated with vocational success. From this review of literature and the various discussions, we decided to focus on nine categories of questions: success, vocation, education, family,

Table 2.1
Geographic Location of the 71 Interviewees

Arizona, 2	Kentucky, 2	North Carolina, 1
California, 12	Louisiana, 3	Texas, 2
Colorado, 2	Maryland, 7	Virginia, 6
Connecticut, 1	Massachusetts, 3	Washington, 1
Florida, 2	Minnesota, 4	Washington, DC, 1
Georgia, 3	Missouri, 1	Wisconsin, 1
Illinois, 1	Montana, 1	Wyoming, 1
Iowa, 1	New York, 9	Toronto, Canada, 2
Kansas, 2		

Note. The participants came from 24 states across the United States and Canada.

Table 2.2
Average Age and Gender of Participants by Group Assignment

	Males	Females	Total
High success	N = 32 Age = 46.5	N = 14 Age = 43.1	N = 46 Age = 45.5
Moderate success	N = 16 Age = 45.2	N = 9 Age = 41.8	N = 25 Age = 43.9
Total	N = 48 Age = 46.1	N = 23 Age = 42.6	N = 71 Age = 44.9

Note. As depicted in the table, the number of males participating in the study (*N* = 48, 67.6%) was more than double the number of females (*N* = 23, 32.4%). Analyzing the data in the table further, males represented 69.5% of the total in the high success group (*N* = 32), with females representing 30.5% (*N* = 14). In the moderate success group, males represented a slightly lower percentage of 64% (*N* = 16), with females a slightly higher percentage of 36% (*N* = 9). We were not surprised that we had more males than females; this disparity is typical of the population of individuals identified with learning disabilities. The ages of participants in the high and moderate success groups, however, were very similar, with the high success group only slightly older (average age of 45.5 as compared to 43.9). The male participants were slightly older than female participants, males averaging 3.5 years older than females (average age was 46.1 for males, 42.6 for females). The average age for all participants in the study was 44.9 years.

Table 2.3
Income Distribution of Participants

Salary Range	Moderate Success N = 25	High Success N = 46
Less than $10,000	3	0
$10,000–$20,000	2	0
$20,000–$30,000	3	0
$30,000–$40,000	5	2
$40,000–$50,000	8	1
$50,000–$60,000	2	8
$60,000–$75,000	0	11
$75,000–$100,000	0	3
$100,000+	1	21
No answer	1	0

Note. Income was a distinguishing characteristic between the groups. The vast majority in the moderate success group fell below the $50,000 salary level (22 of 25 participants), whereas the majority of those in the high success group had salaries in excess of $50,000 (43 of 46 participants). Due to gender inequity across occupation levels, a different set of standards was adopted to equalize income levels for males and females.

Table 2.4
Education Level of Participants

Education Level	Moderate Success $N = 25$	High Success $N = 46$
High school degree	2 (8%)	5 (11%)
Associate degree	1 (4%)	0
High school degree/honorary doctorate	0	1 (2%)
Bachelor's degree	3 (12%)	11 (24%)
Master's degree	14 (56%)	2 (4%)
Courses beyond masters	2 (8%)	1 (2%)
Doctorate	3 (12%)	26 (56.5%)

Note. While a larger percentage of the high success group (11%; see Table 2.4) than the moderate success group (8%) had only a high school degree, a much larger percentage in the high success group had doctorates (56.5% to 12%). The most common degree attained by those in the moderate success group was the master's degree (56%), while the most common degree attained by the high success participants was the doctorate (56.5%). Overall, both groups had highly educated participants (bachelor's degrees and beyond).

social issues, emotional issues, the learning disability itself, daily living, and recommendations for children with learning disabilities (including ideas to help teachers, parents, fellow employees, and employers).

A panel of nationally known experts reviewed the initial instrument.[1] The advisory board offered suggestions for improving the instrument. The project staff then conducted pilot interviews with a total of six moderately or highly successful adults with learning disabilities. These interviews enabled us to refine and clarify the instrument, to determine how long the interviews would last, and to begin to discuss how we would transcribe and analyze the data after each interview.

The final interview included more than 130 questions in the nine previously stated categories. Each question was open ended in format, though probes were provided by the interviewers for many of the questions. At the end of each category of questions, the interviewers encouraged the adults with learning disabilities to add any other information not covered in our questions. The last question in each category asked the participants to identify and discuss any

---

[1]Members of the advisory board were Dr. Laura Lehtinen-Rogan, director emeritus, the Cove School, Evanston, Illinois; Dale Brown, President's Committee for the Employment of People with Disabilities; Dr. Charles Goyette, former principal investigator, National Institute for Disabilities Research and Rehabilitation Project on Adults with Learning Disabilities; Dr. Paul Gerber, professor of special education, Virginia Commonwealth University; and Dr. Henry Reiff, associate professor of special education, Western Maryland College.

Table 2.5
Occupations of Participants

Occupation Type	Moderate Success Group	High Success Group
Education	Director, academic center School director Resource manager Elementary teacher School administrator Principal Special education teacher (2) Education specialist Academic advisor College professor (2)	College professor (6) Founder, LD foundation Director, LD clinic
Business	Insurance clerk Marketing (2) Land developer Sales manager	Accountant Banker Marketing director (2) Marketing VP Economist Entrepreneur (2) Contracting business Management training Owner, insurance company President, insurance company Real estate (4)
Law	Police officer	Attorney (3)
Health	Administrator Vocational rehabilitation counselor	Physician (3) Dentist (3) Psychologist (6) Nursing administrator
Art	Storyteller	Artist Photographer
Science		Biomedical engineer Electrical engineer Paleontologist Statistical quality assurance
Journalism	Journalist (2)	

Note. The most distinguishing characteristic of those in the moderate group was the large number in education-related positions (11 of 25), whereas the high success group had many in the more traditional "high status" professions including physicians (3), attorneys (3), dentists (4), scientists (4), college professors (6), and psychologists (6). There were also a large number of businesspersons (16). While persons in both groups were in important occupations, it is obvious that those in the high success group were in more prestigious positions.

critical incident(s) (Flanagan, 1954) in their lives related to the category of questioning. As discussed in Chapter 9, identification of critical incidents can provide critical insights for understanding individual behavior patterns. At the end of the interview, the participants had an opportunity to provide information not included in any of the question categories. The interviewers all used a common script to begin each interview, explaining the purpose of the research. In this way, all interviews began by providing the same information.

Along with the interview schedule, we developed several other instruments for use in the project. As a part of every interview, we concluded by asking a set of 15 questions that required selecting a response from a Likert scale. These data were analyzed and utilized in order to further substantiate that the highly and moderately successful adults with learning disabilities were similar except for the degree of success obtained. Tables 2.6 through 2.8 indicate that the matching process used in selecting the sample did achieve the goal of having two groups who were similar in terms of self-esteem (from the *Rosenberg Self-Esteem Scale*, Rosenberg, 1965), vocational achievement motivation (from the *Manifest Needs Questionnaire*, Steers & Braunstein, 1976), and workplace relationships (from the *Organizational Diagnosis Questionnaire*, Preziosi, 1980).

What the Interviewers Did

Seven individuals conducted interviews over an 18-month period from 1988 to 1989. The interviewers contacted interviewees and traveled to the home location of the interviewees or another acceptable site in order to conduct the interviews. Interviews were audio taped with permission. Interviewees signed a consent and release form ensuring confidentiality of all information collected.

Table 2.6
A Summary of High and Moderate Success Group
Responses to Rosenberg Self-Esteem Scale

| | Range of Scores | | | | | | |
| | 10–15 (HI) | | 16–21 (MOD) | | 22–29 (LO) | | |
Group	N	%	N	%	N	%	Mean
Highly successful	19	46	16	39	6	15	16.6
Moderately successful	8	37	12	54	2	9	16.6

Note. Possible scores could range from 10 to 40. A low score indicates high self-esteem. Cases with missing data were eliminated from the analysis.

Table 2.7
A Summary of High and Moderate Success Group
Responses to the Manifest Needs Questionnaire

| | Range of Scores | | | | | | |
| | 6–10 (HI) | | 11–15 (MOD) | | 16–23 (LO) | | |
Group	N	%	N	%	N	%	Mean
Highly successful	5	12	21	51	15	37	14.1
Moderately successful	2	9	15	68	5	23	14.1

Note. Scores could range from 5 to 35. A low score indicates high vocational achievement motivation. Cases with missing data were eliminated from the analysis.

Table 2.8
A Summary of High and Moderate Success Group
Responses to the Organizational Diagnosis Questionnaire

| | Range of Scores | | | | | | | | |
| | 5–9 (HI) | | 10–14 (MOD HI) | | 15–19 (MOD LO) | | 20–28 (LO) | | |
Group	N	%	N	%	N	%	N	%	Mean
Highly successful	13	40	12	36	4	12	4	12	11.7
Moderately successful	7	30	13	56	2	9	1	4	11.3

Note. Scores could range from 5 to 35. A lower score indicates better relationships with fellow workers. Cases with missing data were eliminated from the analysis.

All interviews began with a common explanation of the study, which also allowed the participants to raise any questions they might have. The interviews ranged in length from 3 to 8 hours, with the average length of the interviews being approximately 4.5 hours. Questioning by the interviewers followed the interview schedule developed by the project staff, which included probes for certain questions to assist the interviewees in understanding the purpose for those questions. Neither the interviewers nor the interviewees were aware of whether the project participants had been assigned to the moderate or high success groups.

The project codirector, an expert in qualitative research methods and interview procedures, conducted interviewer training in the fall of 1987. Two full days were devoted to interviewer training, although all interviewers had some

prior experience conducting interviews. All interviewers were provided literature on conducting qualitative interviews. The training involved an overview of
qualitative research techniques, qualitative data analysis procedures, information on conducting interviews in general, review of the tentative interview
schedule, practice conducting interviews using the interview schedule, and presentation of the interview transcription process for all interviewers to use. The
practice interviews focused on developing high levels of reliability across interviewers in terms of following the interview schedule strictly. After all interviewers had conducted at least one pilot interview in the field using the interview
schedule, all interviewers reconvened in early 1988 to assist in revising the interview schedule, to review and discuss problems in the interview techniques and
interview process, and to critique interview transcripts prepared by each interviewer based on the pilot interviews. The project codirector also maintained close
contact with all interviewers during the entire project to discuss any interview-
related concerns. All subsequent staff meetings devoted time to discussions
among interviewers related to problems and concerns.

How We Analyzed the Data *or* What Can You Do with 2,000 Pages of Transcripts?

We hoped to identify key themes that characterized the rich descriptions collected in the interviews. To strengthen the reliability and validity of our analysis, we relied on the four criteria of trustworthiness established by Guba (1981):
credibility, confirmability, transferability, and dependability. These criteria were
evaluated in several ways. To establish credibility, the testing of conceptual categories from a variety of sources, and confirmability, the objectivity of the
research and the findings, we carefully compared, explained, and discussed the
findings at project meetings with the interviewers, other project staff, outside
consultants, and the advisory board of experts. We addressed transferability, or
the generalizability of findings, by taking care in selecting the final sample for
participation, matching the individuals assigned to the two groups, and collecting in-depth data from each participant. The care taken in training interviewers, the checks from outside consultants and the advisory panel, as well as the
detailed explanations used in constructing the themes related to the data all
contributed to strengthen the dependability or the reliability of the findings.

The actual data analysis began with standardizing the information gathered in each interview in terms of the reporting format by transcribing the
interviews, assigning a predetermined number, and numbering each page of the
transcripts. Then the transcripts were coded for placement into low-inference
categories, the nine categories of questions from the interview schedule.

The second step of data analysis involved compiling all the data from the high success and moderate success groups into a reasonable form for further analysis. Next, analysis of the master sheets by the three project staff and three outside consultants was undertaken for possible within-category sorting. The same process was followed for both the high and moderate success groups.

These early phases of data analysis, coding into low-inference categories, development of meta-matrices, and sorting, are techniques used to summarize and collapse large amounts of information into relevant clusters for further analysis. The next phase of analysis required us to establish propositions related to vocational success for each group. This process, again done independently for each group, resulted in five categories of variables for both groups. Ultimately, the five preliminary categories were furthered expanded and broken down, resulting in the final model for success. We describe and discuss the model in detail in Chapter 7. Figure 2.1 summarizes the steps of data analysis.

Limitations

As with any research, this project was characterized by several limitations. Self-reported data as collected in the in-depth interviews utilized here are only as good as the information presented. Simply put, the participants may not

---

Step 1: Standardize the information from the interviews:
    a. Transcribe each interview.
    b. Code the transcripts for placement into low-inference categories based on the nine categories of questions from the interview schedule.

Step 2: Compile data from the high success and moderate success groups into meta-matrices or master charts.

Step 3: Analyze meta-matrices for possible within-category sorting.

Step 4: Collapse categories (or parts of categories) into larger, more descriptive units (cross-category sorting) to identify key themes.

Step 5: Establish propositions related to vocational success for each group.

Step 6: Integrate comments of advisory board members, interviewers, consultants, and project staff into a revised document.

Figure 2.1.   Steps of data analysis.

have perfect recall, and certain key issues may have been overlooked or purposely avoided. Given the intensity of our interviews, as well as the use of multiple cases, such concerns are somewhat diminished, although we expressly recognize this common limitation of self-reported data.

Related to this is the potential for a reactive effect to the interviewer in such a study. This may emanate from interviewer bias, or participant reaction to personality or bias, but it is generally recognized as a potential dilemma in such qualitative designs. Our careful training of interviewers and preparation of a standard interview schedule should have minimized the possible impact of reactive effects.

Another problem in this study was the nonrandom nature of the sample. Given the parameters facing us, such as the difficulty in identifying a suitable sample for this research, the problem of nonrandomization in such a study is common. Nonetheless, we do recognize that generalizations from our sample must be made with caution.

In addition, the process we utilized of data reduction, analysis, and interpretation is often cited as a limitation to such qualitative designs. That is, subjectivity in the research process must always be confronted (c.f., Peshkin, 1988). While recognizing this limitation, we attempted to offset it through the training of the interviewers and use of multiple individuals independently analyzing the data. These serve as checks on individual subjectivity in the research process.

Finally, several potentially influential variables or dimensions were not directly examined in this study. For example, no information on individual intelligence (e.g., IQ) was collected, but severity of disability was emphasized. Moreover, some might argue that luck plays a role in anyone's vocational success. Certainly, this research was limited by not attending directly to these and other potentially important variables. We are confident, however, that our matching process did adequately control for many confounding variables, and while luck may be a significant factor, the ability to recognize and take advantage of luck is likely to affect an individual's success.

Up Close and Personal: Five Portraits

To present a picture of the types of individuals involved in this study, we include in this description of the research five vignettes of several of our highly successful adults with learning disabilities. These vignettes are drawn of representative individuals we interviewed and depict the backgrounds and personalities of these amazing people. The source of our study was not an abstract compilation of facts and figures but a group of real, living people. In the following pages, we hope the reader will come to know five of them: KD, MT, KM, DW, and JC.

KD

KD has reached an enviable position. "I feel good about myself. I feel good within my family. I feel good about my relation to the world. I feel recognized and appreciate it. I feel a sense of generativity. I feel that I'm giving something important to the world in the work that I'm doing. It's qualitatively part of me. I feel like I'm giving something in terms of me." KD's multiple successes lend credence to his beliefs. A clinical psychologist with a thriving practice, he has authored a best selling book on men's issues and writes features for prominent magazines, has his own local television show, has appeared on the talk show circuit, and is in demand as a speaker at national and international conferences. His lucrative career has not only brought him material wealth but the freedom to control much of his time. He is able to focus on his family and overall quality of life. To a great extent, he can do what he wants. At present, he tries not to invest too much of himself in his work. His credo is to work "smarter, not harder," in order to give more of himself to his family. His greatest accomplishment is his marriage and being a dad.

Yet bubbling just below the surface of these untroubled waters are "major and ever present difficulties." While one side of him can claim to have found peace and self-affirmation, another side continues to push too hard, to upset the balance he seeks in life and work. "Other obstacles are all those demons coming back and saying, 'You're the impostor here. You're going to get found out. You're a big phony. You're not smart enough.' It's a small miracle that I write with fluidity and proper punctuation."

KD seems genuinely self-assured, a naturally empathic psychologist; it is hard to reconcile this image with such self-doubt and insecurity. Ironically, his vulnerable side plays a role in his success. "I think I identify with people in low self-esteem positions or people who are struggling to believe in themselves because I had that experience so intimately. . . . Initially, I was trying to rescue other people as a way of healing myself."

The pervasive hurt and pain are the legacy of his learning disabilities, or perhaps more accurately, the interaction of his learning disabilities and his schooling. Never formally identified as learning disabled in childhood, he struggled with D's and F's, habitually attended summer school, and was generally regarded as a dummy. School was so exasperating because he had so much difficulty reading. "I never used to be able to read. You could hand me in seventh, eighth, ninth grade something and I wouldn't know what I was looking at. I could read a sentence and I had no comprehension. I could read it ten times and I still wouldn't get it."

This failure did not jive with his father's expectations. KD fit in socially and was an excellent athlete. How dare he be stupid! Eventually his father's criticism became destructive. KD's learning difficulties were treated as a source of embarrassment and largely ignored. "Mostly school was a horrible, humiliating experience of trying to hide somewhere and avoid being picked on and asked questions. And being embarrassed by teachers. . . . I was ridiculed a great deal."

He managed to graduate from high school. His athletic abilities made him attractive to colleges. An injury ended his collegiate sports career, yet he was beginning to discover newfound success in the area that had eluded him, academics. He did not become a stellar student exactly, but he managed to earn a bachelor's degree in sociology, a master's in counseling psychology, and a doctorate in clinical psychology. He did not suddenly learn to read well. Instead, he decided that if he simply worked hard enough, he could meet the requirements. "I never stop trying. I have an incredible amount of persistence. . . . I would adapt by doing extra work. My doctoral thesis, the damn thing was 800 pages. I almost died. It was physically painful, but I was determined."

He needed to prove himself, to be acceptable, lovable, and recognized. Higher education gave him that opportunity because it provided more flexible means for him to show what he could do. He used his wisdom and charm to find people to support and teach him. It was still a struggle, but it helped develop the learned creativity so useful to him in later life. "The ways I've been asked to learn, with very few exceptions, were not native to me. I was always having to change the situation to show what I knew or to show how I learned. So I learned how to struggle adversely with the system." He learned to trust himself and not get too hung up in what others said he could or could not do. "At times it was extremely lonely and painful, but I think I got to know myself in that loneliness. I think I had to really pull for myself. The struggle has taught me something. I'm now drawing from that wisdom to help other people. I draw from that wisdom for perspective. I draw from that wisdom to help my kids cope with a lot of challenges they're facing, and to help my marriage grow."

Today, "the process of reading just still doesn't click with me. I enjoy the process of reading and learning now, but I'm still very slow." He has been cheated, he feels, because he is unable to learn as much as he would like through reading. Ironically, his writing career has blossomed in many ways because of his reading style. He writes at a level that he can read, which turns out to be simple, clear, and accessible—just the ticket for popular success. His writing has also rewarded him with a unique method of improving his reading.

"I'm learning how to read by reading my own writing, things that I'm making intelligible to me. And as I make myself a better writer, I'm going to train myself to be a better reader."

KD considers himself "healed" from the emotional trauma of his learning disabilities. Yet watching his daughter with learning disabilities contend with her education touches apparently sensitive nerve endings. "My worst nightmare [is] to hear my daughter saying, 'I'm stupid.' And I say, 'Oh my God, here it is again.' Now she's going to start believing that she's really stupid, that she's deficient, something's wrong with her. She's going to internalize that belief and she's going to go through the torture that I went through and act and hold herself back from taking greater risks and believing in herself. And it will delay and postpone her development as I believe it did mine." Sharing her pain and understanding her struggle has made him a better father. He shows her tricks and compensation strategies. He's also been very tough with her "because there is a tendency to feel like a failure and start buying into a loser mentality. And I say, 'That's bullshit. You're giving up. Don't give me excuses. That's your way of fooling yourself and that's not going to help you.'"

KD readily admits that he is a man of contradictions. He can be intense, even angry, or he can be soft. He can be difficult, inaccessible, depressed, or he can be nurturing, protective, caressing. In other words, he possesses the wide range of emotions and characteristics found in any complex, thoughtful, and reflective person.

MT

If ever there were a case that illustrates the "impostor syndrome," MT could play the starring role. Today MT is one of the most respected executives of his multinational Fortune 500 corporation. His role is uniquely important. Whenever his company has a problem, other executives turn to him to solve it. These are not trivial issues; they involve product development, marketing, sales, and service on an international scale. They call him the "hit man" because he can solve problems faster, cheaper, and with greater efficiency than others can. His abilities have helped to make his company the envy of the international business community. He explains his prowess by acknowledging, "I can see the heart of the matter." His wizardry constantly amazes his colleagues. They repeatedly ask him how he can figure out the solutions to such complex questions. He responds quite matter-of-factly, "I just knew that."

Why should an individual with such remarkable abilities feel like an impostor? Each workday he is surrounded by colleagues with MBAs and other advanced degrees from prestigious institutions such as Harvard and Stanford.

They all work for him—a man who never attended college. He had and continues to have problems in reading numbers and difficulties in reading and writing. As an adult he has used three tutors who have helped improve his skills and gain self-confidence. Still, MT understandably sees himself as not quite fitting into the rarefied atmosphere of the corporate elite.

His business (and life) education took place in his father's butcher shop in New York City. In spite of his learning problems, he was able to run the shop after his father was not physically able to carry on the business full time. He learned his entrepreneurial acumen from his father who mentored him in the ways of the business world. He was enrolled in the school of hard knocks—the world of retail. It was the best education he could have found. "Retail is feedback! I learned a lifetime of book learning in a short time," MT proudly proclaims.

After working in the butcher shop he got his first job as a salesman for an office supply business in New York City. He quickly established himself as their top performer, or in his words, a "super performer." His apparent lack of immodesty did not spring simply from being number one. His accomplishments filled a burning need to cover up a feeling of inferiority about his learning problems. He compensated via his all-consuming drive to be the best, to prove to himself that he was superior.

How was he able to sell so effectively? He attributes his success to "figuring it out on my own and not following routines." He began to make money, he was praised and reinforced by his clients, and he actually started to *feel* successful. His performance caught the attention of his current employer. The corporation soon asked him to relocate to their headquarters in the Midwest where he could parlay his skills on a grander scale.

MT quickly climbed the corporate ladder. Each time he made a presentation he "shook the room and received a promotion." His approach embodied pragmatism. He could frame complex problems in understandable ways to construct workable solutions. He describes this process as creating "skeletons and my staff puts the flesh on them." His crowning effort was to institute a corporate-wide planning system that affected decisions at all levels. Implemented years ahead of schedule, his system saved the corporation millions of dollars.

MT is successful in every sense of the word. In spite of his humble origins, in spite of his learning disabilities, he has proven that he is not, in fact, an impostor. He has gained respect and admiration at the highest levels of the multinational business community. Discovering new and exciting challenges from former Eastern Bloc countries, he continues to rise in stature and position in his company. He has won awards for distinguished accomplishments of persons with dyslexia. This recognition has motivated him to embark on a new mission of "helping others live fulfilling lives" through speaking publicly about his life as a person with learning disabilities. In relating his experiences, he is validating the experiences of others with learning disabilities. MT is helping persons with learning disabilities to acknowledge and celebrate their accomplishments—and not to think of themselves as impostors.

KM

When KM was a child in school, she was always the first to sit down in the spelling bee. She was the one child in kindergarten who couldn't learn to spell her own name. Math and reading were difficult too. She generally did not fail. Instead, she managed to eke out C's. So she really did not present a problem. She was obviously bright and exhibited a particular talent in art. In the late 1950s and 1960s, parents and teachers probably would have shown concern about a boy with such characteristics. But KM's parents and teachers were not worried. They assumed she would eventually marry and have a husband to support her.

As an adult, KM is not married—and she does not need a husband to support her. She is on the faculty in the Art Department at a major campus of a state university. Students love her courses. She has established a reputation as an innovative visual artist and sculptor who became one of the first artists to receive an invitation from the Chinese government to exhibit her work and participate in an exchange program. She embodies an artistic sensibility. Success to her is not a product per se but being involved in the creative process itself. "Coming up with ideas is rewarding. Making them into reality, the blood, sweat and tears is important." But once the vision is realized, it's time to move on to the next project. Perhaps most importantly, "success is doing something that I like."

She sounds self-assured, proud of her accomplishments, and content with her life. Surprisingly, she describes her self-esteem as being at "around my ankles" for a long time. Now, it's "maybe at knees but edging up to the hip. I can't say it's 100 percent, more at a midpoint." Her self-esteem has improved, at least in part, due to being diagnosed only 3 years ago as having learning disabilities. She has begun to spend time with other adults with learning disabilities. Talking and sharing have helped her to understand herself and to be less hard on herself. "When they start to identify, then you have a common dialogue. I'm just finding out. I'm starting to realize the coping skills or the strategies. I find as I listen to other people, I'm starting to learn myself how to deal with it. The beginning is just to recognize it. For myself that has lifted a great deal of pressure or stress."

Her adult diagnosis has also dissipated some deeply buried anger. Although her academic difficulties did not set off alarms in those around her, her memories are filled with pain, frustration, and humiliation. The spelling bees were "always excruciating" and embarrassing. She remembers looking for the skinniest book to assuage her anxiety about doing book reports. She persevered, buoyed by her talent and interest in art. But when she got to community college, she was almost destroyed by a psychologist's response to her vocational testing. He imperiously informed her, "You have third year college level visual perception. But you are retarded in all other areas." Retarded? She felt as if she had been slapped in the face. During our interview, KM referred to this critical incident a number of times. It was clear that the memory still stings. It has greatly influenced her general outlook: "If some people can't read or write or do mathematics, but they can do art, they're labeled learning disabled. But what about the people who can't do art or music, what are they labeled? They're not labeled anything."

Like many of the adults in our study, however, she refused to let one blow keep her down. Rather, it strengthened her resolve to succeed, to prove that she was a capable and talented person. "I know he's wrong," she repeated to herself. And she got angry. She dropped out of community college and transferred to a well-known art institute. As she began to specialize more and more in art courses and less and less in basic educational requirements, her grades improved. She eventually made the dean's list and went straight to graduate school where she received a fellowship. She has not looked back. She succeeded because she persisted, because she was stubborn, because she refused to allow someone else to tell her that her expectations were too high. She exceeded his expectations, but not her own.

KM believed in herself even though others did not. She credits much of her resolve to her parents. They saw her talent as an artist and nurtured it. They did not fixate on her difficulties in school, nor did they compare her to her brother to whom academics came easily. Instead, they emphasized her artistic strengths, making sure she had plenty of supplies around the house, praising her work, and even sending her to a museum school during the summers. "So although I wasn't feeling good until third grade, from then on, when I started to get this praise with the art, it just seemed to—it clicked for me. If I didn't have art, I don't know how I'd feel about myself."

Her successful career in art has not obliterated the impact of her learning difficulties. She has had a long-time interest in the biomedical field but never felt she was capable of pursuing such a career. In her teaching, she finds it nearly impossible to memorize her students' names. She makes mistakes writing on the board, although she encourages her students to correct her. Her forthrightness not only makes students comfortable but works as an effective strategy to get them to pay attention. She has a large library collection at her home, not because she has become a good reader but because if she does not understand one book she can go to another. Writing continues to be a problem. "If I have to write a letter, it takes me maybe a good week. The ideas are clear in my head, but to get them down the arm—to have it make sense—there are times when I have to write the letter, put it aside for a day, come back, read it, and I'll say, 'Oh boy. That's structurally incorrect.'"

She is not overwhelmed by her learning disabilities in her profession or in day-to-day life. For the most part, her strengths rather than her weaknesses drive her career. Overall, she has created environments that only minimally exacerbate her learning disabilities. Instead, the impact may be greatest in her social and personal life. She is prone to sensory overload: the noise at large social gatherings, the visual stimuli at a department store. She believes that her learning disabilities may have screwed up some personal relationships. Processing and memory difficulties have led to miscommunication and misunderstandings. One boyfriend became exasperated because she didn't talk much. "It takes time for me to sort things out and put them in perspective. It eventually gets worked out but it's not immediate. I don't see the picture right away." Her difficulties with social perception have made her tentative, cautious, and a little apprehensive that others might be taking advantage of her without her being aware of it.

KM is quite satisfied with her career and professional life. She believes she succeeds because she is willing to try many solutions to any problem. If one doesn't work, she switches to another. This approach has worked beautifully in art. Now she would like to apply it to her personal life.

DW

Being born into a family of wealth and privilege usually guarantees certain advantages. But when learning disabilities enter into this scenario, the resulting uncertainty of life events may undermine and erode those advantages. DW found out quickly that his family's power and prestige could not ensure the success that was expected for someone with his background.

He was never a student of note. Always on the brink of failure, he barely got through his private high school program. His family connections did get him accepted as a "charity case" at the prestigious southern university his father attended. But he could not buy good grades. He finished with a 1.9999 grade point average, a performance that pushed the envelope to graduate. Putting his checkered educational past behind him was "the happiest day of my life."

His learning disabilities discouraged him from following in his father's footsteps as an investment banker. Conformity, the valued commodity of old money business, was not part of his repertoire. He simply could not march in the lock-step of the corporate world. When he went to a job fair at the age of 21, he unnerved most of his interviewers when he announced his intention to be president of the company. He did not lack confidence. Endowed with drive and savvy, he needed to find the right fit for his greatest assets, his determination and single mindedness. He found employment in a business where mavericks are usually not welcome, an insurance company; consequently, his job did not last long. He had trouble following rules; he often forgot them. It was too boring.

The key for DW was working for himself. He could live with rules if he made them. He could not envision selling specific insurance products so he opened his own insurance claims business. He began to tailor a business concept to his strengths: the ability to sell and problem solve. The problem-solving situations that arose in selling became his passion. He did quite well in his initial business venture. Moreover, his marriage at the age of 22 gave him extra motivation to make something of his life. "A lot of things became clearer at that point in my life," he reflects.

He parlayed his interests and strengths into even greater accomplishments. Well before health care costs became a political agenda item, his invention of the concept of the preferred physician organization (PPO) propelled DW to the stature of a guru in the health care insurance industry. His pioneering work in managed care has helped to buffer zooming health care costs. His emphasis on consumer choice has revolutionized the concept of health maintenance organizations. He is justly proud of his contributions and believes that, "What I do has social value. There are a lot of sick people out there. There is a lot of dumb capital out there as well."

On the surface, DW seemed to travel a very linear, predictable, and logical path to achieve his highly praised accomplishments. But beneath the surface lurks the chaotic processing of everyday events that continually confronts and often confounds a person with learning disabilities. He may walk into a meeting room, only suddenly to wonder why he is there. His world is one in which "time and space have no meaning," where he often does his best work at 11:59 before a 12:00 appointment.

Paradoxically, as is the case with so many of the adults with learning disabilities in this book, DW has transformed the very idiosyncrasies that would appear to hold him back into his greatest assets. His unconventional ways and his mercuric creativity unfettered by the linear confines of time and space have propelled him to the forefront of his industry. Perhaps newfangled ideas and ways of doing things can only arise from a vision that sees the world in a qualitatively different perspective. He may not be readily able to implement those ideas himself; after all, that tends to be an inherently linear process. Instead, he has learned to rely on colleagues who are implementors, who can translate his visions into actions. Speaking fondly of his right-hand man, he reveals,

"I do the thinking, and my implementor [sic] does the translating. I could not do without him."

He also brings an unexpected ethic to this highly competitive workplace. In the dog-eat-dog business of health care, he is scrupulously honest, because he knows he cannot remember his lies. Failure is of little concern to a person who has to reinvent and reformulate his strategies constantly; it is just another way to learn, to make the idea work.

DW has realized the American dream. A multimillionaire at the age of 40, DW has a beautiful house and the accompanying amenities of financial success. He is happily married with four children, two of whom have learning disabilities. His style is easy, his humor is pixilated, and his imposing appearance is reminiscent of a middle-aged, absent-minded professor. It is the composite DW, his unique ways of approaching all aspects of his life, that has ultimately accounted for his spectacular accomplishments.

But do not be fooled or lulled into surmising that his success just happened to him. He made it happen. DW learned long ago to convert his determination into an achievable reality. In high school he promised himself that he would be in control of his own destiny. He adopted an attitude of "Screw you. I'm not going to let you do this to me." He consciously constructed the means to maintain control. He developed ways to approach and meet challenges his way and on his terms. In this quest for autonomy and control, he has found a way to "call his own shots." Moreover, he has contributed significantly to improving the quality of life for millions of Americans.

JC

JC is an angry man. He has a happy, fulfilling marriage and family life. He is warm, friendly, even gregarious. His self-developed contracting and building business has prospered, enabling him to live in a large, expensive redwood house in Southern California that offers a sweeping panorama of the Pacific Ocean. Writers, journalists, and film producers have approached him about his life story, a compelling vindication of the American dream with a dramatic and poignant twist. Politicians and celebrities invite him to share the podium at prestigious forums. Yet the very source of his renown and his drive to succeed also fuels his anger.

At the age of 47, in spite of immense success in his business, JC had a harrowing secret. "I always had a horrendous inferiority complex. It affected me every moment of my waking hours that I could neither read or write. . . . I don't think I could feel successful unless I could learn to read and write. And in this society learning how to read and write is very basic and you learn it when you're a child. So psychologically and emotionally we're left in our childhood. And we're left in the emotions and fears of our childhood. No matter how much intellectual power and success that people might have, it's always been superficial to me."

As a child, JC started out with a sense of wholeness and confidence. His parents loved him, supported him, and told him he was a winner. Until he was 6, he had no reason to doubt them. Then, "I went to school only to find out that I was a loser." He did not learn to read and write like the other kids. On the one hand, he felt inferior and weak. "I went through a time where they were calling kids like me mentally retarded. I don't even know what the other names were but they all came out being subhuman." Yet he did not give up on himself. Instead, he quickly learned to overcompensate. In fact, he learned to compensate so well that he fooled most people. He acted much too self-assured to have an inferiority complex. He even fooled the system. In spite of not learning to read, he kept on getting promoted. He learned how to survive, how to play the game. He was able to succeed and pass because "I'm an athlete, six foot four, blue eyed, and I had adapted socially."

On the outside, he was making it. He became a fighter who decided he simply was not going to be held back no matter what he had to do. If that meant deception, so be it. "It was easy to deceive the system because they were continuing to deceive themselves. So all I did was to find out where their deceptions were, where their weaknesses were. I was at war every single day with my world. That gave me some discipline. . . . The literate world was my enemy. I wasn't much different than a Jew in Nazi Germany. I took a psychological posture of who the good guys were and who the bad guys were. I wasn't going to let the literate world beat me." Strong words. Strong feelings.

At home, his parents provided perhaps the only consistent source of support and encouragement. They never gave up on the idea that he was a winner. They made it clear that it did not matter what the world said—he was special. Part of him hung on to this belief, and today he credits his tenacity and determination to succeed to the role models his parents provided. Yet he managed to hide his illiteracy even from them. He kept the shame to himself, a shame so devastating that he likened it to the guilt of being molested.

Times were tough. His father worked up to three jobs at a time to support the family. In search of better opportunities, they moved 35 times. He attended 17 different schools. One might be inclined to think that this nomadic instability exacerbated his learning problems, but "to me, it was my salvation. It was my geography. It was my history. It was my escape from being labeled by the teachers." He was never in one school long enough for his illiteracy to be detected, or at least to be confronted. A fugitive from injustice, he always managed to stay one step ahead of the literacy police.

He managed to get through high school, partially through sheer force of will (he took science eight times until he passed it as a senior) and partially through his nonacademic talents. His social charm and obvious brightness may have overwhelmed his teachers and obfuscated his academic deficiencies—and it did not hurt that he lettered in three sports.

His athleticism led to a college scholarship. By now, he had honed his survival skills to a fine edge. Not only did he graduate, he took a job as a high school teacher, still not being able to read. Paradoxically, his strategies to hide his illiteracy may have made him a better teacher. Instead of reading the daily bulletin, he let the kids read it. To cope with taking roll, he used assigned seating, and for the first week of class, the students would introduce themselves to each other each day. JC memorized the roll list, and the students got involved in positive social interactions. Debates and discussions became the hallmarks of his teaching approach. He worked with the students other teachers could not handle, perhaps a sure way to endear oneself to the administration. He told the students that they were his teachers and he did not want to be bored. He challenged his students to grow and learn, and they responded. "A good teacher is somebody that is sensitive and cares, and I was that, even though I was illiterate." But his deception still haunted him. "My conscience was clear, but I still had that terrible fear of being caught."

While he was teaching, JC took a leave of absence, built an apartment building in nine months, and made several hundred thousand dollars. He has never looked back. If he had learned to cope as an illiterate in one of the most literate environments imaginable, he could certainly handle the world of business. "I identify other people's skills and abilities. When I was a teacher in the classroom I found out who the best reader was in the class—and quick! I used those people to read the instructions. So I found readers, and it was my link to the literate world that I would look for other people's strengths. They thought I was the leader. . . . I did everything any good manager would do to tap into the natural resources at his disposal."

He also found that a wide array of his other qualities had a particularly good fit for contracting, developing, and building. "The reason I'm an entrepreneur and have my own business is because I couldn't work for somebody else's system because their system wasn't fixed for me." A man who built his own house with no previous experience, he has a hands-on knowledge and understanding of his business. His natural learning style is well suited to an enterprise that literally requires a vision to turn ideas into tangible form. "I'm a visual person. I'm a conceptual person. That's how I work." His illiteracy may have helped him develop these talents. He had to tap into parts of his brain that many literates never need to discover.

Clearly, the reasons for JC's success are varied. Nevertheless, he believes the driving force is relatively simple to explain. "The key to success is hard work. Tenacity is more valuable than knowledge and skills. The difference between success and failure is that when you fall down a million times and fail and you get up one million and one times and you succeed. That's all you need is one."

He has achieved success. His company has done as much as $50 million worth of business in a year. He likes what he does. He regards the longevity of his marriage and the raising of his children as a significant achievement. But his greatest sense of accomplishment stems from a catharsis that began 2 years prior to our interview. "I define success by learning how to read and write. That's my definition." Slowly, painstakingly, he is entering the previously forbidden literate world. "I think learning how to read and write for me has meant coming home and being able to be whole."

How It Feels To Grow Up with Learning Disabilities

Chapter 3

I'm Not a Child; I'm Maturationally Challenged!

To conduct an ethnographic interview, that is, to see the world through the eyes of the one being interviewed, the interviewer must explore not only the present but the past. Our past shapes our present and our future. From a childhood developmental perspective, we progress through identifiable stages, one leading predictably to another, until we reach adult maturity. Of course, theorists believe that development continues through adulthood, although perhaps not as predictably, sequentially, or systematically. But childhood may be particularly powerful. As Plato contends in *The Republic*, "Anything received into the mind at that age is likely to become indelible and unalterable." In fact, some adult developmentalists view adulthood as a process of resolving a plethora of issues from childhood. For many of us, adulthood is a battle to break away from much of our childhood persona, a struggle recognized throughout recorded history and succinctly articulated in these familiar words in St. Paul's letters to the Corinthians: "When I was a child, I spoke like a child, I thought like a child, I reasoned like a child. When I became a man, I gave up childish ways." At the same time, we stay connected to who we were as children, trying to maintain a sense of consistency or wholeness.

Growing up is not easy for anyone. As soon as we get reasonably comfortable in one phase or stage of development, we are confronted with new expectations. The role we play changes continually and, it often seems, unfairly. Consider Piaget's model of cognitive development: Our first view of the world is egocentric; everything revolves around us. As a kind of cruel joke, we spend the rest of our lives becoming less important! Even the most idyllic childhood hurls one potential trauma after another at the unsuspecting victim—separations, conflicts, responsibilities. Henry Miller, the notorious American novelist, once quipped that we're welcomed into the world with a slap on the ass, and it doesn't get much better after that.

For many of the adults in our study, childhood took on an additional dimension of difficulty. They were saddled with a label, either formally or informally. Their learning disabilities singled them out as different at best, but usually as dumb, lazy, or stubborn. Sadly, many of our participants eventually believed these remarks. They had even more trouble with the part of growing up that almost all kids find difficult: school. Instead of a relatively natural flow through progressively more advanced levels of learning, they hit bumps and wound up with bruises. Occasionally, in specific areas such as reading, they hardly progressed at all. Most of them could not understand why.

The adults in our study did learn to compensate and devise ways to learn effectively, but their experiences of learning in childhood were qualitatively different from those of children without learning disabilities. That history continues to color the way they perceive the world today. Their learning disabilities made indelible impressions on their childhood in at least two ways.

First was the direct impact on learning, of processing information differently. Problems with processing information had an obvious effect on performance in the classroom. More subtly, and perhaps more debilitating, some of these individuals had difficulty with a complex cognitive process that relies on gathering information from a total social field, processing the relative importance of the data, and formulating a direction for social action (Thorndike, 1921). In practical terms, they faltered in their ability to recognize or understand the thoughts, feelings, and intentions of others as expressed in behaviors (O'Sullivan & Guilford, 1976). This phenomenon, often termed (nonverbal) social perception, has been discussed at length in research on students with learning disabilities dating back more than 20 years. (See Reiff, 1988, for a review of this literature.) Because some individuals with learning disabilities either cannot discern relevant and irrelevant information or confuse the two, they do not connect cause and effect. They may not see the "big picture," and they are more at risk to respond and act inappropriately in social situations.

Upon reflection, one participant in our study concluded that problems with social perception may have marred his social interactions. "I wonder how many times I never looked at anybody's body language. I wonder how many times I never noticed anybody's looks in their eyes. I wonder how many times I never heard anything they said, and how deeply embarrassed I might become now if I sat down and thought deeply about it." Interestingly, few participants referred to such a difficulty. It is possible they were not even aware of this potentially insidious deficit.

Equally significant was the secondary or indirect impact of growing up with learning disabilities. Because they did not learn like other children, they often doubted themselves. They became frustrated, angry, aggressive, disruptive, dependent, depressed, or ashamed. Moreover, teachers, peers, and sometimes family members often perceived them as uncooperative, stubborn, unfriendly, or unlikable. They often did not seem to get the same respect as their peers. Understandably, these reactions tended to exacerbate self-doubt and often caused hurt and pain that persist today.

School Daze

For many of our participants, the most vivid memories of learning disabilities begin with school. After all, problems in the classroom tended to be the most visible manifestation that something was different or wrong. It was not unusual to hear remarks about simply hating school, an understandable reaction from individuals who experienced a seemingly unending procession of failure and frustration. "I hated it. I hated school. I think if I had been more like the normal students and able to do things better, the things that they were teaching better, I would have been better off." Another participant remembers having so much difficulty that elementary school was "like a nervous breakdown."

Several of our participants were able to reframe the chronic torture of their formal education by adopting the Nietzschean outlook of "that which does not destroy us makes us stronger." Several reasoned that they could face and succeed at anything in adult life after surviving 16 years of school. Instead of crushing their spirit, these negative experiences and messages often had a positive effect, in that the participants became so determined to prove themselves. One participant credited part of his success to this kind of negative encounter. "The motivating thing that got me through college was the high school counselor who told me I'd never make it through the first semester."

But the majority of these successful adults were considerably less cavalier or sanguine about life in the classroom. The overwhelming memory for some was frustration:

> Tremendously frustrating all the way through high school.

> I was stupid. . . . I couldn't read and was very frustrated and angry about it.

> I was carrying a lot of baggage from high school. My advisor had told me I shouldn't consider doing anything other than picking up a tray because I would never be accepted into college. That was very hurtful. I decided that I was going to do it anyhow; it just took me longer to do it.

Usually, their self-esteem took a terrible beating and, in some cases, never fully recovered. It may be hard for some of us to imagine what it must be like to live in constant fear of failing, a nightmare that came true time after time. For many of our participants, the overwhelming recollections of school were feelings permeated with fear and terror.

> When I made a D in spelling in the third grade he [stepfather] told me that he would give me spelling words every night. When I'd screw up the five- and six-letter words he'd give to me, he really got mad. This bothered me so much that it drove me to actually cheating on spelling tests. I was afraid to bring home a bad grade in spelling.

> It [school] reinforced the "fear cycle" in me. I was put into situations where I couldn't succeed though there was a high demand that I should. Other than the tutoring all of my output was inadequate in their eyes so it reinforced the belief that I was incompetent. I'd trip over my feet in gym and couldn't catch a ball at the age of 13. Teachers and students reinforced my feelings of inadequacy. It made me sensitive to the impatience of educators. I still will transfer negative feelings onto my secretary or people taking dictation, and it's not really there. It's just the old fears that I'm putting on others.

> I would hide and not go out because of my fear of abuse and failure.

> When you're LD you don't want to develop close friendships because you're always afraid of being discovered. . . . Not being able to express your feelings can be very detrimental, especially to kids.

> I remember one time was one of the core humiliations of my life. In upper fourth grade the teacher chose me when we were out on the playground to go look in the window of our classroom and come back and tell her what time it is. It's very important. She needs to know the time, and I wanted to die. I didn't know what to do. I ran and remember staring, staring at that clock. I didn't know how to tell time.

> Sometimes after a vacation or being away from work for awhile, I wake up feeling terror—afraid of failure. I feel that I don't know my job and will have to start all over again. This feeling is instantaneous. Once I get to work everything is OK. I haven't lost anything. This feeling has happened *all of my life*. . . . I am still so terrified by people coming in with a simple question on paper that I am unable to read.

> . . . I was scared. "I can't do this." I would sweat bullets, wanted to faint and play dead. I did get sick all the time. I think it was emotional.

One way of coping with such fear and humiliation was to try to deceive others and pretend that everything was all right. Smith (1992) has referred to the "masks" individuals with learning disabilities wear to hide their deficiencies. The participants in our study often perfected the art of "faking it," not coincidentally the title of a book about growing up with learning disabilities (see Lee & Jackson, 1992).

I was a little bit bad just so I could maintain some "face" in school. Maybe they would think I was doing it just to be bad. . . . I'd rather be bad than stupid.

I knew how to analyze situations and how to avoid a lot of things by conning my way out of different things. . . . I had to fake a lot. I didn't like to study and hated to read so I found that teachers would call on you if you did not maintain eye contact. So I looked right at them like I knew the answers when I didn't. Very seldom was I called.

I perfected ways of cheating. I really perfected fudging in high school. I used to have nightmares about it, that somebody would stop me in the hall and ask me an algebra problem and I wouldn't know it because the person wasn't sitting next to me.

You had the ability to con people so you are going to keep coming back to that ability to con. I just tried desperately to let people not know my grades because they would know I was retarded. . . . I never discussed it with anybody because then I would be blowing my cover. . . . I have five book reports that are due by Thursday. How in the world am I going to read five books by Thursday? I have no intention of reading five books by Thursday. All I have to do is write five book reports by Thursday. There is a difference.

When you are LD you become very defensive and offensive. You know what your weaknesses are and you want to cover them up and you build up a tremendous entourage of ways to get around it and of avoiding different issues. It also teaches you to build on your assets. Instead of trying to improve your weak points, you let them go and build on your strong points.

As a typical dyslexic I was the class clown when it came to spelling. The teacher tried absolutely everything and nothing worked. I built up a shield, and no matter what she said I'd laugh. My handwriting was absolutely atrocious, and I kept it that way so you couldn't tell that I couldn't spell.

Confidence eroded. It became all too easy to buy into the criticism and deprecation. It seemed like the only explanation.

Most people thought I was lazy or stupid. For a long time I thought I was real slow.

I felt that I was retarded.

I still have in the back of my mind that I'm stupid and worthless.

I felt like I was dumb in elementary school because I was interested in things no one else was interested in, because I had a reading problem, and because I had trouble processing information and presenting it. The inability to read restricted me to what exposure I could have to books and other things. It took me a long time to learn how to write and when we had to read aloud, I couldn't do it. I had a lot of problems in math. I'd get all muddled up. I could tell you the answer, but not how I got there. . . . I felt like I was dumb all through elementary school and had a terrible time particularly in high school in terms of grades. . . . Because of the LD I did not have a happy life in high school.

As you grow up you struggle with these kinds of things—why am I different and nobody really has an answer.

I remember the humiliation in the first grade trying to read out loud, because I couldn't pronounce words. . . . I'd read out loud and the kids would laugh. . . . The one thing I'd like to do more than anything else is to go back to that kindergarten and first and second grade teachers and put the degree [Ph.D.] on the desk and say, "See, I wasn't stupid." I needed recognition.

Academically each year got harder. I had secrets. I was really ashamed that I couldn't tell time until the fifth grade and I tried. Or to tie my shoes, I couldn't do that until about fifth grade. And I didn't want anybody to know and I'd have my mom tie my shoes tight, really tight, because they couldn't come undone during the day because I couldn't redo them. . . . I think I really felt dumb, felt inferior.

I went to school to find out that I was a loser. It's that integrity, the human spirit, that gets crushed.

How To Make Friends and Influence People

Research has consistently and clearly indicated that growing up may pose special difficulties for children with learning disabilities. Study after study has concluded that students with learning disabilities are less accepted and more rejected than their nondisabled peers (e.g., Bruininks, 1978; Rosenberg & Gaier, 1977; Schumaker & Hazel, 1984); in sum, many students with learning disabilities occupy a lower social status than other students (Wiener, 1987). Adolescence may exacerbate the already existing social and emotional difficulties of youths with learning disabilities. Researchers have voiced concern on issues such as depression and suicide (Huntington & Bender, 1993), problems with the law (Gregory, Shanahan, & Walberg, 1986), and less-than-satisfactory social lives and peer relationships (Phil & McLarnon, 1984).

Many adults in our study found themselves in these kinds of situations. They were the outsiders, rejects, or nerds. One participant vividly and sadly remembered that other students teased him for not being able to spell anything. Comments such as the following came up frequently in our interviews:

I never was a member of the group in grammar or in high school. I was an outsider, and my best friends were the rather delinquent "rejects."

I really had the feeling of not being accepted.

I knew I was different, and by definition it was wrong. . . . It unquestionably affected my self-esteem.

I was ridiculed a great deal, especially by guys I was competing with in sports.

I would be playing with a couple of other kids and I would be carrying on this conversation with this [imaginary] fellow and the parents would come and take their kids away.

It sucked. I was never invited to anything and never a part of anything.

One participant recalled a particularly painful rejection because it completely undermined his first taste of peer acceptance: "Once in junior high I was going out with this girl and somehow I was voted in as president of the Student Council. In the middle of the assembly she got up and said, 'He can't do it because he can't read and stuff.' It just hurt so much."

The net result of being an outsider often takes the forms of emotional isolation and loneliness. "Growing up, I was the only LD in the family and I had different goals, desires, and emotional needs than they had. They weren't restrictive but were unaware and unempathetic to my frustrations. I was going in an opposite direction in my interests." Margalit and Levin-Alyagon (1994) found that 60% of students with learning disabilities in their study could be classified as being lonely. As we have seen, many of our participants were overtly rejected. Others may have isolated themselves for innumerable reasons—fear, insecurity, frustration, and so on. "I felt defensive and awkward. That's why I didn't want friends. I didn't feel like the rest of the gang; I felt different. I didn't want to be compared to my friends." This participant repeated throughout the interview that her best, and only, friends were her dogs. At least they did not criticize or pass judgment on her because she had so much difficulty reading.

No wonder that poor self-concept and inadequate social and interpersonal relationships plagued so many of our participants in childhood. Yet some of the participants of our study adapted well to being outsiders. Even as children, they accepted the fact, or at least rationalized, that they marched to different drummers.

Kids thought I was odd. I thought that they had a lot to learn. I just liked doing the things I liked to do like having a telescope and collecting fossils.

> When I was very young I hung around with kids who'd go out looking for fossils. In high school I chased women, drank beer, and got thrown in jail, which was normal for my group of baby boomers.

> Basically I am a loner. I was not unhappy about that. I loved wandering around alone as a kid.

Clearly, many students with learning disabilities do have assorted problems with social competence. However, the degree of social competence or incompetence may change from setting to setting or from observer to observer. For example, although general classroom teachers in one study rated the social behavior of students with learning disabilities lower than that of their nondisabled peers, special education teachers did not see the students with learning disabilities as being different (Morrison, 1985). Furthermore, there is no definitive etiology for social skill problems. Social difficulties may result from a primary causal relation to learning disabilities (e.g., a breakdown in the processing of social information), a secondary causal relation (e.g., frustration, anger, etc.), a perception based more on preconception than actual behavior, a coincidence, or, in most cases, some combination of these and perhaps other variables. Bryan (1989) speculated that because of social skill deficits, the way they perceive themselves, or the way others perceive them, children with learning disabilities are often emotionally and socially vulnerable. Many of the adults in our study could relate to feelings of vulnerability growing up with learning disabilities.

Even though many of the participants felt that they were different, for better or for worse, others recalled fitting in comfortably with their peers. They had academic difficulties, but apparently not social difficulties. These perceptions are consistent with much of the research investigating social status; some studies that have reported social difficulties in children with learning disabilities have also indicated that half or more of children with learning disabilities have at least average peer status (Conderman, 1995; Wiener, Harris, & Shirer, 1990). Social difficulties may not constitute a defining characteristic of students with learning disabilities. Haager and Vaughn (1995) concluded that students with learning disabilities tend to have problems with some, but not all, aspects of social competence. Moreover, some students with learning disabilities do not experience any noticeable social difficulties.

One participant felt that her social abilities were a tremendous and unique asset: "I could always get along with all sorts of different people. In high school I never ran with a clique, yet I could sit with the real popular folks or with the unpopular. It didn't make much difference to me." Rourke (1989) has suggested that the population of individuals with learning disabilities consists of several subgroups, including one that may be characterized as having wonderfully adept social skills. In many cases, a gregarious, likable personality serves to compensate effectively for educational shortcomings. "My personality and bullshit could get me through. . . . That was very deliberate, premeditated from the earliest time on" was not an uncommon self-analysis of our participants. Another participant remarked, "I guess I tended to be the leader or the instigator of my group of friends. So, in that way, maybe there was some relationship to success. . . . My personality has probably contributed to my success. . . . What makes me different is that I've always felt good about myself, which has made success much easier. I never felt that I couldn't do things. I never got beat down in school."

Another key to maintaining social–emotional intactness was discovering and nurturing strengths and abilities. Even as children, a number of our participants developed ways to compensate for their academic shortcomings. They did not necessarily find ways to become successful students. Instead, they explored other areas where they could feel successful.

> I knew something was wrong, though I didn't know exactly what. I started to develop the idea in my mind that I needed to find what I could do well and then stick to it. As a child when told to do things, I did what I could very well, and things that I couldn't do, I sought help for in order to get them done properly.

> When I was 14, the minute my father was in the drive on Fridays I was washing and polishing his car, and he'd say, "Good job." When cutting grass I'd always go one step beyond what I was asked to do. If they'd say, "Do the lawn," I'd also cut the shrubbery just for the three seconds it would take someone to say, "That's the greatest job I've ever seen."

All in the Family

Overall, the participants in our study grew up in supportive and nurturing families. Many attribute much of their success to this kind of environment. One participant recalled, "My mother never gave up on me. She would never ask how many I got right on the test, only how many I had finished. . . . She explained that it never hurt to keep trying. She just refused to believe those people who called me a dummy or retard." In the world of school where acceptance was often conditional and based on doing what is inherently difficult for children with learning disabilities, unconditional acceptance at home took on extraordinary significance.

Yet some of our participants did struggle to be accepted by their teachers, friends, and families, particularly by their fathers. "My dad wrote me off," concluded one participant who remembered being called "the retarded son." Often they had to compete with siblings who did well in school. "I was always at odds with [my sister]. She was the brainy one who worked hard and got all A's. I hated that because I got bad grades."

Parents frequently report behavior problems in their children with learning disabilities (Haager & Vaughn, 1995), but perhaps some of those problems evolve from parental expectations of appropriate behavior. Many of our participants recalled unrelenting criticism, unreachable standards, and unending disappointment. "As I would speak to my mother she used to correct my grammar and I wouldn't want to talk anymore. She was very harsh and perfectionistic in some ways, mostly about grammar."

The emotional toll remains heavy for many of the adults in our study. As one participant revealed, childhood memories of being criticized for having learning disabilities continue to cause pain in adulthood: "My father said, 'P, that isn't what it says. If you can't read it right don't read it.' I'm 50 years old, and I was 16 when it happened, and I've never forgotten that. What message does your father tell you when he tells you that kind of stuff?" Another participant, a successful psychotherapist, remembered bluntly that her family gave her only "negative motivation. They told me they never expected me to succeed. They weren't a support at all. I was the abused child. I was the one who was a disappointment. I wasn't succeeding in school. . . . If I hadn't had the learning disability, I question whether I would have been the abused one. I think it made me, in their eyes, the failed one and, therefore, the vulnerable one."

One participant finally demanded unconditional acceptance from his father. "Especially through high school, my dad was always correcting me: 'You misspelled this' or 'that's not the proper usage of that word.' 'You didn't pronounce this correct. Can't you hear the s?'. . . . I still to this day remember I wrote my father a letter when I was in college and he corrected it. He sent it back and the whole thing was red so I wrote this little postcard that said, 'Dear Dad—Accept me as I am or not at all.—Your Son.' For about the three next consecutive days I'd send a postcard, 'Hi.—Your Son.' Finally I got this letter that said, 'OK, I accept you as you are.'" This person's persistence in his efforts to gain acceptance most likely reflects the determination that led to his success. Yet we can also imagine the emotional pain that must have precipitated such a need.

A select few of the participants did not share negative memories of growing up with learning disabilities. Childhood provided an optimal mix of support systems, or favorable social ecologies as we call them in this book. Learning problems were identified early and effective interventions followed. A highly successful banker recollected a childhood largely unintruded by learning disabilities:

I was in second or third grade at a private school in Boston when the headmistress told my mother that she would have to take me out of the school because I was incapable of keeping up. I can look back on that without a moment's pain because my mother let me know that I was plenty smart and that the headmistress was nuts. . . . I was lucky because way back in the 40s no one knew much about LD. I went through a course for a year and a half to learn my way around it and it took! From that point forward, I never had any problems in school. I did very well in boarding school which is my earliest memory of doing good and succeeding. I got good marks and was on the student council and football team. I was captain of the tennis team and on the wrestling team.

I had an unbelievable mother. She made me believe that I could do anything, and I don't know how she did that. . . . She was supportive and never made me feel inadequate. Dyslexia was never considered a defeat by me. I really cannot remember anything in my life that represents a defeat, which is pretty damn fortunate.

A professor of finance and real estate remembered a childhood that worked for him because of a set of factors. Some of those factors would not seem to constitute typical ingredients for success, but the combination worked for him. "Why did I succeed and so many others didn't? I think probably a combination of things. The loving concern of my parents when I was little; they didn't take the advice of people and just lock me away. Some very special teachers that found something that I could do well and were willing to recognize me for that. I think also the timing, the timing of the moves. We moved from one school to another. The fact that I could leave things behind and start over and nobody knew."

It is possible to grow up happily with learning disabilities, but it was unusual for adults in our study to describe their childhood as happy. In addition to favorable social ecologies in childhood, other factors had to align into an optimal confluence. Many parents of our participants were unquestionably supportive. They sought diagnosis and treatment, encouraged their children continually, and provided a multitude of opportunities to experience success. Nonetheless, these efforts were not enough to ensure a childhood development unruffled by learning problems.

Back to the Future

Many of the adults in our study clearly feel better about themselves today than they did as children. On the one hand, it is encouraging that adulthood can provide more satisfaction for individuals with learning disabilities. Other research has given credence to this phenomenon. For example, Spekman, Herman, and Vogel (1993) suggest that getting beyond the academic demands of the school environment often has a positive effect on persons with learning disabilities.

Most of the individuals in our study would certainly agree. It is also evident that many of these adults carry a great deal of emotional baggage from some very troubling experiences in childhood. We cannot dismiss the concerns of growing up with learning disabilities simply because things might get better later in life. And once again we must remember that our participants are a special group, the ones who have exceeded expectations and reached lofty levels of success. They are characterized, at least partially, by tremendous resilience, a determination that inspired them not to give up in spite of all the messages that they should. Yet, as children, so many of them believed they were dumb, stupid, or lazy—and quite a few continue to fight the demons of that self-perception today. As interviewers, we were struck by the degree of anger expressed by many of our participants, especially about their schooling. We sensed that these feelings continued to shape the emotional architecture of their adult lives. It was not unusual for these adults to refer to being in a process of "healing" from their childhood wounds.

What's wrong with this picture? Think about some of the implications. If the "best and the brightest" can be convinced that they are "dumb and dumber," what has happened to so many other individuals with learning disabilities? The literature suggests that social–emotional problems in childhood result in negative outcomes for individuals with learning disabilities (Bender & Wall, 1994). We must ask how many other adults with learning disabilities have bought into the negative messages of childhood and are now resigned to lives lacking in satisfaction and a sense of self-worth. How many capable persons who happen to learn differently have been permanently scarred by feelings of incompetence, incompleteness, or downright worthlessness? Would these outcomes be different if childhood had been more positive?

What Can We Do?

Find Out What's Going On

As we consider children with learning disabilities today, we may have some reason for cautious optimism. Self-esteem tended to deteriorate when the participant did not know what was wrong. "I knew that something was wrong, I knew that something was causing the problem, but I didn't know what it was or that other kids were having problems," related one participant. It was the not knowing that led to feelings of aloneness, rejection, insecurity, and self-doubt. From the retrospective of adulthood, some of our participants resented the lack of concern or unwillingness of parents and/or teachers to investigate why they were having such difficulties.

On the other hand, most of our participants felt relieved when they learned that they had an identifiable disorder. A weight had been lifted from their shoulders, a metaphor that we heard a number of times in our interviews. They were no longer dumb or stubborn; they simply had a different learning style. Most importantly, it was not their fault:

> I was called dyslexic in high school. It helped me because it sort of pinpointed it for me and gave me something to slough it off on rather than to blame myself. Though it was hard to reconcile, it was better to know than not to know.

> It [diagnosis of dyslexia] was really wonderful because there was something to hold onto. I could say this was what was wrong with me. . . . I didn't think I was stupid or dumb anymore. Rather than being global, it isolated one part of my ability and disability. Previously I thought God was punishing me for something.

> We can explain all the history of this person with one word. What a difference a little label made.

> Initially, just wonderful relief. This is what was going on all those years and no one recognized it. "I bet you're just as bright as your brothers." It made me feel real good. . . . To have a really thorough evaluation to understand your disabilities, it really tells us how to function and directs us a lot.

> Relief that I wasn't stupid but had a mechanical problem. It made me feel better.

Thus, the experiences of the individuals in our study indicate the potential benefits of early assessment, diagnosis, and identification. These formal procedures represent merely the beginning of a lengthy process of self-actualization. The results of the evaluation provide an initial opportunity to help the student understand his or her strengths and weaknesses, learning style, and needs. Both professionals and parents need to take part in these discussions. The dialogue not only increases understanding but may lay the foundation for building positive self-esteem. The focus should not be placed so much on what is wrong as what is right. This early discovery period offers a chance to acknowledge that the child is OK.

Question the Status Quo

Many of our participants were averse to schooling. One reason was the unrelenting emphasis on the kinds of academic demands intrinsically sabotaged by learning disabilities. Having learning disabilities should not act as an excuse for eschewing basic academics. Nevertheless, a narrow focus on academics and basic skill remediation is unlikely to serve as the best practice for educating children with learning disabilities. In Chapter 10, we use the experiences of these adults to offer specific suggestions for new approaches to curriculum and instruction. Simply from listening to these remembrances of what it feels like growing up with learning disabilities, the reader may already concur with Spekman et al. (1993) that focusing on "adaptive behavior and coping, authentic life preparation, and family, community, and other aspects of each individual's social context" (p. 63) would greatly enhance the educational process.

Support, Support, Support

Perhaps the most "alterable" variable of childhood is the way that parents, teachers, and significant others respond to children with learning disabilities. As we have related, some of the adults perceived their childhood as being affected, but not overwhelmed, by learning disabilities. They had optimal social ecologies. We might be naive to think that all children can be afforded such environments. But many of our participants who did experience rocky moments growing up with learning disabilities found they were able to survive, persevere, and move on because they had some kind of significant support. Some of our participants specifically identified their parents as sources of support:

> The motivation factor came from my mother who would never let me quit. I would have quit if she hadn't been there to keep me going.

> My dad was very influential. He challenged me and made me responsible. He saw my talents at a young age and because I was a girl, I had a lot of responsibilities. I felt I was put into a lot of situations earlier in life as being the one responsible or the rescuer.

> He [psychologist] said that if my mother supported me and let me handle things in my own way, I would find a way to do it. I remember this clearly. [Participant was in first grade.] This was helpful to know that. He put this in a report. Whenever I went from school to school, teachers knew I was not screwed up. . . . My mother was influential because she said I could do it if I wanted to.

> It goes back to my family environment. My parents really had a strong belief in self-determination and that every decision that was to be made was my decision. Every decision that was made was the right decision and there wasn't a wrong decision. What had to be done was a commitment to a decision.

> During high school and college my parents were very supportive. They never let me fail or give up. They supplied a disciplined and positive atmosphere.

They never compared me to my brothers who did much better in school. They truly believed that I could do it and instilled this belief in me.

I feel that I'm very lucky because at a young part of my life it made me appreciate hard work. I was able to get over it because I had a lot of support. . . . With any disability if you don't have the right support, I think it's tough. You can go so many ways.

I always had a great deal of confidence and I attribute most of that to my family.

A lot of people have come my way. Teachers and family members have provided wonderful support.

The preceding quotations implicitly suggest some ways that parents may be able to make life a little easier for their children with learning disabilities. Recently, a mother of a son with learning disabilities published a very personal parental perspective on growing up dyslexic in a journal usually devoted to academic research, which, nevertheless, realizes the importance of multiple vantage points. From her experience, she concluded that her successful parenting efforts took the form of three strategies:

1. Remove the negatives and stress-makers;

2. Break every piece of information into its smallest components;

3. Find something at which he could really excel. (Donawa, 1995, p. 325)

We would imagine that many of our participants would agree completely with this approach. In Chapter 12, we offer advice from our participants to parents of children with learning disabilities.

Other participants cited the influence of teachers. In some cases, they could remember a host of teachers who supported, inspired, and demanded, but demanded fairly. The reminiscence of a successful psychologist is typical: "There was that sixth grade teacher who was wonderful. He was very humanistic. You felt good. He was lovely. He gave untimed tests and he really encouraged people to succeed and he was great."

We cannot underestimate the importance of teachers on the overall development of children with learning disabilities. A particularly vivid reminder of both the positive and negative impact of teachers comes from the following comparison: "In grade seven there was an English teacher who really took an interest in me. She'd ask me to go in after school and it wasn't a punishment; it was a treat. We'd discuss books and she really made things come alive. That same year I had a gym teacher who did the complete opposite. He would torture me in gym and humiliate me in front of the class because I was a spastic.

My parents had insisted on oral exams, and he'd get up in front of the class and say that, 'We have a dummy in our class who can't read or write. Who wants to help him?'"

A New Appreciation of Learning Disabilities

How does it feel to grow up with learning disabilities? Obviously, the experience was different and unique for each participant in our study. As the quotations throughout this chapter have illustrated, our participants faced the good, the bad, and the ugly. Although a true heterogeneity of experiences is represented, some generalizations inexorably bubble to the surface. Some of the participants had relatively happy childhoods; the majority did not.

For many years, the research on learning disabilities emphasized primarily academic and educational deficits. More recently, social–emotional issues have assumed increasing prominence. The histories of our participants confirm the importance of addressing this concern. Learning disabilities are a legitimate disabling condition that can impair more than simply one area of functioning. Interventions that do not take the social and emotional implications of learning disabilities into account may fall alarmingly short of therapeutic intentions. On the other hand, efforts to meet the needs of the whole child may lay a foundation of emotional strength and security. Armed with a sense of self-worth and dignity, of social competence and acceptability, children with learning disabilities just may grow up into adults who exceed expectations.

Part II

Creating a Context

What It Means To Have Learning Disabilities: The Insider's Perspective

Chapter 4

No Simple Answers

What are learning disabilities? If this book were about people who are deaf or blind or have physical or mental disabilities, such a question would hardly be necessary. Most of us probably have a shared understanding of visible disabilities. Even when conventional wisdom does not adequately describe all essential constructs of a given disability, a uniform and consistent definition is usually present to clear up any confusion. But when we try to describe learning disabilities, confusion continues to reign about the specific meaning.

In this chapter, we do not intend to resolve the controversy about defining learning disabilities. The successful adults in this book have widely varying ideas, insights, and perspectives about the meaning of learning disabilities. This divergence should not be surprising, because the impact of learning disabilities tends to differ with each individual. Effects range on a continuum from mild to severe. For some, learning disabilities are a minor inconvenience; for others, an omnipresent and sometimes overwhelming catastrophe. Learning disabilities affect different areas of functioning in different individuals. Moreover, what we call learning disabilities may be a "general term that refers to a heterogeneous group of disorders" (National Joint Committee on Learning Disabilities [NJCLD], 1989, p. 1). Consequently, one person may characterize his or her learning disabilities as making reversals when reading, another may be concerned with problems with expressive language, another may describe difficulties with short- or long-term memory, attention or concentration, and so on. The adults in this book offer a plethora of perspectives, sometimes at odds with one another. We will not find a firm sense of consensus. This is not surprising. We never expected to find one. Instead, we will begin to meet individuals with unique viewpoints. And in listening to how they describe learning disabilities, we will begin to know them.

A discussion of issues surrounding definitions of learning disabilities provides a context for the perspectives of the adults in this book. In spite of their individual differences, these successful adults share much common ground with the theoretical orientations of the fields that take an interest in learning disabilities. In fact, both the convergence and divergence of these individual perspectives with existing definitions may lead to a more holistic understanding of what is meant by the moniker "an adult with learning disabilities."

Although the term *learning disabilities* is relatively recent, it has become part of our common vocabulary. Yet even the most eminent authorities do not agree on its exact meaning. Reaching a consensual understanding poses even more difficulties when the focus is on adults. How has this relatively new area in the field burst forth unto the national consciousness only to find itself grappling with an identity crisis?

Part of the identity crisis stems from the diversity and, at times, the divisiveness of the traditionally distinct disciplines that took interest in problems with learning. A developmental perspective may characterize learning disabilities statistically as two or more standard deviations below the mean for normal learning behavior (assuming we can operationalize this construct). As a cultural and social phenomenon, the term *learning disabilities* fulfills cultural and social needs, not the least of which is the need for a sanctioned label that delineates us from them, that is, people who are different. In another sense, the ecological perspective denotes a "lack of fit" between the person who is disabled and his or her environment. At the same time, our individual needs may create unique and personal perspectives about learning disabilities that do not necessarily conform to conventional wisdom or professional judgment.

The fields of medicine, biology, psychology, sociology, anthropology, education, language, and even politics have all offered differing perspectives about the nature of learning disabilities. Whether learning disabilities are a developmental, educational, psychological, sociopolitical, cultural, or individual construct depends on one's theoretical orientation (or "whom you talk to"). To make matters more confusing, disagreement about theory and practice are endemic within many of these fields. The study of human behavior and its theoretical constructs, such as learning disabilities, is a low-consensus endeavor (Reynolds, 1986).

The conceptual fuzziness of the very concept of learning disabilities, often referred to as the "hidden disability," has played a significant role in sustaining this confusion. The hidden nature evolves not only from the lack of visible and direct characteristics—after all, we can only infer learning difficulties through performance-oriented tasks—but also from the presumption that the learning problems arise from some undetectable brain dysfunction. As a result, attempts to characterize, identify, and understand learning disabilities generally have met with only limited success or acceptance. A brief history of the field provides a measure of insight about the ongoing struggle to define the term adequately.

The Conceptual Evolution

The first researchers to study phenomena now associated with learning disabilities shared a common interest in discovering links between brain functioning and human behavior and consequently developing commensurate theoretical constructs. In 1802, Franz Joseph Gall, a Viennese physician who had worked with adults with language problems, published perhaps the first study of what is now termed *aphasia*, a language disorder with characteristics similar to some learning disabilities. As a practitioner of phrenology, Gall tried to locate the area of the brain related to language disorders by feeling for bumps on the skull. Phrenology ultimately garnered as much scientific acceptance as the modern-day "psychic hot line," but Gall's efforts have assumed their rightful place as a significant contribution to scientific understanding, not because of the method or results, but because of the direction of his research. Yet as recently as 1987, some "diagnosticians" practicing avant-garde methods were identifying students with learning disabilities by sticking their thumbs near the eye socket and feeling for certain orbital bone patterns.

Theoretical differences regarding behaviors now associated with learning disabilities arose in the early twentieth century. Describing poor adult readers who were not educationally deprived, Scottish physician James Hinshelwood coined the term *word blindness* in 1917. The theory that visual language processing difficulties lie at the root of reading difficulties inspired researchers in the 1930s such as Samuel Orton who developed specific remedial approaches for dyslexia, the reading disorder usually included under the present rubric of learning disabilities. In contrast to a focus on reading and visual perceptual processing, Goldstein's work, *The Organism* (1939), describes behaviors of impulsivity, distractibility, and hyperactivity in brain-injured World War I soldiers. Goldstein's work greatly influenced two of his disciples, Alfred Strauss and Heinz Werner. Strauss and Werner noted the same types of characteristics in some children having significant difficulties in school, observed that these behaviors could account for learning difficulties, and hypothesized that the behaviors resulted from some kind of brain injury. In 1947, with the help of Laura Lehtinen, Strauss and Werner offered a definition for this type of child, which, after much controversy in professional circles, later became known as *Strauss syndrome:*

> A brain injured child is a child who before, during, or after birth has received an injury to or suffered an infection of the brain. As a result of such organic impairment, defects of the neuromotor system may be present or absent; however, such a child may show disturbances in perception, thinking, and emotional behavior, either separately or in combination. These disturbances can

be demonstrated by specific tests. These disturbances prevent or impede a normal learning process. (Strauss and Werner, 1947, p. 4)

By the 1950s, researchers in a number of fields began to turn their attention to two relatively distinct phenomena, dyslexia and brain injury, in children exclusively. Over time, however, a theoretical, if tenuous, relationship between dyslexia and brain injury developed. While dyslexia has remained an acceptable term and theoretical orientation for many people over a number of years, the use of "brain injury" engendered debate and dissatisfaction. Not only did the term reflect an unsubstantiated theoretical orientation, it seemed offensive to label students who were simply having difficulty in school as "brain injured." Different theoretical orientations offered alternative terms, which included minimal brain injury, brain dysfunction, minimal brain dysfunction, perceptual handicap, educational handicap, developmental aphasia, and slow learner. Nomenclature from other disabilities, such as autism and mental retardation, was also used.

With such a complex mix of theory, practice, and terminology, the need clearly existed to negotiate a degree of consensus. Parent groups actively vocalized their desire for professionals to offer an understandable explanation and acceptable term for their children who were having trouble learning. In 1963 at the Conference for the Perceptually Handicapped Child, largely attended by parents, Samuel Kirk delivered an historic address that began to unite the diverse perspectives:

> Recently, I have used the term learning disabled to describe a group of children who have disorders in development of language, speech, reading, and associated communication skills needed in social interaction. In this group I do not include blindness or deafness, because we have methods of managing and training the deaf and blind. I also exclude from this group children who have generalized mental retardation. (Kirk, 1963, p. 2)

In formulating the term *learning disabilities*, Kirk did refer to possible cerebral dysfunction but clearly focused on a developmental language deficit that did not include Strauss syndrome characteristics. Instead, the identity of learning disabilities was largely a matter of what it was not. Determining the balance of what to include and what to exclude in the definition continues to be a perplexing problem. Kirk also presented a perspective that was more educational than medical, with a concern toward "effective methods of diagnosis, management, and training of the children" (p. 2). In addition, he focused the field on the school-age years and on children and youth. For the time being, adults with learning disabilities were not part of the learning disabilities agenda.

Nevertheless, proponents of a central nervous system function etiology developed increasing support for this orientation. The construct of a deficit in "psychological processing" provided a broad and logical descriptor of learning problems, tacitly linked brain function and human behavior, and, in essence, included the theoretical orientation and characteristics of Strauss syndrome. In 1968, under Kirk's guidance, the National Advisory Committee on Handicapped Children (NACHC) revised and expanded Kirk's original concept to accommodate a broader orientation:

> Children with specific learning disabilities exhibit a disorder in one or more of the basic psychological processes involved in understanding or using spoken or written languages. These may be manifested in disorders of listening, thinking, talking, reading, writing, spelling, or arithmetic. They include conditions which have been referred to as perceptual handicaps, brain injury, minimal brain dysfunction, dyslexia, developmental aphasia, etc. They do not include learning problems which are due primarily to visual, hearing, or motor handicaps, to mental retardation, emotional disturbance, or to environmental disadvantage. (Kirk, 1968)

In reflecting Kirk's language orientation, the NACHC definition incorporated the construct of dyslexia. It increased both the inclusionary and exclusionary criteria, clearly demarcating learning disabilities as a unique condition while remaining so broad as to allow various interpretations about the essential nature of the condition. Perhaps this definition did the best job of satisfying many diverse constituencies. The framers of P.L. 94-142, the Education for All Handicapped Children Act of 1975, used this definition to act as the guideline for conceptualizing learning disabilities within the educational system and, to a large extent, within society at large.

Federal legislation may have attempted to end the debate about definitions by obligating the public education system to adopt this particular perspective. In spite of this new doctrine of learning disabilities, numerous professionals from a range of fields continued to grapple with developing more satisfactory definitions. Cruickshank (1975) felt that an adequate definition should incorporate perceptual processing deficits as a central construct. Other positions were proffered over the years. In 1987, a group of researchers contended that social skills deficits belonged in a comprehensive definition of learning disabilities (Interagency Committee on Learning Disabilities, 1987).

The federal definition of P.L. 94-142 did not expressly address the issue of intelligence (only obliquely in the exclusion of mental retardation). However, a separate set of regulations constitutes what is considered to be an operational and second part of the federal definition (Lerner, 1993). The regulation states that a student has a specific learning disability if (a) the student does not achieve at the proper age and ability levels in one or more of several specific areas when provided with appropriate learning experiences, and (b) has a severe discrepancy between achievement and intellectual ability in one or more of seven areas: oral expression, listening comprehension, written expression, basic reading skill, reading comprehension, mathematics calculation, and mathematics reasoning (U.S. Office of Education, December 29, 1977). Consequently, identification procedures used by most states employ the criterion of average or above average intelligence as requisite for the existence of learning disabilities. This practice has led to a continuing argument surrounding whether IQ testing should be used as part of the operational construct of learning disabilities. A number of researchers have questioned whether the presence of learning disabilities may adversely affect *performance* on IQ tests, potentially precluding identification based on these regulations (c.f., Siegel, 1989).

Advocates for the use of IQ testing have cited historical, social, political, and practical reasons for this practice (Wong, 1989). This line of reasoning is perhaps emblematic of the current identity crisis of learning disabilities. While educational, psychological, and medical researchers have sought to develop scientifically supported theoretical constructs of learning disabilities, the term has fulfilled other agendas, most notably by making a substantial impact on educational policy. Definitions can be chosen or manipulated to increase or decrease the number of students likely to be identified. From 1978–79 to 1986–87, the number of students with learning disabilities increased from 3.9 to 4.4 million, more than all other categories combined (National Center for Educational Statistics, 1988). In less than 30 years, the learning disabilities program has become the largest single disability program in the United States with a growth rate unparalleled in any other area of special education (U.S. Department of Education, 1989). Particular historical, social, political, and practical circumstances have all played roles in determining the use or development of a given definition. Definitions of learning disabilities do more than conceptualize learning disabilities; they may determine identification, placement, and services. Moreover, the issue of defining learning disabilities has had a profound and personal impact on the lives of persons with learning disabilities.

What are the implications of having diverse definitions of learning disabilities? On the one hand, a number of researchers support this situation. Reynolds (1986) has suggested that a continuing discussion on definitions is largely productive and perhaps necessary to prevent the field from growing stagnant. Lerner (1993) contends that because learning disabilities, as a construct, do not represent a single condition, a single definition may not adequately capture the inherent heterogeneity of the condition. Further, the various professionals, populations, age levels, and degrees of severity require different definitions in order to pursue various agendas.

In contrast to these justifications, Silver (1988) has warned that the lack of a uniform definition limits the value of epidemological, clinical, basic, and educational research. In practice, the multiple and sometimes conflicting meanings of learning disabilities may result in alarming consequences. Because professionals who are empowered to diagnose and label students disagree about what does and does not constitute a learning disability, they frequently circumvent official identification criteria, which has contributed to the perception of learning disabilities as a "wastebasket" term or "catchall" for all types of problems (Smith, Osborne, Crim, & Rhu, 1986). While allowing for the heterogeneity of learning disabilities, many professionals express a need for a consensual definition that is broad enough to include a range of characteristics common to persons with learning disabilities, yet specific enough to validate learning disabilities as a defensible construct.

Finding Common Ground

As we enter the latter part of the 1990s, on what issues do we agree and not agree concerning a definition of learning disabilities? Hallahan and Kauffman (1994) assert that two definitions are the most popular. The federal definition is the most commonly accepted. In addition, the definition formulated by the NJCLD has received widespread attention and acceptance. This definition states:

> Learning disabilities is a general term that refers to a heterogeneous group of disorders manifested by significant difficulties in the acquisition and use of listening, speaking, reading, writing, reasoning, or mathematical abilities. These disorders are presumed to be due to central nervous system dysfunction, and may occur across the lifespan.
>
> Problems in self-regulatory behaviors, social perception and social interaction may exist with learning disabilities but do not by themselves constitute a learning disability.
>
> Although learning disabilities may occur concomitantly with other handicapping conditions (for example, sensory impairment, mental retardation, serious emotional disturbance) or with extrinsic influences (such as cultural differences, insufficient or inappropriate instruction), they are not the result of those conditions or influences. (NJCLD, 1989, p. 1)

Those who crafted this definition believe that it offers several distinct advantages over the federal definition (Hammill, 1990): (a) It does not refer exclusively to children but recognizes that learning disabilities occur across the life span; (b) it deletes the term *basic psychological processes* that, in spite of a legitimate intention to delineate the intrinsic nature of learning disabilities, became a source of confusion and led to much criticism as the basis for dubious "perceptual–motor" training programs; (c) it rectifies the redundancy of listing spelling as a specific disorder by subsuming it under the term *written expression;* (d) it eliminates the confusion inadvertently generated by listing terms formerly associated with learning disabilities (e.g., brain injury); and (e) it recognizes that learning disabilities may exist simultaneously with other disabling conditions or environmental disadvantages. Additionally, the phrase "a general term that refers to a heterogeneous group of disorders" refutes the assumption that people with learning disabilities are a homogeneous group (NJCLD, 1981).

On the other hand, the fact that nine definitions other than the federal definition and the NJCLD definition have achieved some degree of popularity (Hammill, 1990) would appear to indicate a striking degree of disparity. Nevertheless, Hammill (1990) contends that the field is reaching an emerging consensus. Basically, definitions fall into one of two categories. Four of the lesser used definitions focus primarily on disorders in learning or basic psychological processes, often generically referred to as processing difficulties. The majority tend to emphasize specific functional limitations such as language and academic deficits (Hammill, 1990).

Learning Disabilities in Adulthood: New Questions with No Easy Answers

The search for a workable definition becomes even more complex when we try to understand learning disabilities in adulthood. Most definitions of learning disabilities per se tend to focus primarily on educational difficulties. Generally, students are identified as learning disabled if their educational achievement is not commensurate with their presumed abilities. The term describes students who, in the absence of a primary disabling condition, fail to negotiate the demands of the educational system. The most visible practical use of a definition of learning disabilities was (and is) to categorize students who do not fit into other educational categories (Mercer, King-Sears, & Mercer, 1990). Traditionally, only children in the educational system were likely to be diagnosed with learning disabilities. As a result, many persons assumed that learning disabilities simply disappeared as a child grew up. This school-age emphasis and academic skills orientation resulted in a lack of awareness about the adult population and raised a perplexing question: Once the student exited the system, did learning disabilities continue to exist?

By the early 1980s, the post–P.L. 94-142 special educational population included significant numbers of adolescents and young adults. Thus the issues of life span adjustment and adults with learning disabilities had returned as important agenda items. Beginning with the federal initiative of transition from school to work (Will, 1984), the special education system has gradually addressed the issue of what happens to students with learning disabilities when they grow up. The NJCLD formally initiated an awareness of learning disabilities in adulthood with its "Call to Action for Adults with Learning Disabilities" in 1987. This process has included a universal acknowledgment that learning disabilities do persist into adulthood. Deciding how to define learning disabilities in adulthood has proven to be more elusive.

Clearly, many persons with learning disabilities have significant difficulties with one or more areas of adult adjustment. During the school years, the educational manifestations are usually clear. Expectations and outcomes become more multifaceted in adulthood. Learning disabilities can be construed as a syndrome of characteristics having different manifestations at various developmental periods, including adulthood, and within differing environments. The same processing deficits or underlying characteristics that caused problems in school may undermine vocational adjustment, social and emotional functioning, and daily living. According to Smith (1988), "Learning disabilities in adults can be viewed as a psychoeducational phenomenon that can seriously impair vocational and social effectiveness" (p. 52).

In some cases, the effects of learning disabilities become even more debilitating in adulthood. We asked the adults in our study to indicate if characteristics found on the most commonly used definitions of learning disabilities remained stable, got better, or got worse over time. Many rated their specific problems as getting worse rather than better when comparing school-age to adult years (Gerber et al., 1990). Instead of affecting academic grades, persistent problems in adulthood with reading and writing may preclude the activities of reading manuals, writing memos, letters, and reports, and writing and cashing checks (Johnson & Blalock, 1987). Difficulty with math interferes with paying bills, maintaining records, reconciling bank statements, filing income taxes, and handling money (Siegel, 1974), reading graphs and charts, estimating, approximating, predicting, making change, determining the price of sale items, calculating tips, following recipes, using measuring devices (e.g., thermometers and gauges), and setting alarm clocks (Johnson & Blalock, 1987).

When adulthood is viewed from a developmental perspective, manifestations of learning disabilities may be different in different adult developmental stages (Gerber, 1993). Learning disabilities may figure significantly into life stages such as moving away from home, establishing an occupation, selecting a mate, starting a family, beginning a career, parenting, retirement, and so on

(Havighurst, 1972). The degree of impact will depend on a constellation of factors, which are difficult to predict in individual circumstances.

The debate about definitions has been waged largely without regard for adults with learning disabilities. The paucity of research in this area, the dearth of programs designed specifically for adults with learning disabilities, and the relatively recent acknowledgment of the importance of the issue itself have all contributed to the relative lack of concern about defining learning disabilities in adulthood. Exceptions to this oversight include the 1982 National Institute for Handicapped Research (NIHR) conference, which formulated a research agenda about adults with learning disabilities, including the development of a definition (Gerber & Mellard, 1985). Although this conference generated significant momentum in addressing the needs of adults with learning disabilities, it did not fulfill the goal of formulation of an agreed-on definition. The Rehabilitative Services Administration (RSA) has adopted a formal definition, largely adapted from the federal definition, in order to establish eligibility for services. This definition is concerned with employment and vocational functioning, yet it does not really distinguish specific adult characteristics:

> A specific learning disability is a disorder in one or more of the central nervous system processes involved in perceiving, understanding, and/or using concepts through verbal (spoken or written) language or nonverbal means. This disorder manifests itself with a deficit in one or more of the following areas: attending, reasoning, processing, memory, communication, reading, writing, spelling, calculation, coordination, social competence and social maturity. (RSA, 1989, August)

The California Community College system has also attempted to formulate a definition aimed at young adults (Mellard, 1990). While incorporating three components found in most definitions (IQ, processing, and discrepancy), this definition addresses unique adult issues by examining adaptation to adulthood. Most notably, the criterion of a "measured achievement deficit" (p. 79) that includes vocational areas moves beyond the traditional focus of academic or educational difficulties. Moreover, the definition does not preclude success in areas other than the specific deficit.

The manner in which learning disabilities in adulthood are defined has a significant impact on diagnosis and identification practices. The RSA definition clearly grants much latitude in the ways clinicians may choose to diagnose and identify learning disabilities. To receive reasonable accommodations for learning disabilities in college and university courses, in entry-level tests in education and business, in licensure examinations in careers and professions, and in fulfilling certain job requirements, adults must present verification that a learning disability is present. In the absence of a widely used definition for adults with learning disabilities, clinicians must rely on their best judgment.

McCue (1993) recommends the use of a recognized diagnostic system, such as the DSM-III-R. However, the DSM-III-R does not address learning disabilities specifically; instead, clinicians assign the diagnosis of learning disabilities based on interpretation of the diagnostic options of academic skills disorders, developmental language disorders, motor skills disorders, and nonspecific categories of developmental disorders. Three criteria, reflecting both P.L. 94-142 and RSA definitions, act as the foundation for clinical interpretation: exclusionary criteria, ability/achievement discrepancy, and a substantial impact on the individual's ability to function.

Adults with learning disabilities range from being extremely functionally limited to exceptionally functionally capable. Functionally limited adults with learning disabilities are typically unemployed or underemployed, live at home with parents, and have limited social opportunities and less-than-satisfying interpersonal relationships (Reiff & Gerber, 1990). At the other end of the spectrum, the adults in this book (and many like them) have achieved eminence in their chosen professions that would be the envy of anyone, and many have been able to maintain stable and happy marital and family relationships. They typically are satisfied with the quality of their lives.

How do we characterize those adults, perhaps identified as learning disabled in school, who show no signs of being disabled in adult life? A definition emanating from a pathologic model perhaps excludes adults who do not evidence functional limitations. On the other hand, a definition based on a "difference" model where learning disabilities "is viewed as representing an extreme position within the normal range of variation in human information processing strategies" (Aaron, Phillips, & Larsen, 1988, p. 537) incorporates adults who have managed to compensate and become functionally intact. Aaron et al. (1988) remind us that the resolution is largely a matter of personal perspective.

Who Are the Experts?

We have discussed this controversy about definitions as a framework to encourage the reader to appreciate the subjective meaning of the term *learning disabilities*. One method of validating learning disabilities lies in listening to the experiences of persons who wear the label. Formerly, self-appointed representatives of persons with learning disabilities have played the role of decision makers about issues such as definitions, while the persons identified as having learning disabilities were virtually excluded from the process. As we embark on an emerging paradigm shift that focuses less on what professionals can do for persons with learning disabilities and more on what persons with disabilities can do for themselves (Reiff & deFur, 1992), the insider's perspective lends a critical element to the discussion.

Asking adults with learning disabilities to define learning disabilities provides one method of determining the range of characteristics included in the term while offering additional insights about what distinguishes learning disabilities from other conditions. The experiences of adults may help us understand both what learning disabilities are and what they are not. As we interviewed the adults with learning disabilities in this book, we felt more than a little uncomfortable labeling them as handicapped or disabled. Their remarkable accomplishments challenge, at some level, the conventional wisdom about the very meaning of the term *disability*.

The Insider's Perspective

At the end of the lengthy interviews with each of the adults in this book, the interviewer asked the following question: "We have sometimes addressed the issue of your disability in each of the sections, but now I'd like to focus on your learning disabilities specifically. The feelings you share regarding your disability can have a significant impact on others who may feel that they are the only ones who are different. Let's talk a little about your learning disabilities. There are many different definitions of learning disabilities. How would you define learning disabilities?"

As the reader might expect, the responses were varied. Some were expansive; others were laconic. Some offered quite complex explanations; others responded parsimoniously. Some demonstrated a sophisticated knowledge of current research in the field; others admitted to naïveté and a lack of awareness. Yet all the participants who responded to this question had their own definitions of learning disabilities. Of even greater interest, despite the wide array of responses, the definitions essentially mirrored four themes or components from current definitions that we discussed earlier in this chapter. That is, the adults in this study basically conceptualized their own learning disabilities as related to one of the following phenomena: (a) processing difficulties; (b) specific functional limitations; (c) a discrepancy between ability and achievement, sometimes referred to as underachievement determination (Hammill, 1990); or (d) learning disabilities as more of a difference than a disability, a theme that challenges traditional models of pathology.

A Processing Problem

Fifty-seven of the 71 participants offered their own definitions of learning disabilities. More than a quarter of these adults (16) conceptualized their learning disabilities as some kind of processing difficulty. They felt that their brains somehow process information in ways that make it hard to perceive and interpret stimuli. Many of these adults specifically used some version of the term *processing* to describe this condition:

> Any interruption in the learning process that makes it difficult for that person to achieve goals.

> Brain is not programmed to process information like most people's brains are programmed.

> Not a learning disability; it's a processing disability.

> Probably a central nervous system condition that interferes with a person's ability to process information.

> A breakdown in processing.

> Definitely not sensory; interpretation and perception process that is involved.

> An obstacle to processing information in the normal way.

> An inability because of natural causes with a person to accomplish thought processes, speech and language processes, educational processes.

> Inability to process information and utilize it.

> Not mental retardation. Higher IQ, processing problem. You work hard and you fail.

A number of the preceding quotations interweave other concepts found in many current definitions. Some type of central nervous system dysfunction is directly addressed by one participant, and is perhaps alluded to by another's description of "natural causes." We will see similar references, particularly to the term *neurological*, in further definitions. The definitions that stated "definitely not sensory" and "not mental retardation" call to mind the exclusionary component of learning disabilities, that is, defining a learning disability by what it is not. Another response referred to "higher IQ," and another mentioned that learning disabilities make "it difficult to achieve goals." Both these remarks touch on underachievement determination, another component of most definitions.

Clearly, most of these participants perceive their learning disabilities as a problem with processing information. In many ways, this may be the most common everyday explanation to the question, "What are learning disabilities?" It is not unusual in initial class discussions, for example, to try to understand learning disabilities as a phenomenon where, after information enters the brain, something different happens. The result is that the individual does not perceive or understand the information in the same manner as a person without learning disabilities.

This description also recalls the term *basic psychological processes*, a concept that the NJCLD (1989) definition deleted as being confusing and potentially misleading. The use of this idea may reflect the era in which many of these adults became aware of their learning disabilities, when the overwhelmingly predominant definition was the one adopted in P.L. 94-142. On the other hand, we cannot be certain that all of these adults had ever come across a formal definition. Their responses may represent an intuitive and truly personal portrait of the effect of learning disabilities. In this case, we might wish to reconsider summarily dismissing the term *basic psychological processes* from a viable definition and instead concentrate on clarifying and operationalizing it.

Perhaps one way to operationalize the term lies in more descriptive accounts of what a breakdown or difficulty in the basic psychological processes is like. A number of respondents utilized a metaphorical approach to describe their processing styles. While necessarily subjective, these descriptions offer a true insider's perspective and allow us to begin to have a more meaningful and vivid understanding of psychological processes. We are able to look at the world from the eyes (and maybe the brain!) of persons with learning disabilities. Here are some of the ways that these adults tried to convey what happens when they try to process information:

> Physical manifestation of the brain malfunctions and it is associated with behavioral aspects, like dysgraphia, but also the psychological adjustments that one has to make when one knows one can't break stuff out very well.

> Someone who can't concentrate on more than one thing at a time. Difficult time breaking your train of thoughts, analyzing different things.

> Some areas of the brain or the neuropathways are jumbled, missing, in a mess, kind of stretched.

> Blocks that can occur in a person's ability to sense or perceive information and to spit it back out for a combination of neurological reasons, psychological reasons.

> Not able to learn in the conventional way because of a technical problem in their brain that makes them unable to visually or orally remember or both.

The beauty of these definitions lies in relating learning disabilities to feelings or sensations that most of us have experienced and can understand. Certainly we all can recall not being able to break a train of thought; perhaps the distinction of learning disabilities centers on the degree or significance of such a problem. Similarly, we probably have an inkling of what it feels like when our cognitive processes seem "jumbled" or "in a mess"; when there are "blocks" to our thinking; when we "can't break stuff out very well." In other words, the "basic psychological processes" depicted here appear to be concentrating, attending, and remembering, traits long associated with learning disabilities. Further, the reference to "psychological adjustments" reminds us of the social and emotional difficulties that may accompany learning disabilities.

In spite of these more colorful and metaphorical descriptions, we probably will continue to have a limited understanding of psychological processing. As we have seen, professionals have struggled with this concept. Even these successful adults find it difficult to clarify what is going on inside their heads. Perhaps the insider's perspective cannot provide a clear focus on the deeper workings of the human mind. Yet knowing that it is hard for even successful, articulate individuals to explain and describe their learning disabilities may sensitize us to the impact of such a phenomenon on one's psyche.

A Functional Problem

On the other hand, the adults in the study who described learning disabilities in terms of functional limitations present relatively concrete and operational definitions. For them, the impact of learning disabilities is not so much related to an internal thinking/learning process as to the visible effects of learning disabilities on their everyday lives. Many definitions attempt to operationalize learning disabilities by delineating specific deficits in receptive and expressive language, academics (e.g., reading, writing, and math), reasoning, or even in areas of adult functioning such as vocation and social relationships. One factor for the heterogeneous nature of learning disabilities may lie in the multitudinous ways that learning disabilities are manifested. Almost a quarter (23%) of the definitions employed a depiction of a functional limitation to convey the meaning of learning disabilities. Many of the participants focused on problems with reading, writing, and math—perhaps an indication of a strong association with school experiences:

> Specific block in the attainment of academic skills that are not accounted for by mental retardation and tends to be specific to reading, math skills.
>
> Inefficiency in reading.
>
> All kinds of problems like reading and writing.

Difficult time with written word, comprehension, handling numbers . . . time factor . . . slow reader, poor decoding, poor writing.

Person who's been diagnosed as having reading, writing, spelling, auditory, or visual problems.

Very specific like in reading or math when IQ is normal or above.

Individual difficulty in reading and writing in the accepted way.

We should not be surprised that the primary response of these adults recalls academic difficulties. In most cases, students are not referred for an evaluation of possible learning disabilities unless academic concerns exist. Clearly, these adults feel that their learning disabilities were responsible for problems at school. One respondent pointedly recollected the educational setting: "People who have trouble functioning in a classroom, comprehending, trouble staying with it." This statement almost suggests that, regardless of the implications of learning disabilities in adulthood, the most vivid realization of learning disabilities remains in the classroom.

These responses, however, do not limit the effects of learning disabilities to the classroom. These definitions may also remind us that difficulties with reading, writing, and math have not abated in the adult years. Perhaps the deficit areas are less exposed to public scrutiny, but they continue to pose obstacles to some extent in adult life. We are aware that some manifestations of learning disabilities do change in the adaptation to adulthood. As our participants told us at the outset, however, some basic problem areas may remain constant or even worsen (Gerber et al., 1990).

Two adults emphasized a functional limitation specifically in the area of language:

Lose meaning—inability to string words or syllables together.

A language disorder.

These conceptualizations certainly hearken back to Kirk's notion that learning disabilities are, in fact, rooted in difficulties in processing language. We may think of this perspective as a "dyslexia" orientation, which focuses on dysfunction with words (dys lexia). Learning disabilities and dyslexia have long been linked; many students who are classified by the educational system as learning disabled have also been evaluated as dyslexic. But learning disabilities represent a broader constellation of learning problems of which dyslexia may be a subset. A number of the adults in the study did not seem to experience functional limitations in language per se. Instead, they depicted more generic learning problems, sometimes termed *conceptual problems* (Hammill, 1990). Some theorists have even suggested specifying these problems as "dysrationalia." Three responses suggest this more global concept in describing functional limitations:

> Difficulty with learning.
>
> Difficulty in learning in some area. Could be general due to low IQ or specific like dyslexia.
>
> Makes it more difficult for you to understand or do something you should normally be able to do.

These responses may capture the sense of a conceptual disorder. Rather than describing specific ways in which thinking, conceptualizing, or processing information may be different or deficient, these adults focus on the most generic manifestation of conceptual disorders, problems with learning. One participant sees problems with learning as so general as to include "low IQ," a construct normally associated with exclusionary criteria. At the same time, few definitions explicitly address or operationalize the common opinion that persons with learning disabilities have average or above average intelligence. If some individuals with learning disabilities continue to believe that low intelligence affects their learning difficulties, then a need exists for a definition that can definitively resolve this issue.

In many ways, we might expect vocational or social difficulties to be a focus of functional limitations for adults with learning disabilities. After all, these are perhaps the two areas in adulthood where learning disabilities are likely to have the greatest impact. However, the make-up of this particular group of adults with learning disabilities accounts for lack of attention to these areas. Due to the very nature of our study, the adults who spoke with us were uniformly successful in their careers, and most had satisfying social interactions. Rather than acting as a lightning rod for the difficulties of learning disabilities, their careers have provided the venue where learning disabilities have not sabotaged their goals and aspirations. In this sense, they are not typical of all adults with learning disabilities, many of whom struggle to find vocational and social satisfaction. On the other hand, these adults have made it abundantly clear that problems in areas such as reading, writing, math, and so on have persisted in adulthood. We would suspect that at least some of these shortcomings must have had some functional impact on their careers. Apparently, these adults have learned to cope, compensate, and achieve, perhaps to a point where their limitations do not have any kind of negative bearing on their careers.

A Discrepancy Between Ability and Achievement

Central to many definitions of learning disabilities is the notion of under-achievement, or a discrepancy between ability and achievement. These adults have constructed careers that stand in direct contradiction to this concept. Consequently, most of the responses are not concerned with a discrepancy between ability and achievement. Nevertheless, a surprising number (6) of the participants did perceive themselves as underachievers due to their learning disabilities. They alluded to a discrepancy between expected and actual achievement:

> Prevents one from developing one's potential.
>
> Not being able to do something in the normal manner when the basic ability is there.
>
> Disability doesn't affect your intelligence but affects your ability to perform sometimes as intelligently as you could; can affect a variety of areas, almost anything.
>
> Disability other than the norm, whatever the norm is, that creates a limitation in an individual with restriction to not allow him to achieve to his full potential.
>
> A difficulty, sometimes an inability, to achieve at one's potential.
>
> Smarter than can illustrate to others.

Even within our successful sample of adults with learning disabilities, some obviously feel that learning disabilities have held them back. They do not label themselves as underachievers, quite possibly because the issue is not about a lack of trying. Instead they seem to see learning disabilities as a kind of immutable force: It teases them with possibilities that somehow through diligence and desire they can reach their potential. It may allow them to get close and take a good long look. But ultimately it denies the satisfaction of seeing the journey completed. Ironically, having learning disabilities has made them more cognizant of a potential that seems impossible to reach.

We may question whether these adults truly have been held back. In some cases, the anger and frustration about having learning disabilities became the driving force that propelled them to extraordinary success. They might not have been as motivated to succeed if they did not have learning disabilities. Learning how to deal with learning disabilities provided the foundation for learning how to deal with the challenges of life. Learning disabilities may have actually catalyzed greater resources of determination, persistence, resilience, creativity, and goal orientation. They may not have followed the prescribed route, but they did reach their destination after all.

In spite of this attempt to reconstruct the meaning of perceived under-achievement, for many people, perception is a kind of reality. That is, if these adults perceive that they have not reached their full potential, then there is a reality that learning disabilities have, at the least, caused them to undervalue or even overlook their own accomplishments. If we receive messages, particu-larly during the critical developmental periods of the school-age years, that we are somehow less than adequate, we may come to believe that we are less than-adequate-adults—and no amount of empirical evidence to the contrary can change our minds. A dependence on academic achievement to validate one's potential may severely limit a full realization of strengths and abilities. Defini-tions of learning disabilities in adulthood must determine whether academic deficits are a relevant component of adult functioning and achievement.

One of our participants took a more introspective posture by examining intra-individual differences rather than a discrepancy between aptitude and achievement. This adult saw learning disabilities as making it difficult to suc-ceed in some areas while not affecting others: "Those areas in my life, aca-demic, social, that are quite a bit suppressed in relationship to the other abili-ties and functions in my life." Presumably those other areas include vocation, where this individual has been quite successful. While continuing to reflect a sense of underachievement in some areas, this definition makes it clear that learning disabilities in adulthood do not preclude achievement, a qualifier noticeably absent in most definitions.

A Problem, Yes; A Disability, No

Overall, the adults who associated learning disabilities with underachievement represent a small minority of our sample. More than twice as many took an almost defiant stance by rejecting the notion of disability altogether. For these adults, learning disabilities are nothing more than individual differences:

Can't learn the way everyone else learns.

Anything that gets in the way of the normal process of learning, whatever normal means.

Learning is different. The capacity for learning is the same as normal but the way they learn is different and not normal.

Activities that are harder for you than the normal person.

Different way of learning, having to learn in a different way, an unconventional way.

Problem that you experience in a particular way.

Most of these definitions depict the "difference" as a difficulty. A learning disability "gets in the way," is a "problem," and makes things "difficult." Nevertheless, the term *disability* does not arise. Rejecting the notion of disability should not be surprising. Disability traditionally denotes incapability or a deprivation of mental strength (Morehead & Morehead, 1972). These individuals have convincingly demonstrated that they are neither incapable nor incapacitated. No wonder they find the term irrelevant, insulting, or simply erroneous.

A number of our participants pushed the rejection of the term a little further. While recognizing that learning disabilities do account for individual differences, those differences are not necessarily difficulties. They are neither good nor bad. They are simply differences:

Not a disability as long as you realize that you will have to work a little harder than other people.

Not learning disabled; it's learning different.

Normal variation of learning, of how people go about learning and communicating. Word that should be gotten rid of. Ought to find a new term.

Mind operates differently than the normal. Does not mean that it doesn't work right, just different.

Not only do these adults explicitly refute the notion that they are disabled; one individual presents learning disabilities as "a normal variation of learning" and concludes that the term is misappropriated. This perspective calls to mind the work of Howard Gardner on multiple intelligences. Gardner (1983) contends that at least seven distinct types or variations of intelligence exist. In many cases, the learning disability profile of individual weaknesses and strengths may fit into one of these variations, simply not the most common variations.

Two of our participants did not hesitate to use the term *disability*, but not about themselves. They were victims of someone else's disability:

Not a learning disability, but a teaching disability.

Teaching disability.

At first, we might recoil slightly at the idea of blaming someone else for learning difficulties. But let's try to see the world through the eyes of these adults.

Are they incapable of learning? Yes, they did have significant difficulties learn-ing in the traditional ways. They did not respond well to teaching that, admit-tedly, may have been effective for many of their peers. As adults, however, they discovered that they could learn, and learn well. They may not have depended on the means that most of us use, such as reading, but the knowledge, under-standing, and applications they acquired have proven to be more than ade-quate to meet the demands of the adult world.

To what extent are learning disabilities just a difference in style that becomes a disability because of our lack of understanding about individual learning differ-ences? Poor teaching surely may exacerbate the behaviors that are associated with learning disabilities. Some theorists go further and claim that ineffective teaching may account for up to 90% of students identified with learning disabil-ities (e.g., Engelmann, 1977). Consequently, much of what we call learning dis-abilities could be prevented, if only teachers knew how to respond more effec-tively to diverse learning styles (Hallahan & Kauffman, 1994).

These adults have additional reasons to reject the term. From the school-age years to adulthood, the emphasis on what might constitute a functional limitation changes dramatically. In school, our world of work revolves around academics, the foundation for building skills for successful adult adjustment. In adulthood, the focus obviously changes to success in one's chosen vocation. As we have mentioned before, definitions of learning disabilities in adulthood should incorporate functional areas relevant to adulthood. Conversely, perhaps we should place less emphasis on predominantly school-age issues. While these adults may still have trouble reading, writing, or doing math, those areas have little impact in their day-to-day adult lives. Further, in an area where learning disabilities could have a significant negative impact, their careers, they have achieved beyond (not below) expectations. No wonder some of the adults in our study question the presumptions that have labeled them learning disabled. A definition of learning disabilities that refers to a discrepancy between ability and achievement may simply not fit these adults.

A Conclusion and a Beginning

In this chapter we have provided insights and new perspectives about the issues surrounding definitions of learning disabilities. We believe that the adults in our study lend unique and useful voices to the ongoing discussion. It would be a little naive or simplistic, however, to accept every comment literally. Our participants are not typically professional experts in the field of learning dis-abilities. They simply live their disability every day. Readers familiar with the accepted nomenclature of fields such as education and psychology have undoubtedly noticed simplified, generalized, or incorrect use of some terminology and constructs in the remarks of some of the participants. We should exercise caution in interpreting such comments when the participants may not fully understand the meaning of terms they are using. At the same time, technically inaccurate conceptualizations should not be disdainfully dismissed as ignorant piffle. For example, some of the participants used the term *psychological* loosely or colloquially, probably referring to their general emotional state. Definitions have tended to separate emotional issues as being distinct from learning problems per se. While clinical perspectives may be theoretically justifiable, the insider's perspective suggests that how we learn and how we feel cannot always be distinguished in real life. The experiences of these adults should remind us that learning disabilities often have a global impact on individual persons.

We are also aware that the whole method of this project may raise concerns regarding both the reliability and validity of definitions based on such personal perspectives. We address methodological issues in detail in Chapter 6. The nature of this particular sample obviously plays a critical role in the types of responses we received. Their perceptions surely differ from those of adults with learning disabilities who have not been successful. Yet, in spite of their success, the vast majority of our participants presented a rather striking portrait of the persistence of learning disabilities into adulthood. Thus, achievement does not preclude learning disabilities, and learning disabilities do not preclude achievement. In order to achieve, however, one must recognize, accept, and understand the impact of learning disabilities. Even those that rejected the label or the construct of disability acknowledged that the condition, however it may be defined, has an adult impact.

The voices of successful adults with learning disabilities are essential in gaining an overall understanding of learning disabilities. If the field is to develop a valid conceptualization of learning disabilities in adulthood, then the direct and personal experiences of persons who live with the condition represent the true empirical database. The degree of overlap between the personal responses of our participants and the constructs found in most definitions offers a kind of validation or reality check of current definitions. The divergence of opinions within the sample not only reminds us of the individual nature of learning disabilities but also parallels much of the theoretical dialectic. From the eyes of these adults, we see medical, educational, psychological, social, and political perspectives, often reflective of the professions of the individual respondent. The participants who reject the term convey an iconoclastic perspective, an outlook that also reflects a segment of professional orientations.

On the one hand, the insiders' perspectives are as varied as the persons themselves. Most of us would probably agree that each individual with learning disabilities is unique and, consequently, the construct of learning disabilities is, to some extent, unique to each individual. But as individuals, we do share commonalities, and these successful adults are no exception. In aggregate, the responses and experiences of these individuals can help us to understand the meaning of learning disabilities in adulthood. In closing this chapter, we present our attempt to synthesize these data into an operational definition of learning disabilities in adulthood. We bear in mind that this definition reflects the perspectives of those who have found the road to success. We hope that it may serve as a signpost for those who are struggling with the directions:

> Learning disabilities in adulthood affect each individual uniquely. For some, difficulties lie in only one specific functional area; for others, problems are more global in nature, including social and emotional problems. For many, certain functional areas of adult life are limited compared to other areas. Adults with learning disabilities are of average or above average intelligence, but intelligence oftentimes has no relation to the degree of disability. Learning disabilities persist throughout the lifespan, with some areas improving and others worsening. Specific deficits associated with learning disabilities are real and persistent and may pose significant difficulties in vocation and career. Nevertheless, such deficits do not preclude achievement, and in some cases, may have a positive relationship with achievement. In almost all cases, learning disabilities necessitate alternative approaches to achieve vocational success. (Reiff, Gerber, & Ginsberg, 1993, p. 124)

Outcomes on Employment: What We Know So Far

To place the achievements of the adults with learning disabilities in our study in context, it is important to provide a discussion on employment about all individuals with learning disabilities. We can truly see how far many of our participants have come in spite of their learning disabilities when we consider what we know so far about employment outcomes for persons with learning disabilities. Throughout the literature on employment and learning disabilities, researchers have made numerous attempts to hone in on employment outcomes and declare success or failure. From these data they have offered suggestions and new initiatives in the areas of vocational preparation, training, placement, and policy.

This strategy has given the field some markers to live by. But at the same time a case can be made that outcome studies, while helpful for the field, need to be placed in a conceptual framework that does not separate the population with learning disabilities from the general population or from the entire population of individuals with disabilities themselves.

Similarities can be seen when individual comparisons are made between the three groups. First, the vast majority of the learning disabled population is similar to the general population because they are destined for competitive employment without the help of caseworkers, placement specialists, or job coaches. Second, individuals with learning disabilities, being considered a segment of the population with disabilities, are able to utilize Section 504 of the Rehabilitation Act of 1973 and the Americans with Disabilities Act of 1990 to gain access to employment and ensure a wide variety of rights in the workplace.

Dissimilarities are seen as well, especially when individuals with learning disabilities are compared to the general population. First and foremost are the negative perceptions and misinformation attributed to learning disabilities. In addition, despite existing laws, overt and covert discrimination practices persist in employment settings that affect workers with learning disabilities. Second are concerns from employers about whether persons with learning disabilities can really do the job. Ultimately, "individuals are hired and promoted on the basis of what an employer perceives to be their potential for producing goods and services. Employers want to select the most productive workers from a pool of applicants." (Collignan, 1989, p. 205).

We need to view success and failure in the workplace through the lens of market forces. The data on the employment of individuals with learning disabilities must be judged in relation to time of data collection, geography, demographics, labor supply, school resources, and legislation (Collignan, 1989). Most important, it also needs to be judged for its methodological rigor.

We should view the data from a longitudinal perspective because of the long-term implications of learning disabilities both personally and in the workplace (Gerber et al., 1990). Moreover, the assessment of employment outcomes, whether a person is disabled or nondisabled, is a complex mix of an individual's profile and job market variables (including governmental intervention). With so many variables to consider, we might understandably wonder, "When individuals with learning disabilities find success in the workplace, is the success experience idiosyncratic in nature or is there a pattern of behaviors and variables that clearly explain the reason for vocational adjustment?" To address that question, we present the available data in a manner that provides balance, methodological sensitivity, and a clear understanding of the issues.

Economic and Demographic Trends in the Workplace

The success of individuals with learning disabilities is dependent to a large extent on the larger market forces in the workplace. When the economy is expanding, greater numbers of jobs and more choices for employment are available. Employers are also apt to be more liberal in the way they attain their human resource goals. Conversely, when the economy is contracting, the process of finding a job can be protracted and the chance of being employed diminished. Unfortunately, a visible segment of the learning disabled population is not fluid in those market dynamics. These persons are considered to be structurally unemployed, individuals whose chronic unemployment never gets addressed and who become a permanent drag on attempts to reach the ideal of full employment.

Will (1989) found that two thirds of all persons aged 16 to 64 with disabilities were not working, and of the one third who were, approximately 24% of them were working full time and 10% were working part time. Of the unemployed group, 66% wanted to work. Embedded within those figures is the learning disabled population, but they were not separated out for analysis.

In 1990 the President's Committee on Employment for People with Disabilities reported that, in comparing 1970 and 1988, there was a drop of 8% of people with disabilities employed. Whereas the data were reported in the aggregate, it was reported that there were unacceptably high rates of unemployment and underemployment (people working below their capabilities) in the learning disabled population (Brown, Gerber, & Dowdy, 1990; White, 1992). During that time frame the availability of labor in the 15- to 24-year-old category diminished, which should have created more opportunity. However, the shift from a manufacturing to a service economy and from a labor-intensive to a technology-driven economy diminished the need for workers. Thus the pool of entry-level jobs for people with and without disabilities went down.

On the other hand, an increase in job mobility may lead to greater opportunities in the job market. Will (1989) reported that only 1% of employed people remained in their job for more than 10 years, and they expected to work for more than 10 employers during their working years. Harris (1987) reported that 39% of workers said that they did not intend to have their same job in 5 years, 31% intended to leave their job, and 25% said they did not know what they would be doing in 5 years. All in all, Will (1989) characterized the job market as being noted for job change and mobility rather than permanence. Although job mobility creates opportunities and possibilities, it is not certain whether people with learning disabilities will be able to capitalize on this labor trend. In fact, this trend may be negative for individuals with learning disabilities because of the flexibility needed in all areas of employability from job entry to job advancement.

Post-School Follow-Up Studies: Rate of Employment

Each year large numbers of students with learning disabilities leave school-age programs. In 1990, 2,064,892 students were in learning disabilities programs across the country. This number represented 48.5% of students with disabilities. Of the students with learning disabilities in 1990, 75,000 were 18 years old, 125,000 were 17 years old, and 16,000 were age 16 (U.S. Department of Education, 1991). Today, all of those students are out of school and have completed their transition to the workplace. Moreover, the demographic trend remains steady for the learning disabled population. We can safely assume that well over 100,000 young adults with learning disabilities are attempting to enter the workforce every year. This trend has many implications for transition to employment and long-term employability. Important questions arise such as "Do these students ultimately find work?" and "What is the quality of that work when they find it?"

In studies that track employment rates, mixed results emerge. In reviewing 11 follow-up studies between 1985 and 1990, Wehman (1992) found the average employment rate of persons with learning disabilities to be 70% with a range of 57% to 89%. Six other studies on unemployment of people with learning disabilities averaged 2% with rural localities having a 15% unemployment rate. At the time when these studies were done the national unemployment rate for individuals 18 to 24 years old was 13%.

A study done in the state of New Mexico of former self-contained students with learning disabilities from self-contained classrooms (Haring, Lovett, & Smith, 1990) found a 31% unemployment rate that was more than twice the national youth (16 to 24 years old) unemployment rate of 13.6%. In Ontario, Canada, 80 adults considered to have learning disabilities were studied by Malcolm, Polatajko, and Simons (1990). They found that there were similar employed and unemployed percentages, 38.5% and 34.6%, respectively, with 24.4% of the sample still students. Unemployment figures were markedly higher than in the general population in the area where 4% to 5.5% were unemployed according to the Canada Employment Center. In addition, Sitlington and Frank (1990) in their study of 911 randomly selected students with learning disabilities in Iowa found 77% of graduates were working part or full time with 9% "otherwise meaningfully engaged" (p. 45). The employment rates were similar for individuals who had like severity of disability, but an analysis by gender told a different story. About 15% more males were employed than females. Moreover, males made an average of more than $1 more per hour. This finding caused considerable concern for the investigators because of fewer employment opportunities as well as inequities in pay for females with learning disabilities compared to males with learning disabilities. Nevertheless, both these issues also affect female workers without disabilities compared to their male counterparts.

Bruck (1985) found that the unemployment rate of students with learning disabilities was the same as the control group, which was comprised of siblings. This middle class group of participants held a variety of jobs, and very few were working in unskilled employment. D'Amico's study (1991) on individuals with learning disabilities 1 to 2 years after high school corroborated Bruck's findings. The employment rate for the group with learning disabilities was 58% and the employed group without disabilities was 61%. Interestingly, over a 2-year period (from 1987 to 1989) the employment rate of individuals with learning disabilities rose from 62.7% to 75.8%.

In the studies reviewed there was a significant relationship between the number of years after leaving high school and the rate of employment when participants were followed over longer periods of time. In essence, the older the former student with learning disabilities, the higher the rate of employment. For example, Edgar, Levine, Levine, and Dubney (1988) studied individuals with learning disabilities in Washington State and found an employment rate of 65% after 6 months, but an employment rate of 75% after 2 years. DeBettencourt, Zigmond, and Thornton (1989) found an employment rate of 80% in a rural sample after 1.5 years. Scuccimarra and Speece (1990) found an employment rate of 89% after 5 years. These "positive" findings have not received widespread attention probably because few studies have employed longitudinal and follow-up methodologies.

Most disconcerting was the finding that wages for those with learning disabilities who graduated or received a certificate of completion showed little difference from those who dropped out of school (Peraino, 1992). What clouds the data is the lack of specificity about the job, typically an entry-level labor or service worker position—which brings the issue of underemployment into question. White (1992) in his review of research on post-school adjustment raises the issue after tracking the kinds of jobs listed in the research on learning disabilities and employment. He states:

> Underemployment was also seen to be a problem. Most studies stated that the largest percentage of workers in their samples held low level service, fast food, laborer, production, and helper occupations. . . . In a comparison of an LD sample with a nonlearning disabled sample, White et al. reported that the jobs held by the adults with learning disabilities had significantly less job status than the jobs held by the nonlearning disabled adults. (p. 451)

Follow-Up Studies on Employment Attainment

In SRI International's National Longitudinal Transition Study (Valdes, Williamson, & Wagner, 1990) the population with learning disabilities showed a diversity of employment outcomes during transition. The percentage of youth working for pay after being out of school between 1 and 2 years was 76.6%. (*Note:* All percentages reflect data for individuals with learning disabilities 1 to 2 years beyond high school.) The percentage who were currently unemployed was 23.6%. The average wage was $4.60 per hour (just above the legal minimum wage). Individuals with learning disabilities worked in jobs such as manual labor (27.2%); skilled trade (19.8%); other (17.9%); and waiter, busboy, cook (13.7%). Other jobs that ranged from 9.7% to 2.3% were farm work, sales, cashier, factory work, and child care.

In 1993 SRI International reported subsequent findings on post-school outcome (Wagner, 1993). This study followed former students with learning disabilities longer into their working years. In the general population youths who were out of school less than 2 years were employed 59.1%; youths out of school 3 to 5 years were employed 69.4%. Compare that to youths with disabilities employed at rates of 45.7% and 56.8%, respectively, and youths with learning disabilities at 59.2% and 70.8% respectively. In fact, youths with learning disabilities lead the list of 12 disability categories in less than 2-year and 3- to 5-year employment rates. We should emphasize that the learning disabilities figures are better than those of the general population. Still the untold story in the numbers revolves around such items as pay, job, status, job satisfaction, advancement, and the issue of underemployment.

Other studies' findings shed light on the cited outcomes of the SRI International study. Rogan and Hartman (1990) did a follow-up of the population of adults with learning disabilities that they used for their previous follow-up study (Rogan & Hartman, 1976). In this study the range of ages was from 30 to 50 years old. Employment data were similar to the 1976 study. Seventy-nine percent were employed full time. Twenty-nine percent were in the same or a similar field as in 1976, several had advanced in their jobs, and others had changed their careers after seeking additional training. Seventy-five percent of the college graduates rated their job satisfaction as high. As in 1976, there was still a range of employment. A large number of college graduates held professional and technical positions, but the continuum of employment spanned from managerial to unemployed. A wide diversity of jobs was held by the high school graduate–only group (production machine operator to military to service and custodial to unemployed). The self-contained special education students worked in jobs such as clerical, laborer, and unemployed. Many of those who did not complete high school were employed as clerical workers and drivers. In summing up the employment part of the study, Rogan and Hartman observed:

> The successful ones in this group were judged to be those who had found relatively secure and satisfying occupations, had made a comfortable move into independent living, and had cultivated a variety of interests. Once having found positions they liked and could do well, they tended to remain employed for long periods of time. They are, however, vulnerable to changes in the workplace and limited job opportunities. For two (subjects) the (sheltered) workshop experience concomitant with social work assistance made a transition possible from total dependence on the family to employment and independent living. (p. 101)

In 1994, the Learning Disabilities Association of America's Adult Issues Committee surveyed the adults with learning disabilities who attended their

1994 annual conference. In total 587 people responded. The data revealed that "70 percent had held a job, but only 57 percent were currently employed . . . incomes for 27 percent were below 12,000 dollars [50 percent between 12,000 and 20,000 dollars] and 23 percent earned 20,000 dollars or more. Of the currently unemployed respondents, 25 percent were supported by parents and 11 percent by SSI/SSDI" (p. 3).

Adelman and Vogel (1990) focused on employment attainment and career patterns when they surveyed 36 graduates with learning disabilities from a small Midwestern liberal arts college. The greatest number of graduates went into business, but others held a wide array of jobs such as education, chemistry, computer programming, health services, and performing arts. Adelman and Vogel concluded that even though learning disabilities affected the work of these graduates, they were successful because they developed compensatory strategies. Moreover, their success was commensurate with how well they compensated.

Gerber (1992a, 1994) studied a graduate of a teacher education program (TJ) who had learning disabilities. He followed him every working month through his first 2 years of teaching an elementary-level learning disabilities resource class. His experience was characterized by a series of trials and tribulations in each year. In his first year he succeeded for a number of reasons. He had chosen a teaching job that was fitting to his capabilities and skills, and he developed a professional and personal support system that complemented his efforts. However, he struggled to acclimate himself to a school where change was difficult and to a faculty that was resistant to his advocacy posture. Ultimately, he prevailed because of his desire to succeed and his persistent style in doing his best for his students. He was able to reframe his learning disability (despite ongoing self-doubt) and through that process adjust to the many challenges and issues endemic to his profession. At the end of his first year many of his students were doing well in their regular classes, and more students were being served in his resource room. He had developed a credible program and, for the most part, established his credibility with students, parents, and colleagues.

The following year, which should have been an easier one, became more difficult because of a total change in his teaching situation. He had a larger caseload of students with more severe problems and more difficult behavioral problems (some very severe). His school had a new principal who had a different style from the one the previous year. He had a new special education supervisor who had a hard time accepting TJ's somewhat unconventional style. This set of changes taxed his reframing capabilities and called on a different set of professional and personal supports. In essence, he was starting all over again. His success in year 2 was overshadowed by a constant struggle to master the new challenges of his work.

In the ethnographic study of nine adults (ages 21 to 55) with learning disabilities that we briefly described in Chapter 1, Gerber and Reiff (1991) found a range of employment outcomes, from highly successful to moderately successful to marginal vocational adjustment. The highly successful group had done relatively well in school and higher education despite their learning disability and were working in professional settings. Those participants who were moderately successful were stable in their work life and aspiring to higher levels of vocational achievement. The group who were the least successful had an erratic work history and worked in unskilled jobs. The highly successful group, not surprisingly, had a very good understanding of their learning disability and their strengths and limitations. The middle group showed somewhat of the same profile, but they had not yet received the education or training to move them to higher levels of vocational achievement. They also were younger than the highly successful group and had not yet spent enough time in the workplace to reach high levels of success. The marginally adjusted group lacked a plan for vocational advancement, had not sought significant postsecondary training, and seemed to be overwhelmed by their learning disability and its daily manifestations.

Gerber and Reiff for the first time told the stories of highly successful adults with learning disabilities who beat the odds and became exemplars for coping with a persistent problem that had implications for employment as well as global adult functioning. Most important, the authors made the qualitative case for a diversity of employment outcomes, which was shown quantitatively by the seminal study of Rogan and Hartman (1976) of former Cove School students.

What Are the Data Worth?

Numerous studies on learning disabilities and employment before and after enactment of the Americans with Disabilities Act are available. In total, the data on employment of individuals with learning disabilities are worthwhile because they explain what is happening in the workplace. No doubt the field profits from the findings and observations of investigators from across the country. But to a large extent what we see individually and in the aggregate is only a snapshot of what is really happening. For example, the data from the most comprehensive study yet, the SRI International study, focus on transition and, in part, job entry. The data are quantitative and, while extensive, tell only part of the story (for which the data are designed). Certainly, the national sample makes the data unique and very valuable.

Most studies have a very select focus. They concentrate on individuals from one program, one geographical or metropolitan area, one secondary or postsecondary program. The data focus primarily on the first few years of employment or the transition years. Few studies research employment post-transition. That is what makes the Rogan and Hartman (1990) study, the Gerber and Reiff (1991) qualitative investigation, and other studies like them so very valuable.

Fourqurean (1994) reminds us of the limitations of follow-up studies. After reviewing numerous follow-up studies he concludes that "the data tell relatively little about the specific idiosyncrasies of local communities, each of which may be vastly different from other areas in the United States." Halpern (1990) in his methodological review of studies investigating outcomes of special education students has shared his perspective on studies that are helpful to the field. He comments that "past studies generally have drawn samples to describe the studied population rather than for explanatory purposes. It is important to understand what produces adjustment success." He goes on to say "that broad and diverse outcome measures, rather than employment variables are needed. Such areas as social integration, post secondary education and personal and social adjustment are needed" (p. 25).

Oftentimes the variables measuring employment outcomes are limited within the age range of young adulthood. Infrequently do the data reach beyond the 30s. Certainly focusing on young adulthood and the early years of employment is important in discovering vocational attainment and employment outcomes. But it is important to account for the complexities of adulthood throughout the entire life span to capture its myriad of development issues. Employment as one of the chief tasks of adulthood should be placed in its proper context. We often have to remind ourselves that adulthood is a stage of development that can last for up to 70 years. Of those 70 years, 50 can be spent in the working world. Moreover, at this point we have no longitudinal data that chronicle or explain the trends and issues of a lifetime of work for people with learning disabilities.

One overriding issue that calls some of the recent follow-up data into question is the past effectiveness of the transition movement for students with learning disabilities. Reiff and deFur (1992) have pointed out that the original transition policies were developed with severe and complex disabilities in mind and that learning disabilities–type students would find their way via "the no special services bridge." That observation gives us a particular view of the original data on outcomes after transition. We can hope that the current, more intensified and sophisticated transition efforts on behalf of students with learning disabilities will yield improved intermediate and long-term employment outcomes.

The workplace is a complex setting to study. When mixed with employment issues of individuals with learning disabilities it becomes even more complex. Add in the ongoing changes due to technology and legal issues and the study of employment becomes still more complicated. Studying this area is no easy task, but the effort is worthwhile. What we find out in these studies can make the difference between vocational adjustment and vocational failure, job advancement, and underemployment in business and industry. Chances are that no study will become the quintessential set of information that will guide us in our thoughts and practices. But it is incumbent for us to seek out what works, why it works, and how that knowledge can affect the lives of adults who are currently taking their rightful places in the workplace.

Part III

A Conceptual Framework of Employment Success

What Is Success? Perspectives of Adults with Learning Disabilities

Chapter 6

A ny study focusing on success faces the difficult challenge of defining the term. What at first may appear to be a routine research-related process of identifying, defining, and operationalizing a variable quickly evolves into a much more onerous task. Why? Because success is in the eyes of the beholder. Whereas making a great deal of money may signal success for some, enjoying one's work, working for a prestigious company, or having a happy and healthy family may be more important for others.

Our study examined the vocational success patterns of adults with learning disabilities. As discussed in Chapter 2, we defined success as a mixture of attainment in five areas: income level, education level, prominence in one's field, job classification, and job satisfaction. High success for this study meant that a participant attained a high rating (on a scale of low–moderate–high) for at least four of the five variables, with a moderate rating in the other variable. We also controlled for possible gender differences by differentiating the income levels related to success for males and females. Our moderately successful adults with learning disabilities included those who had a majority of moderate ratings and no more than one rating of low.

Success is a seductive concept that has generated a wide variety of literature. Influential books such as Covey's (1989) *Seven Habits of Highly Effective People*, or Peters and Waterman's (1982) *In Search of Excellence* are examples of the popularity of works related to success. W. Clement Stone even founded *Success Magazine*, capturing the public's fascination with this concept. Studies have focused on success by examining a variety of people and variables, including successful female executives (Halcomb, 1979; Wilkens, 1987), successful black women (Sims, 1982), successful businessmen (Caddes, 1986; Garfield, 1986; McCormack, 1984), highly talented individuals in specific artistic, psychomotor, or cognitive fields (Bloom, 1982), overachieving community college students (Easton & Ginsberg, 1985), and various achievement-related factors (Griessman, 1987; Jencks, 1979). Literally hundreds of success strategy guides have been produced. Many of these recent works are the kinds of quick-fix approaches that Covey (1989) categorized as the "personality ethic," which emphasizes influence techniques, power strategies, consumer skills, and positive attitudes. For example, note the titles to just some of these works: *Roger's Rules for Success: Tips That Will Take You to the Top* (Rogers, 1986), *Making It in America* (Jasinowski & Hamrin, 1995), *Succeeding in the World of Work* (Kimbrell & Vineyard, 1992), *Skills for Success* (Soundview Editorial Staff, 1989), and *Getting Ahead: Career Skills That Work for Everyone* (Andersen, 1995).

The actual definition of success has been an area of contention among scholars. Dictionary definitions are succinct, focusing on ideas such as "the achievement of something desired" or "favorable termination of a venture." Such definitions usually are extended to include notions like the gaining of wealth or fame. Scholars in the area of vocational success, however, raise various issues confounding the more simple dictionary definitions. Some recognize that gender differences must be accepted, as many women, according to Horner (1972), avoid success or carry a "fear of success." A similar concern, a fear of failure, appears to intensify as one becomes more successful (Harvey, 1985). Probably the most contention in the literature has centered around the issue of including both objective and subjective components in the definition of vocational success.

According to Peluchette (1993), until recently, most studies of careers used a narrow societal-driven set of standards for evaluating success that focused on objective criteria such as income or job title. Simply put, a person who made a lot of money or had a high status job was considered successful. More recently, scholarship has suggested that career success consists of both these objective criteria as well as subjective criteria (Phillips-Jones, 1982; Van Maanen & Schein, 1977). The subjective component of these definitions involves issues such as how one feels about job-related accomplishments and prospects for future achievement (Gattiker & Larwood, 1986). Betz and Fitzgerald (1987) describe this concept of subjective career success as a combination of internal and external factors, involving internalized evaluations of self by significant others, as well as evaluations of self in comparison to peers and one's achievement regarding age or career expectations.

Research implies that this subjective side of success is particularly important. This recent focus on subjective career success derives from studies indicating that some seemingly successful people do not feel pride or success in their accomplishments (Korman, Wittig-Berman, & Lang, 1981; Platt & Pollock, 1974; Van Maanen & Schein, 1977). Korman and Korman (1980) term this phenomenon "career success/personal failure." They argue that if individuals do not feel successful, the result may ultimately be negative performance consequences or interactions with others in an organization. Such individuals may attain a high level of income or status but nevertheless experience feelings of disappointment, personal and social alienation, burnout, or other negative consequences. Clearly, success, however defined, may carry a heavy price tag in terms of psychological harm (Harvey, 1985) and family and personal relationships (Burke, 1986).

In our highly achievement-oriented society, cultural norms regarding the value of hard work and the success that may follow are widely shared. Psychological literature related to this achievement orientation of our culture, what has been labeled *achievement motivation* (McClelland, Atkison, Clark, & Lowell, 1953), suggests that highly motivated persons perform better on a variety of tasks (Atkinson & Litwin, 1973; Lowell, 1955). An area of research closely tied to the achievement motivation literature, locus of control (Rotter, 1966), underscores the importance of internal and external factors as they relate to performance. Specifically, the locus of control research suggests that individuals view success as dependent on either their own behavior or the result of chance, luck, or significant others. The more inclusive definitions of success that encompass both objective and subjective criteria more directly capture these psychological features of individual behavior.

In the exceptionality field, most studies addressing issues of success avoid much of the complexity of defining the term by relying on "conventional wisdom" or by adopting definitions that are either implicit or are directly related to the focus of their study. Thus, Pines (1979) studied "superkids" who were noted for their achievement in academics, extracurricular activities, and leadership. As we previously mentioned, Baker (1972) studied famous historical figures with disabilities, and Maker (1978) studied notable scientists with severe handicaps. Terman and Oden (1947) examined the success of gifted individuals. Rogan and Hartman (1976, 1990), in their follow-up study of former Cove School students, found that a number had gone on to highly successful careers in the military and business; others had completed terminal degrees. Kokaska and Skolnik (1986) studied the successful vocational adjustment of adults with learning disabilities, and Adelman and Vogel (1990) focused on college graduates with learning disabilities who were successful in the workplace. Several autobiographical accounts of success with learning disabilities focused more on the reasons for success rather than expounding an explicit definition (Wambsgans, 1990; Brobeck, 1990).

Our definition of success encompasses both objective (income, job classification, education level) and subjective (job satisfaction, eminence) criteria. Although our definition does not include any psychological profile variables, we did find that all those in our sample were highly motivated and internally driven. This chapter examines the specific definitions of success offered by the adults we interviewed. Means they suggest for maximizing that success are also presented. Our hope is to capture how closely the adults with learning disabilities define their success in relation to our preconceived ideas and the extant literature and to offer specific feelings they share about their success.

Definitions of Success

As we began each interview, we asked the participant to define success. Remember, we chose this group of individuals with learning disabilities because of either moderate or high degrees of success across the five variables we selected: income, education level, job classification, eminence, and job satisfaction. Despite the fact that they all had significant attainment in the objective areas of income, level of education, and job satisfaction—though there were variations between the two groups—the definitions of success they shared with us were strongly driven by more internal concerns. Both the highly successful and moderately successful adults with learning disabilities presented very similar definitions, emphasizing the more subjective elements of success. The only differences in the definitions we discerned were that the highly successful participants emphasized the need for balance in life more often, while those in the more moderately successful group more often defined success in terms of just getting by in life. Nonetheless, these differences were only a matter of degree, because both groups did tend to underscore the importance of personal satisfaction as the main component in their definitions.

What is personal satisfaction? For these adults with learning disabilities, personal satisfaction refers to issues such as finding a proper balance in life between work and family, accomplishing goals, and being happy. The more objective or externally driven criteria for success in our culture, such as making a lot of money or earning an advanced educational degree, were not as powerful as these more personal perspectives. The idea of being recognized as good and competent was also important to many of the adults we interviewed. But the internal side of success was the preeminent theme for these successful adults. We consistently heard comments such as these:

Success is internal happiness, peace.

Success means achieving a goal that you set for yourself. It has nothing to do with how the world views it, because the goals are always defined from your inner world.

Success is setting goals for yourself and attaining them.

How well you accomplish whatever your objectives are is success.

Success is something that's just for you.

Success is personal concern defined by yourself.

Success is being able to be yourself.

Success is achieving everything I set out to do.

Success is in the eyes of the beholder. If you think you are successful at what you are doing, then you are.

Success is being comfortable in knowing I'm accomplishing things that I think are right and good.

A successful person is someone who is happy with themselves and with what they've done in life.

Success is fulfilling yourself, not necessarily monetary reward. The success that made me the happiest was raising my children.

To me success is doing something that makes you feel good and you provide services to others.

I define it [success] fairly personally. A sense of accepting, liking and trusting myself and my intuitions in battling with the environment. A successful person is someone who's happy with themselves and with what they've done with their life.

Obviously, these remarks reflect a group of individuals who define success on their own terms. Success to adults with learning disabilities was not primarily driven by the objective cultural norms, which encompass a major set of the components we used originally to identify the people we interviewed.

Among the more highly successful participants, a key aspect of this internally driven definition of success involved the idea of balance in life. This balance involved a proper mix between home, professional, and other parts of life. For example, remarks we heard included the following:

Success involves different parameters including life success and professional success. It means feeling successful yourself even if others don't. One doesn't have to make a lot of money, but there must be a balance of family life and friendship with professional success.

Success is a sense of wholeness, feeling good about self and family. . . . I don't have to be necessarily wealthy, although financial success is important to improve the standard of living for my family because good things cost money.

Success is achieving the ultimate goals in my life, in my personal life, business, and all areas.

Success is not money. It's about how people think about you when you leave this earth. It involves achievement in parenting, business, community, and self. Also good relationships with other people.

Success is someone who works hard, has gotten some type of training or education, and earns a good living, perhaps has a nice home, is a decent person, helps others . . . that type of thing. Ideally, success should be defined by how valuable you are to society, not what you have gotten from society.

At one time in my life I might have defined success strictly from a financial standpoint. Now . . . I feel that there is more—such as family success, success with people, and success with communication. A successful person is one who has a good mix of business, family and recreation. A successful person is one who has gotten his life together.

The older I get the more the words success and happiness coincide. Therefore, I may not be as focused on economic success as some of my contemporaries. To have a good job and a good marriage is my definition of success. A successful person is one who is able to obtain and maintain these things.

My definition of success is a life that is balanced, a life that is satisfying. It's not a life that I'm compulsively striving after. It's a life in which I'm moving at a pace which is healthy and satisfying and productive. But the priorities and goals of my life are clear—those goals being maintaining a loving, good, functional set of relationships with my family members. It means maintaining a level of my health.

Thus, while the specific components of the proper balance shift from person to person, the highly successful adults with learning disabilities focus their idea of success on balancing a variety of aspects of what they considered important in life.

Related to the idea of personal satisfaction as achieving balance in life, the highly successful adults with learning disabilities also talked of two other ideas: accomplishing goals and feeling happy. Although accomplishing goals probably affected their happiness, the highly successful adults consistently mentioned goal achievement and happiness as ingredients of their definition of success. We were told that success was "achieving a goal," "establishing a realistic goal and achieving it, which brings happiness," "overcoming overwhelming odds," "setting goals and attaining them," "accomplishing whatever your objectives are," "being happy in whatever you do," "feeling that you accomplished what you set out to do," "a sense of personal satisfaction," and "someone who's happy with themselves and with what they've done with their life." All of these comments reflect their notion that personal satisfaction as success involves accomplishing goals and feeling good about it. Thus, along with seeking a balance in life, success was goal and happiness oriented. Given that these adults struggled so much in their youth, the idea that success encompasses achievement and happiness is understandable.

The moderately successful adults had similar ideas about the meaning of success. As already suggested, the idea of success being subjectively driven was equally powerful for both groups. But to the more moderately successful adults, a sense of just getting by and learning to be content with themselves was much more pronounced in their conception of personal satisfaction than the notion of balance in life that is so powerful for the highly successful adults. Note, for example, the following definitions of success shared by some of the moderately successful adults:

Doing a good job.

Moving along in life.

Feeling good about yourself.

Leading a reasonably happy life without any serious problems.

Satisfied with how life is going, a feeling of well-being.

Being happy, being content.

Being able to do the job you want to do.

Being able to be yourself and not trying to conform to other people's norms.

Contentment, liking one's self, and being honest with one's self.

Someone who knows what they want from life.

If you think you are successful at what you are doing, then you are a success.

Being able to deal effectively with changing circumstances.

Doing a good job, feeling happy and confident in what I do.

A feeling of well-being.

Self-satisfaction in what you are doing.

Such ideas about self-satisfaction and contentment certainly are true of the more highly successful adults as well. Again, both groups defined success as being personally satisfied. But to the more moderately successful adults with learning disabilities, the definitions of success are clearly more a function of just feeling okay about themselves. And the importance of chance or luck, never mentioned by those in the highly successful contingent, was commonly referred to by the moderately successful group. "Much success" one moderately successful adult explained, "is achieved through good luck." Another concluded, "a lot of luck is just fate."

Conclusions

Our foray into the thinking about success of 71 adults with learning disabilities suggests that they define the term much more personally than either the literature or our definition suggests. While the recent scholarship on career success does recognize the importance of including both objective and subjective criteria in a definition of the term, these broader definitions still largely encompass internalized work-related issues such as job satisfaction or prospects for future career advancement. Indeed, our own operationalization of success includes both objective and subjective criteria, though the subjective criteria of job satisfaction and eminence in one's field are both job-related subjective concerns. The definitions of success provided by the adults with learning disabilities, even in the context we provided to them of focusing on their vocational success, include more personal or humanistic components. Thus, while the definitions are obviously driven by their personal sense of success, suggesting a very powerful inner locus of control (Rotter, 1966), the thrust of the definitions focuses on a range of factors unrelated to their jobs. Instead, personal satisfaction meant having a balanced life or just being happy. Many of the adults we interviewed talked about their family and personal life as significant contributors to this more encompassing notion of success. Interestingly, through flexible scheduling, job sharing, career breaks, sabbaticals for employees, and other concessions to the changing needs of employees (Halcrow, 1989; Solomon, 1991), businesses are beginning to recognize the importance of this more holistic and humanistic conception of work success. Future research on vocational success for any employees should consider this broader definition of the term.

As we discuss in Chapter 7, we found slight differences in the responses provided by the moderately and highly successful adults with learning disabilities. In the case of the definitions of success, although both groups offer very personal definitions, the highly successful adults appear more inclined to see a balanced and happy existence as the keys for success; the moderately successful adults more often suggest that success relates to just being content or getting by in life. Though these differences are a matter of degree, they are distinct. In any case, personal satisfaction requires that individuals with learning disabilities and those with whom they work and live understand their disability, and it requires that individuals with learning disabilities seek and utilize support in their environment. These themes of understanding and support will surface again as key ingredients in our discussion of the alterable patterns we describe in our model for enhancing vocational success of adults with learning disabilities.

A Model of Success

You have to decide that whatever you want to do, go for it. Don't worry if people say that you can't do it ... there must be some way to achieve. You have to accept failure, recognize that the route you take may not be right, and accept the fact that you have to start over again. But if you want it bad enough, you'll do it.

—*From interview with highly successful adult with learning disabilities*

There is something about successful people that captures the imagination of most Americans. The visibility of highly successful businessmen such as Ross Perot, Donald Trump, or Lee Iacocca, or the great interest in the potential presidential candidacy of highly regarded General Colin Powell are examples of the attention and respect that success breeds in America. Successful persons in a variety of fields promote products, grace magazine covers, and are held up as role models for children and adults alike. Why this love affair with success?

Americans tend to share a common admiration for careers that offer what sociologists describe as high levels of status, wealth, and power (Etzioni, 1969). Those in the "true" professions, such as medicine, law, university teaching, science and engineering, high finance, accountancy, even high-powered business entrepreneurs, are held in higher esteem than people serving in many other occupations. Generally, anyone who makes a lot of money or achieves some notoriety or eminence is highly regarded. Along with earning a high income, such individuals usually have a good deal of control over their daily work environment and go through rigorous training and intense experiences to develop their talents. They are respected for the work they perform. Such people have attained significant employment success.

The road to success is never easy. It is filled with trials and tribulations, coupled with a lot of hard work, dedication, and risk. For those who must face challenges above and beyond the ordinary, however, attaining success is particularly elusive. People with learning disabilities struggle on a daily basis with common basic skills such as reading, writing, calculating, concentrating, or

97

short-term memory. They just aren't able to process and conceptualize like the rest of us. As a dyslexic economist exclaimed during one of our interviews, "[we] are left-handed learners and thinkers in a right-handed world." Yet, despite the odds, despite the pain and frustration that undoubtedly accompany their striving for success, many adults with learning disabilities overcome the numerous hurdles and move on to greater heights. Indeed, many realize a level of success that would be the envy of any person.

This chapter presents the model for employment success we derived from entering the world of 71 adults with learning disabilities. They beat the odds in that research suggests that learning disabilities do not disappear after schooling (Blalock, 1981) and that factors such as low reading levels, poor written language, feelings of inadequacy, fear of failure, attention disorders, organizational difficulties, and social learning problems can impede performance, no doubt curtailing efforts at success (Johnson & Blalock, 1987). Follow-up studies indicate that although the majority find jobs and support themselves and their families, they continue to drop out of school at higher rates and face greater unemployment and underemployment than the general population (Wagner, 1989). Often many have problems maintaining and/or obtaining positions (Cruickshank, Morse, & Johns, 1980; Lewis, 1977; Rogan and Hartman, 1976), and they express dissatisfaction with personal and occupational outcomes (Okolo & Sitlington, 1988; Reiff & Gerber, 1991).

The model described in this chapter goes beyond examining the personality dynamics and demographics of successful adults with learning disabilities. Instead, the focus is on what we consider the alterable variables and systems of interaction that have fostered high degrees of employment success. In other words, the model inculcates patterns of behavior that we feel are transferable to other individuals with learning disabilities. Derived from research on especially talented individuals undertaken by Benjamin Bloom (Bloom, 1980, 1982; Bloom & Sosniak, 1981), alterable variables are special circumstances in self, situation, influence, and interaction that may have had either an individual or a cumulative effect on success and are susceptible to change. Easton and Ginsberg (1985) used this same approach to study overachieving community college students.

As we mentioned in Chapter 1, in the field of exceptionality, studies have focused on famous people with disabilities in history (Baker, 1972), scientists with severe disabilities (Maker, 1978), and gifted individuals (Terman & Oden, 1947). Findings generally indicate that persistence (of motive and effort), self-confidence, and strength or force of personality characterize success. Other studies have followed up on individuals with disabilities in adulthood (Rogan & Hartman, 1976), although actual reasons for success were not examined. What is conspicuously absent, however, is a clear analysis of how individuals with disabilities actually achieved vocational success. It is such a model that this chapter elaborates.

A Model for Successful Adults with Learning Disabilities

When the focus turns from investigating how learning disabilities interfere with adult functioning to how individuals with learning disabilities succeed in the workplace, one overriding factor emerges. The key underlying the success of those in our sample of adults with learning disabilities was the quest to gain control of their lives. Successful adults with learning disabilities were able to take control of their lives, and the greater the degree of control, the greater the likelihood for success. Our analysis suggests that this pursuit of control involves a variety of considerations that we grouped into two categories: internal decisions and external manifestations. The internal decisions include what we call desire, goal orientation, and reframing. The external manifestations we depict as adaptability, and include persistence, goodness of fit, learned creativity, and social ecologies. These themes interact with one another, and the degree of control and, ultimately, the level of success are related to each individual's attainment within the areas of internal decisions and external manifestations.

Perhaps the most striking finding of our research was how well persons who are labeled as learning disabled are able to learn and, ultimately, succeed. Although it may be true that they don't learn in the well-accepted ways of our culture, they can and do learn. Given the differences in their styles, the road to success was often rocky, strewn with pain and frustration. But the patterns we discerned were common to all our successful adults and therefore suggest a model for others to follow. Most significantly, although both our high and moderate success groups shared the patterns or themes we identified, the attainment levels within the high success group were always more exceptional, meaning that they achieved more fully than the moderately successful individuals within each of the key factors.

Figure 7.1 presents the model for success for adults with learning disabilities. As seen in the model, control was the overriding theme that characterized all efforts geared at success. A set of interacting variables, the internal decisions and external manifestations, characterizes control. Success is a dynamic process, which spans numerous years, and must begin with a conscious set of decisions. Individuals must take a personal stance to devote time and energy to trying to gain better control of their existence. This beginning process we describe as the internal decisions. They are the internal components of gaining control.

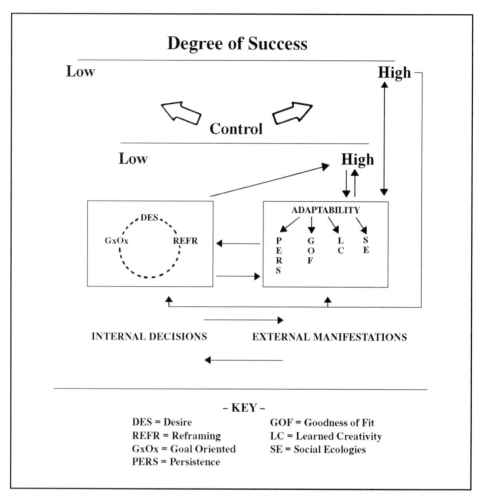

Figure 7.1.   A model of vocational success for adults with learning disabilities. *Note.* From "Identifying Alterable Patterns in Employment Success for Highly Successful Adults with Learning Disabilities," by P. J. Gerber, R. Ginsberg, and H. B. Reiff, 1992, *Journal of Learning Disabilities, 25,* p. 485. Copyright 1992 by PRO-ED, Inc. Reprinted with permission.

But such internal decisions are not enough. The adults in our sample took other steps, undertaking certain activities that helped foster control and success. Thus, the internal decisions must be translated into actual behaviors. These coping strategies and techniques we refer to as the external manifestations, and all fall under the category of adaptability.

The model of Figure 7.1 suggests that these variables interact closely with one another. As one masters the internal decisions (which are pictured in a circle to reflect that there is no clear beginning point, and that these three factors are all closely interrelated), greater adaptability is possible. But improved adaptability also fosters stronger internal decisions. And as might be expected, as more control is achieved, and more success, the internal decisions and adaptability continue to strengthen and improve. The following discussion examines each of the factors—control , internal decisions, and external manifestations—depicted in the model. Implications of the model are also briefly discussed.

Control

Control refers to the drive to manage one's life. This control involved a set of internal decisions (conscious decisions to take charge of one's life) and external manifestations (adapting and shaping oneself to move ahead). Attaining control is the key element for success. Adults with learning disabilities work throughout their lives to learn how to take control of their existence. It undergirds their ultimate success.

Control is so important because individuals with learning disabilities do not learn or even think in traditional ways. They must forge an individualized path in order to accomplish something. Interestingly, just as the federal government in P.L. 101-476, Individuals with Disabilities Education Act of 1990, requires an individualized education program (IEP) for all individuals classified as exceptional, our successful adults informally created their own plans to move ahead. Throughout their lives, these successful adults found that the traditional culture they confronted sought to deprive them of their natural ways of learning and doing. After all, their approach was not acceptable to those without learning disabilities. So often the adults with learning disabilities were reminded that their way was wrong! One adult in our sample described himself and others similarly situated as a "peculiar lot." Another said that individuals with learning disabilities are "obviously weird." A statistician from our high success group described the frenzied nature of his existence as always "feeling like I was in a Chinese fire drill!"

As we listened to the highly successful adults in our sample, we were continually reminded of the specific ways that they reached for control. A noted dentist said that "I feel most confident when something is in my hands . . . when I have total control." A highly successful school director explained, "Being dyslexic and having 75 cents can buy you a cup of coffee. . . . There is no percentage in being dyslexic unless you work to make it better." A female executive stressed the need to anticipate problems to attain control. She reported, "If you can be an anticipator and look ahead and try to anticipate . . . you're ready." Other comments we heard further substantiate the point about the primacy of control:

I like to be in control. If things don't work out, okay, but if I lose control, I get terribly anxious.

Being in control makes me most confident.

I feel the need to control my destiny.

Thus, control was a necessity. As we listened to adult after adult, the significance of this theme of control was unmistakable. It may have been described differently to us, but the idea of the need for control was always present. As the model predicts, high control is needed for high degrees of success, although success is still not automatic. Certainly, an array of uncontrollable factors (e.g., good or bad luck) can affect an individual's level of success. Nonetheless, without a high degree of control, success for the adult with learning disabilities is unlikely.

In our interviews it was clear that the higher degree of control attained clearly distinguished the high success group of participating adults with learning disabilities from the moderate success group. Ultimately, the moderately successful adults with learning disabilities did not acquire the level of control that characterized the high success group. For example, many of the moderately successful adults with learning disabilities sought control only as a means to cover up weaknesses, instead of seeking control as a means to improve themselves. Such a feeling of fear related to the disability was common across most interviews, but it was almost an end in itself for the moderate success group. One moderately successful adult explained the situation this way: "I have so much fear in me about being found out. . . . I need to control that so much." Another said, "You find that you build up a tremendous entourage (repertoire) of ways to get around it (the learning disability) and avoid issues. . . . I'm never very open. . . . I just want to disguise my feelings."

The high success and moderate success groups were also distinguished by their perception of where they were headed in life. The moderate group was clearly less goal oriented and driven. As one moderately successful woman explained, "Much of what happened to me just sort of happened." Another credited his success purely to luck. Members of the high success group, conversely, were very driven and more certain of where they were headed. These differences are clarified further by developing the parallel attainment in each of the factors within the themes of internal decisions and external manifestations.

Internal Decisions

Success for the adults with learning disabilities whom we studied evolved over numerous years. Success begins, however, with a conscious set of decisions. At first, these decisions may simply relate to personal matters and later involve decisions related to striving for career excellence. Nonetheless, individuals must succinctly decide that they are going to try to gain better control of their existence and, ultimately, succeed in life. Success, very clearly, does not just happen. The starting point is an internal, very personal set of decisions. Adults with learning disabilities must want to succeed, must set achievable goals, and must confront the learning disability so that appropriate measures can be undertaken to heighten the likelihood for success. These internal decisions involve what we have labeled as *desire, goal orientation*, and *reframing*. Success is heavily dependent on mastering these internal decisions.

Desire

Desire is an essential element for anyone hoping to excel. At some point, the adults in our sample took a stand for themselves and decided it was time to move ahead. Desire is always a necessity for success, as we were vividly reminded by several of the highly successful adults in our sample who similarly quoted the famous words of former President Calvin Coolidge:

> Talent will not; there is nothing more common than unsuccessful men with talent. Genius will not, unrewarded genius is almost a proverb. Education alone will not; the world is full of educated derelicts. Persistence and determination are omnipotent.

But given that succeeding involves such enormous challenges for the adults with learning disabilities because of the uncommon hurdles they confront, this desire was especially significant and was very conspicuous and powerful. In describing this perception, a number of individuals invoked metaphors related to fire. Their desire to prove that they could succeed felt like a fire was burning within. Thus, we heard "I've always had a kind of burning feeling . . . kind of like being on fire to succeed." "You fight until you can't fight anymore, and then you fight some more . . . you take the hurt and turn it inward and it becomes part of the burn . . . it has to burn." "If the fire of your drive goes out, you will lose your self-respect." One adult we interviewed described this fire-like drive this way: "You've got to have that inner sense that you're going to do it, want to do it. If you don't want to do it, you are not going to be successful. You might have to do one step at a time and go slower. But . . . you have to be determined in life if you are going to make it." Another succinctly explained, "I made up my mind I'd never fail anything!"

For some of those we interviewed, this desire for success came early. For others, it developed more slowly over time. But among the more highly successful adults, this desire was a powerful determinant of their life style. A female physician said that she has always been driven: "Just tell me I can't do it, and I'll do it." A college professor of finance, who told us of his desire to be a top person in his field, described his desire this way: "If you want me to fin-ish something, challenge me and say you can't do it. . . . I'll be damned to prove you wrong, [to show] that I really can do it." The desire of a highly successful dentist was described through his explanation that "I use every angle, every part of my being so I can accomplish what I want to accomplish." "If I play," one highly successful adult concluded, "I play to win. . . . I'm driven to beat them."

The tone of the desire among those in our moderate success group was much more tempered. As one fellow described it, "I'm really just someone who is plodding along." Another from the moderate group described his discomfort with what it takes to really get ahead. "I'm not comfortable with the politics of moving upward in the field," he said, "I'm not comfortable with the competi-tive nature." Such attitudes would be foreign to those more highly successful adults with learning disabilities we interviewed. Another moderately success-ful adult told us that "most successful people have specific plans, and they know what they are going to do . . . not me . . . not me." This sense of concern or despair related to desire clearly distinguished the moderately successful from the highly successful adults.

Goal Orientation

Closely related to the decisions made concerning desire was the conscious goal orientation of the successful adults with learning disabilities. Although some may argue that all human beings have a need for goals and feelings of success, this is especially significant for those with learning disabilities. These individu-als are apprehensive about the all-too-common possibility of a continuing pat-tern of failure. Thus, they set explicit goals to work toward and guide their activ-ities. Goal setting allows persons with learning disabilities to have practical, realistic, attainable aspirations. It also provides needed focus for individuals who have experienced considerable difficulty in learning and other customary daily activities. Our participants did not waste a lot of time pursuing ends that would lead to failure. Finally, goal setting feeds on itself, much like a snowball increas-ing in circumference as it rolls down a hill. Once even minimal goals can be met, the resulting feelings of success can be the basis for undertaking greater challenges. As a highly successful female explained, "I have my goals . . . any kind of movement toward my goals feels very successful. Anything I am doing better than I did last week or three years ago feels successful."

The goal setting for the highly successful group resulted in either short-term or long-term goals. But the key was that they set goals. One entrepreneur explained it this way: "Successful people have a plan. You have to have a plan, goals, strategy; otherwise you are flying through the clouds and then you hit the mountain." A psychologist offered the the idea that "you should link efforts to outcomes . . . stay in your areas of strength." A businessman said, "I had my goals and set out to do them. . . . I didn't care how long it would take." A retired professor said, "When I choose a goal, I stick to it and accomplish it. . . . I'm a very goal-oriented person." A highly successful female businesswomen described her approach as follows: "If I have goals and structure, then I'm okay . . . something like mapping." Similarly, an IBM executive said, "I could clearly see a career and I knew what I had to do to move up the career ladder . . . that was the goal setting process."

The moderate success group differed from their more successful counterparts in several ways. Some set many more short-term goals than the more successful individuals. Others appeared to be much more easily diverted from goals. Still others were much less goal oriented. Clearly, their goals were far less ambitious. One of the moderately successful adults, in explaining his thoughts about goals, remarked, "Successful people have goals . . . much of what happened to me just happened." Similarly, another moderately successful adult said that "I didn't start with any specific goals . . . I didn't beat my head against the wall." Still another sadly confided to us that "I have set goals much too low." This sense of the moderate success group is captured in the words of one adult who explained, "I tend to be much less goal oriented. I think it has been easy for people to not take me seriously or even for me not to take me seriously."

Such comments reflect the tendency for the moderately successful adults with learning disabilities to have fewer clear goals with less ambitious aspirations than their more highly successful counterparts. Thus, as with desire, while all successful adults with learning disabilities were goal oriented to some degree, the high success group is clearly distinguished from the others.

Reframing

The final component of the internal decisions was probably the most significant. A process we refer to as *reframing* is the set of decisions related to reinterpreting the learning disabilities experience from something dysfunctional to something functional. It is the acknowledgment that the major obstacle facing those with learning disabilities is not the disability itself but instead the ability to brave the various challenges endured as one learns to live with it and overcome it.

Scholarship in a range of other fields has referred to this phenomenon of reframing. In the psychological literature, it is conceived of as a change in reality. Bandler and Grinder (1982), for example, define reframing as "changing a frame in which a person perceives events in order to change meaning. When meaning changes, the person's responses and behavior change" (p. 2). Similarly, Watzlawick, Weakland, and Fisch (1974) characterize reframing as "changing the conceptual and/or emotional setting or viewpoint in relation to which a situation is experienced, and place it in another frame that fits the 'facts' of the same concrete situation equally well or better and thereby changes the entire meaning" (p. 211). In the leadership literature, Bolman and Deal (1991) discuss the challenges of those refusing to reframe. "They live," argue Bolman and Deal, "in psychic prisons because they cannot look at old problems in a new light and attack old challenges with different and more powerful tools—*they cannot reframe*" (p. 4). Recently, the school reform literature has adopted the idea of reframing as a key ingredient for successful change (Carlson, 1996).

In our interviews with highly successful adults with learning disabilities, we found this process of reframing to be a powerful component of the set of internal decisions. We discovered a number of stages to this process of reframing. Some moved through the stages almost in unison, while others systematically moved from one to the next. Clearly, the four stages interact very closely with one another.

The first stage we refer to as the need to *recognize* the disability. It is impossible to overcome a disability and devise strategies to overcome it unless the disability itself is recognized. For many of those we interviewed, this recognition was simply the realization that they did things differently and that it was okay to be different from everybody else. Some realized this at an early age; others did not come to this recognition until later. But before an individual with disabilities can begin to discover ways to learn successfully or succeed in other areas of life, a recognition of who and what an individual is must occur. One successful adult with learning disabilities said, "You are your best teacher. You have to be your best teacher. You need to find out who you are, and you are not going to succeed out there if you can't look at yourself in the mirror. If you can't deal with who you are and recognize your gifts and your disadvantages, you are not going to make it." Another concisely concluded, "The beginning is just to recognize it."

Then, a degree of *acceptance* must be attained. Recognition and acceptance go hand in hand. This acceptance can involve both the negative and positive ramifications of having a learning disability, but it is a need that it is real and must be confronted before moving ahead is possible. A part of this process is just learning to accept that despite a disability, a person can be considered worthwhile with something important to offer. Without acceptance of the disability, undoubtedly a great deal of frustration is likely. As a highly successful college professor explained, "I needed to be proud of myself. As long as I was ashamed of being LD, it was difficult to succeed." A school director was equally specific: "I had to face myself in order to help others. This was a peak experience in my life . . . that night I looked at myself in the mirror and said, 'You know, you're not so bad after all.'"

An aspect of acceptance that must be considered is the decision as to whether or not one will share information about the disability with others. Some of the successful adults readily talked about their disability ("Sure, it's no big deal"), while others were not so open ("I don't wear it on my sleeve"). Many times, this decision on how open to be related to the type of work one did. For example, a doctor and a dentist discussed their reluctance to be open in terms of the potential concerns that their clients might have. On the other hand, several adults who worked with others with learning disabilities readily discussed their disability. But the key in terms of acceptance was that a specific and conscious decision had been made about how to deal with what they accepted as real. Acceptance does not mean that everyone handles the disability in the same way, but that there is a common practice, a pattern of decision making related to deciding how to deal with the acknowledgment of having a learning disability.

Third, there is a need for *understanding* the disability and all its implications. An understanding of one's strengths and weaknesses is a prerequisite for success. A lawyer described this component of reframing as follows: "As a dyslexic, you have to accept the degree to which you will and won't succeed in life. The biggest advantage is that once you realize you can't do all these things, you become good at finding alternative solutions and at making the best of what you have." Similarly, a professor explained, "I realized in the areas I'm good, I'm great . . . in the areas I'm bad, I'm terrible." Yet another successful adult, a university administrator, captured several of the stages of reframing: "A successful LD person will never walk in the normal world. And I think you have to accept that. And after you accept that, then you can figure out how you can help other people to understand what's going on."

Finally, one must be willing to take *action*. All the recognition, acceptance, and understanding in the world are irrelevant without a conscious decision to take specific actions toward goals. Obviously, all the successful adults with learning disabilities whom we interviewed chose to do something about their circumstances in order to foster their career success.

All the highly successful adults with learning disabilities moved through the four stages of reframing. Though for many it was very tedious and emotional, they were able to reframe the learning disability experience to enhance their likelihood of greater control, which ultimately led to greater success. The complex and interwoven nature of the four stages of the reframing sequence are captured in remarks from several other highly successful adults with learning disabilities:

> There was something in me that drove me to find something I was good at. A project helped me understand that there were many people with the same problem and they helped me understand the characteristics that accompanied my disability. Therefore, it helped me understand myself a little better. It was a big awakening in myself.

> I think it is almost this—once you can look in the mirror and say "Okay, I can live with you," . . . maybe then you are on your way to success. You can't get other people to respect or love you if you can't do the same yourself.

> It is vital to get over being embarrassed by it. Only when you've done that can you start to make real progress. No matter what it takes or how hard you have to work at it, you have to deal with that learning problem so you can learn to learn. Until you've dealt with it, the world is an impossible place.

> You have to look within yourself. Accept that your brain may be mechanically handicapped, but you can optimize or give up. Try to look at success around you . . . you have brain power . . . use it.

> If you change the perception, you change the problem. Overcoming the handicap was my gift. It was peace plus power. I was destined to fly with one engine, and now I have the other one so I think I'll just try some new altitudes.

Obviously, all the quotations from our interviews depict a very proactive and thoughtful group of individuals. These adults had recognized and accepted their disability, they worked to understand its implications for their lives, and they moved ahead by taking appropriate steps on the road to success. Nonetheless, the pain that many experienced during the process of reframing cannot be minimized. Reframing did not come easily. A psychologist told us that he was "omni-conscious" of his problems during his school years. He used to refer to himself as a JIT—a janitor in training. One woman very emotionally described her youth this way: "I knew something was wrong. I was scared. I knew that 'I couldn't do this.' I would sweat bullets. I wanted to faint and play dead. I did get sick all the time." A businessman told us of a terrible time when he was forced to read out loud to his class: "I had this little voice talking to me. It said that what I was saying was wrong, but the other side of my brain just kept moving and making mistakes." A businesswoman described a similar experience: "I was scared. I can remember having to read out loud and we'd stand up and read and I would have such trouble. I thought my mind was processing so quickly. I just couldn't understand. We were reaching points in class where we were progressing to the next level and I was stumbling . . . I felt inadequate. I would take a test and there would be one word. . . . Oh, my God . . . I would get everything wrong!"

The highly successful adults with learning disabilities, then, weaved their way through the reframing process despite significant hurdles and painful experiences. But the key was that they always moved on. The moderately successful adults reframed as well. However, they generally did not progress through all four stages to the degree of the high success group. They did much more blaming, avoiding, and held back more than the more successful adults. They were an angrier lot and tended to have more trouble with acceptance, perhaps even avoiding complete acceptance. Their understanding was often incomplete, and they did not take the decisive action so characteristic of the more successful adults. A school director in our moderate success group summed up this sense by explaining that "I literally have approached life like I was a second-rate human being. Dyslexics don't feel as good about themselves as other people." Another in our moderate success group told us that being a person with a learning disability was like being "a prisoner unto yourself, locked into yourself." "Success," he explained, "has been so brutal. . . . I've been beaten up so much." A teacher even said she wanted to go back and "spit in every teacher's eye that she had in school." The anger of the moderate success group was obvious, as was the fact that their degree of reframing was less extensive than the more successful adults.

External Manifestations

Certain activities fostered control and success. The internal decisions had to be translated into actual behaviors. These approaches, behaviors, and techniques, which we call adaptability, were the keys for unleashing the potential within each person. Having strong desire, setting goals, and reframing the learning disability experience in a more positive way were necessary beginning points. But the action strategies and various techniques the adults utilized as the means for adapting their abilities to the realities they faced each day were necessary to actualize and optimize success. Many of these external manifestations were quite simple, others very elaborate, creative, and sophisticated. This adaptability, so characteristic of the adults we interviewed, made it possible for these unorthodox learners to excel in a world biased in favor of the population without learning disabilities.

As was true with the three subthemes discussed as part of the internal decisions, the high success group of adults with learning disabilities was more exceptional in their attainment of the four components we depict that make up adaptability. These include *persistence, goodness of fit* with one's work environment, coping behaviors we call *learned creativity*, and the support of individuals in the development of success we refer to as *social ecologies*. All of the successful adults with learning disabilities we interviewed discussed behaviors related to each of these components of adaptability.

Persistence

Successful adults with learning disabilities work extremely hard. Although desire was a necessary internal decision, its external expression resulted in high levels of persistence. Thus, the desire to succeed was not enough; one had to be willing to sacrifice and persevere toward goals. This persistence became a way of life, and no doubt was an outgrowth of having a learning disability. We were continually told that for success to come, the adults with learning disabilities had to do whatever was necessary, and this often meant working harder than everyone else.

For the high success group, this persistence was an acknowledged part of life. Comments indicated what an incredibly resilient group of people this was. For example, we heard "I overcame my problem with sheer grit and determination." "I made accomplishments by working harder than others and gutting it out." "I would adapt by doing extra work." "The learning disability positively affected my success. . . . I learned to persist, to deal with pain and frustration . . . things don't come easy to me, but I work long and hard. This is central to my being." "I never stop trying. . . . I have an incredible amount of persistence." "I'm a real believer in determination. It is three quarters of the battle. There are tons of geniuses in the world who never make it and there are lots of people with personality who don't. The difference between making it and not is determination . . . you absolutely have to stick with it."

Some of the stories we heard related to this issue of persistence underscore its centrality to the adaptability process. One scientist, when looking for a new position as a technician, recalled that he wrote to "every museum in the English-speaking world." A businesswoman described her approach to a new job: "One of the managers just worked with me until 10:00 p.m. or 11:00 p.m. at night and beat it into me. He made me rehearse and practice and present and present and present and finally it clicked . . . once it clicks I have it. But it was that perseverance." Another adult reflecting on college told us that "I took Chemistry 121 five times and never passed it. But there were certain parts of that class I really liked and wanted to learn. I took almost everything twice." This common pattern of extra hard work and resiliency in the face of hurdles and frustrations highlights the unpleasant reality of the cost of persistence—that the adults with learning disabilities had to go beyond the norm in order to learn and prepare for success. But they did it, and the persistence seemed to work to their competitive advantage in the workplace. Several other comments from the highly successful adults further portray this theme:

> I worked harder than others to compensate for my reading problems. I would try to know and learn everything. [The LD] made me compensate. . . . I just worked much harder.

> One of the reasons for my success is that everybody gets 110% from me. I start early in the morning and work late.

> The learning disability taught me how to work, it taught me not to get discouraged, and even though I read much slower than everyone else and things like this, I keep plugging away and I eventually finish. . . . It isn't so important how fast I did it as long as I did it.

> I'm not the type to take no for an answer, not the type to give up on something, not the type to tire of something. I have some energy and am willing to go after something to try and accomplish it.

> I knew that either I was going to be a nothing or I was going to be a something. I wasn't going to be a middle of the road. So I had a choice. . . . I have one advantage; I've got to work harder, so I might as well go for it. Don't build the foundation of the house and not build the rest of it. I feel that I appreciate things more because I have to work so hard for them.

These highly successful adults with learning disabilities were very persistent. This meant hard work and often some pain. But whether it was in school or on the job, they were willing to extend the extra effort demanded by their disability in order for them to succeed. The difference between the highly and moderately successful adults with learning disabilities was distinct. Although persistence was obvious for both groups, the moderates did not push with the tenacity of the more successful adults. The highly successful adults displayed more drive, took more risks, and appeared more tenacious, whereas the moderately successful adults were more easily distracted from their goals. As one moderate explained, "My nonassertiveness hinders my getting ahead."

Goodness of Fit

Along with persistence, an integral part of adaptability for the successful adults with learning disabilities was the goodness of fit they sought with their environment. They tried to fit themselves to surroundings and environments where their chances for success were heightened, where their skills and abilities could be optimized and their weaknesses minimized. These adults found work that they enjoyed where they could be both comfortable and successful. Some were in positions where they could actually create or orchestrate the environment to fit their needs. Because they had reframed and understood their disability well, they took account of themselves and tried to match their attributes and abilities to appropriate jobs. The environments they either selected or created allowed them to maximize their strengths while compensating for their areas of weakness or need. Oftentimes, the assistance they utilized came in the form of people or technology.

In interview after interview, the successful adults explained to us how they carefully chose work that would allow them the chance for success. It was an empowering experience. Most were proud of finding work that they enjoyed. The highly successful adults displayed an evident passion for their work. Their enthusiasm for their chosen careers was the biggest distinction regarding goodness of fit from the more moderately successful adults. Also, the highly successful adults more often selected work contexts in which they could be their own boss or had greater flexibility to control their destiny by making significant decisions about their work. Even as children, many of the more successful adults with learning disabilities sought or created environments in which they could be both comfortable and successful.

One highly successful lawyer, for example, developed his own position within the field of public law, which allowed him to define the kinds of tasks he performed. A female physician described her decision to specialize in dermatology because there was little writing required and the medical textbooks had lots of pictures, so, in her words, "You could see it." Another successful adult explained, "For most of my life, I realized that I could not do what most people could; therefore, I sought to be able to do things that others could not. With an aptitude in mechanics and a fascination with the human body, I chose biomedical engineering." A businessman started his own public relations firm, using his strong verbal skills to his advantage. A businesswoman, who had a self-described "strong personality," succinctly told us, "Capitalize on your strengths. . . . Look at what you can do best and enjoy most."

Goodness of fit, then, was a significant adapting mechanism for the highly successful adults with learning disabilities whom we interviewed. Both control and success were clearly dependent on working in an environment that allowed these adults to succeed. The pattern of goodness of fit differed from individual to individual, but it was always very prominent. Other comments from the highly successful adults with learning disabilities underscore this consistent theme:

> In my field, the devices you create have to work the first time. So I can be careful, I can be deliberate. I think I knew I could survive here. Nobody ever rushed me because they knew I was eventually going to get it right.

> I'm in a field that is very rigid, and once you learn the rules you don't have to worry about too much else. I am a legalist and I like to know the rules. . . . In

accounting, things must add up and you can double check them. It is a field that is containable, with a beginning and an end. You know exactly what you will do day to day. I have no problem with spending enormous amounts of time to get something right . . . a perfect fit for this straightforward job.

One of the reasons I write simple things [articles for *Reader's Digest*] is that I can understand them. I can put them into the simplest, third grade language, which is what *Reader's Digest* requires.

I hate having to contact people. If they come to see me that's fine, but if I have to contact someone I dread it. As a youngster it was nice in terms of my paper route. The newspaper billed people directly and they paid the newspaper so I didn't have to deal with people. I could just deliver my papers. . . . That worked out fine.

As indicated, far fewer of the moderates created their own work environments. Their autonomy was far more constrained in the workplace. Fewer were in supervisory roles. In addition, they did not express the passion for their work so characteristic of the highly successful adults.

Learned Creativity

The essence of adaptability was learned creativity or the various strategies, techniques, devices, and other mechanisms devised by the successful adults to enhance their ability to perform well. Because they had experienced some difficulty operating in the "regular" system, they bucked the company line and realized (probably as part of their reframing experience) that there was little incentive to conform to a system that exposed their weaknesses. Instead, they came up with unique and personal ways to accomplish tasks. Thus, they manipulated the system to avoid highlighting what they could not do, and they tried to anticipate potential problem areas so they could compensate for themselves. Success required that they become "quick studies" in the art of reacting to stimuli so they wouldn't be embarrassed. They learned to develop various systems that played up their strengths, just as a blind person sharpens other senses due to the loss of sight. They learned that there were many ways to solve most problems, and that their idiosyncratic method was equal to anyone else's approach. They did not just cope—they creatively excelled!

For many of the highly successful adults with learning disabilities, the early learned creativity was a means of manipulating the system to avoid exposing their weaknesses. We repeatedly heard the word "manipulate" when discussing how they managed to get by as children. For many in the moderate success group, this manipulation was the most significant form of learned creativity they displayed. Their desire to protect themselves from being exposed was a common theme:

I manipulate myself in such a position that I can't make a mistake.

I still feel anxious in situations where I might be found out . . . that I'm faking it.

When you are learning disabled you become very defensive . . . you know your weaknesses and want to cover them up. You find you build up a tremendous entourage of ways to get around it and avoid the issues.

I have so much fear in me about being found out, so I protect.

The high success group members were protective as well, especially in their formative years. And nearly all of the successful adults with learning disabilities used technology such as spell checkers, tape recorders, dictaphones, and the like. But the high success group exhibited a more sophisticated and creative pattern of coping tactics as part of their mission for success. They more fully built on their inborn strengths. Several of the highly successful adults spoke to the need for developing anticipatory skills. An engineer explained, "I create scenarios of what I will have to do under certain circumstances." A businesswoman boasted about how she could "run rings around well-educated people because I'm faster on my feet and in my mind. I respond when they may still be thinking about it."

Being a good anticipator was only one of the many skills the highly successful adults used to foster their work success. A lawyer explained how he devised his own forms for reporting data, and he even put clients' pictures on each form to help him recognize the clients when they came for an office visit. A dentist described his self-taught lip reading process to help him visualize words during conversations. A college professor talked about his system of inventing names and words for towns and characters when he reads to lessen his possible confusion with the actual text. An accountant revealed how he makes a game out of everything to force a challenge on himself. He explained: "Getting to work on time, catching the right train, being in the right place, they're all games. It doesn't mean that I don't take things seriously, but it makes things a challenge and breaks up the monotony."

Other highly successful adults revealed many different creative coping strategies:

Other people don't seem to look at the possibilities available to accomplish a task. When I have been able to handle tougher jobs, it has always been because I could approach a problem in a different way, a little easier way. I have always tended to think of ways to do things that are a little unusual.

When I read, it has to be aloud. I have to hear it as well as see it to know if I am reading the right words. So, in college, I asked professors to allow me to sit in the corner of the room so I could read aloud without disturbing the others.

I am terrified of people coming in my office with a simple question on paper that I will be unable to read. To deal with this, I focus on one noun and repeat it with a question, "Smith?," which prompts the other person to talk. This breaks down the barrier and I can begin to actually read the paper.

To this day I don't read a roster in my classroom because I can't pronounce the names. I pass it around and have people initial it to indicate whether they are there or not. Passing back exams I just put the score inside the front cover so no one can see the score, then I stack them up in the front of the room and say "Okay, come up and grab your exam." I avoid having to read the names.

My working conditions may seem unorganized and cluttered. But I work like "random access." I jump in and solve problems. I may jump in the middle or the end. I will ask what do you want it to look like at the end.

I also practiced public relations from the start. I knew that there couldn't be a conflict situation with teachers. It's hard enough without having someone dislike you. So I would carry their books to the car or bring them an apple. I tried to be nice in class. With homework, I always tried to do the best I could. That all made a difference in my life.

I have developed a very prosthetic environment. I have a telephone log; I use my tape recorder extensively. I even have a maintenance log in my car in such a way that there is no way I can miss getting the oil changed.

I learned to read by going to a lot of sporting events. Then I could read about them over and over again in the *New York Times*.

These highly successful adults with learning disabilities used an array of coping strategies. The more moderately successful adults tended to focus much more energy on manipulation as a means for avoiding exposure of their disability. The highly successful group was far more creative and attempted to build on their personal areas of strength.

Social Ecologies

Finally, successful adults with learning disabilities willingly utilized supportive and helpful people. Also, they sharpened their skills by designing personal improvement programs. We call these support and improvement-oriented processes their *social ecology*. Most of the successful adults established support networks with a spouse, a family member, a friend, or someone else on whom they could rely. In addition, they purposely selected their mentors. Some were luckier than others— their support came from family members or close friends so they did not have to solicit it. But having support readily available and actually accepting it and utilizing it are not always synonymous. In the case of successful adults, they recognized the need for support and took advantage of help to overcome hurdles. Whether it was in the form of human support or training they purposely sought in areas of weakness, they got the help they needed to succeed. They avoided dependence by achieving a balance between support and autonomy.

Many of the more highly successful adults with disabilities designed apprenticeship-like programs for themselves in order to bolster certain skills. For some, this meant hiring helpers for direct support: tutors, secretaries, support staff. For example, several dyslexics who had written books used coauthors to do the writing, which the highly successful adults in our sample dictated to them. But the need for surrounding oneself with good people was a constant theme we heard. Most often, personal relationships were key—wives for males and friends for females. Many discussed the mentors they had relied on over the years. Regardless of its form, support was important to guarantee that they could move ahead. As one highly successful adult explained to us about support, it kept him from just "gathering dust!" Others were equally direct in substantiating the importance of support:

> It's basically the issue of knowing exactly the types of support you need . . . so it's knowing what it is that you can't do and when you need to call on help to perform.

> Success is a lot of trying to get the right people around you to help you make sure it gets done.

> My success was contingent upon other people doing things for me.

A common theme among the males in our highly successful group was the help their spouses provided. Several explained how their wives read to them, did various household or routine tasks that their disability made difficult, or even whispered names of good friends or business associates to them at social gatherings because of their memory problems. One highly successful male adult explained that "My wife is very important. We are a team, we work together." Another said, "By the end of a year and a half into college, my wife was in a sense whipping me into shape. She was the one who got me to apply myself. Once I started applying myself, then I was able to teach myself how to learn. Nowadays, she kicks my butt if I do something wrong." Still another told us "My wife has been very supportive. While I was in public accounting, it was very high pressure. She deserves the CPA as much as I do." A lawyer summed up the importance of his wife this way: "The original adaptive device was to marry someone, who in addition to having a B.A. in psychology, was a crackerjack secretary!"

Obviously, a spouse was very important for many of the married males in our sample. For others, it was a parent, a teacher, a friend, or a carefully chosen mentor. But the key point is that support and even guidance are invaluable aids to success, and one must be willing to seek, appreciate, and accept what others may offer. Many other comments we heard sustain this point:

> You need other people to help . . . to help you believe in yourself. But you must be willing to accept some help, from a secretary or anyone. Otherwise, you will waste too much time. You must learn to depend on others to a certain extent.

> (My success) is the result of the conscious effort my mother put into working with me with the reading problem.

> I had a teacher, Mr. S. He didn't think I was such a dummy in reading. He convinced me I could read. Suddenly, it made such a difference having someone give me the confidence to go and do the work.

> My boyfriend does the grocery shopping. We would eat potato chips all the time if I did the shopping. I was very thin when I lived alone . . . I always bought ten of the same item, then found out I already had ten at home!

> My wife allows me the freedom I need to work as I do. She prepares the meals around my schedule and puts up with my computer books at home.

> If I don't have a manager that helps me, I swing off. I will know my goal and objective clearly, but I'll drift off. Currently I have a great manager who sets limits for me. . . . It's the discipline that I can't self impose.

> I've had the same collaborator, a science writer, on the two books I've written. I give him all the information and he turns it into English. I similarly use mathematicians for help figuring math problems.

> During high school and college my parents were very supportive. They never let me fail or give up. They supplied a disciplined and supportive atmosphere. They never compared me to my brothers who did much better in school. They truly believed I could do it and instilled this belief in me.

It is apparent that the highly successful adults with learning disabilities relied on the support of others on the road to success. This support gave them more control over their lives. The distinction between the highly and moderately successful adults concerning social ecologies revolved around two key factors: the level of support employed, and the willingness to embrace support. These two factors are closely related to the degree of reframing the moderately successful adults achieved. The moderates were far more dependent on others than were the more highly successful adults. The highly successful adults utilized support to help them gain control of their lives, whereas the moderately successful adults often relied totally on others. One even told us that "I have had to rely the majority of my life on other people."

In addition, the highly successful adults were far more willing to seek support and help than their moderately successful counterparts. One moderately successful adult explained, "If I could do it all over again, I would ask for more help." Another said, "If I had had a little more support, I could be on an equal basis with anybody." Thus, while all the adults with learning disabilities agreed that support was important, the high success group utilized support more to their advantage, they sought it out more readily, and they accepted it more easily when it was available.

Conclusions

The implications of our model are closely aligned with findings from studies on multiple intelligences (Gardner, 1983; Gardner & Hatch, 1989) and variable thinking styles (Sternberg, 1990). Such studies suggest that individuals think and learn in different ways, and that schooling and training must be sensitive to these differences. Our model implies that persons with learning disabilities do think and learn differently, *but* they can and do learn; they just learn in a different way. Our model implies that with the right grit, determination, thought, application, and help, adults with learning disabilities can be very successful in the workplace.

We also believe that each of the internal decisions and external manifestations that make up our model of success are variables susceptible to training. Individuals can be taught about desire, goal orientation, and reframing, and as a result enhance the possibility of excelling in these areas. Similarly, people can be taught about the need for persistence, goodness of fit, learned creativity, and social support. Although training in these areas may not always be effective, presenting how these themes can interact for control and success may play a significant role in altering children's lives. We discuss the implications of the model of success for teaching and learning in Chapter 10.

Personal Perspectives on the Model

A s we began to write and talk about the "model of success" from the preceding chapter, we intuitively felt that we had captured, at least to some extent, commonalities in the process by which adults with learning disabilities become successful. As qualitative researchers, however, we were especially conscious of the potential for bias, subjectivity, and even distortions in our own reactions. We heeded McCall's (1969) admonition that "distortions may . . . arise from the observer's personal characteristics, such as mood, prejudices, or blind spots. And, of course, the observer's intellectual frame of reference may adversely condition perceptions by leading him to pay selective attention to certain aspects of the phenomenon rather than to others" (p. 129).

We were acutely aware of the importance of checking the validity of inferences and conclusions related to the model of success. Notable researchers such as Goetz and LeCompte (1984) and Lincoln and Guba (1985) have devoted considerable discussion to identifying means for heightening the validity of qualitative conclusions. A fairly consistent theme centers on cross-validation, or the use of multiple sources to comment, respond, and react to the findings of the researchers.

We presented findings from the study at various conferences across the United States. Invariably, adults with learning disabilities from the audience told us that we were describing the very things they did. They would often add that they had never conceptualized the success process in such a structured fashion, but that our analysis helped *them* understand or clarify what they had been doing to be successful.

Such responses provided only a modest degree of validation. In many cases, these audience members focused on a specific component of the model. They did not tell us whether the other components made sense. They did not evaluate the comprehensiveness of the model: Did it describe *everything* about the success process?

Fortunately, we had the most logical source available to us for substantiating the validity of the courses of action the model suggests—the participants in the study. Before we could generalize our findings to the general population of successful adults with learning disabilities, we needed to be sure that our findings made sense to our participants. We realized that even our participants, the most logical "experts" to provide cross-validation, were themselves vulnerable to a degree of subjectivity. As Vidich (1969) explains, "Data collection does not take place in a vacuum. Perspectives and perceptions of social reality are shaped by the social position of both the *observed* [italics added] and the observer as they live through a passing present" (p. 86). Nevertheless, we reasoned that, coupled with the means we had already utilized during the process of analyzing our data to strengthen the validity and reliability of our findings, asking several of our participants to critique our work would provide the most direct means for substantiating the validity of the model for success. Such "member checks" are a common practice in qualitative studies, because they provide what Bronfenbrenner (1976) terms "validity." This chapter presents four such reactions to the model. We conclude with *our* reaction to these reactions. We simply could not resist getting in the final word!

A Model and a Case: Some Personal Reflections

Elisabeth H. Wiig, Ph.D.

A native of Denmark, where she received her B.S., Elisabeth H. Wiig completed her professional schooling in the United States with a Ph.D. from Case Western Reserve University. She is currently professor emerita at the Department of Communication Disorders of Boston University. In addition to holding a CCC in speech language pathology and audiology, Wiig is a member of the International Association for Research in Learning Disabilities, the American Speech–Language Association, and the Texas Speech and Hearing Association. She has published more than 60 articles and has made numerous conference presentations dealing primarily with language-learning disabilities. Her research focus on the language problems of children and adolescents with learning disabilities is reflected in tests and texts, including Language Assessment and Intervention for the Learning Disabled, CELF–Preschool, Test of Word Knowledge, Test of Language Competence–Expanded, *and* CELF–3. *She resides in Arlington, Texas, with her husband.*

As I reflect on my activities of the past years, I acknowledge that I have played a small part in an exciting process of developing a model to account for success among individuals with learning disabilities. It started when Dr. Gerber and Dr. Reiff asked me if I would be a participant in an ethnographic study of professionals with learning disabilities. Next, I found myself talking about my experiences of adapting to and coping with LD. Some time went by and then a model of patterns in employment success, abstracted from the various accounts, appeared in a popular professional journal (Gerber, Ginsberg, & Reiff, 1992). I read the account of the model, found major points of recognition and agreement, but thought that was the end of the story for me. Obviously it was not, since I was asked to converse with you about my personal responses to the scientific model. Before you read my reactions, I need to point out that I will react to selected features of the model related to control, internal decisions, and external manifestations—adaptability.

Taking Control

The model states that control in the form of "making conscious decisions to take charge of one's life . . . and adapting and shaping oneself to move ahead" is essential for success. I agree fully at the levels of emotion, reasoning, and experience. In my case taking control of my existence was learned early and not in the context of my learning disabilities. I lived in Denmark during Nazi occupation from 1940 to 1945 (I was five when the war started). My experiences of the occupation and war and reactions to them were in line with the national feelings of commitment to freedom. My parents taught me to take control emotionally and behaviorally. They expected me to accept physical hardship, keep public and personal secrets, to aid in the resistance efforts, and to move ahead as if survival and life were sure outcomes. During it all they shared their emotions and gave support when I was paralyzed by fears.

The type of taking control I learned from war experiences served me well later on, when my fears and frustrations were about reading, math, geometry, and gym, to mention a few dread subjects. However, from kindergarten through grade three I gave in to the impact of my disabilities. I was unable to apply what I had learned about taking control in real life to lie in the structured and competitive academic setting. I lost my sense of being able to generate fun, being creative, and being capable of handling adult secrets and situations. In school I was fragile and distrustful, and was out of touch with myself as a learner and with others in the school setting. Life began when I got home from school—in school there was only submission, failure, and inefficient coping. My real-life ability to take control was not transferred and applied to learning until I received help from external sources.

Favorable Social Ecologies

More than anything else the people around me fostered my development. They helped me reestablish conscious control. There were several people that were essential in the process. My father, a physician, and my uncle, a neurologist, realized when I was 4 or 5 years old that I developed to a different drummer. They anticipated that my uneven abilities might give me problems in school. They discussed among themselves that I exhibited evidence of brain dysfunction—there was no term for a learning disability then. When my learning disability symptoms began to show in kindergarten—I had problems with anything that required visuomotor integration—my parents were contacted and I was called a slow learner. My father and uncle went into action at that point. I was given a neurological examination and several signs of neurological involvement were established. I was also given a psychological evaluation. It showed high-level verbal abilities associated with below average nonverbal abilities. Later on, when I doubted my ability to learn, my father would quote my verbal IQ—he gave the actual number—to remind me of my strengths and bolster my motivation and persistence. My father and uncle remained stable supports throughout my education. When I failed geometry three semesters in a row in high school, they told me to focus on my strengths—foreign languages and social studies—get good grades in those subjects and wait until the system got some sense and realized I was geometrically illiterate for life. Eventually the system gave me a waiver for geometry. When I failed basic college math, they gave me the same kind of advice. They counseled me to take symbolic logic and to focus on getting a top grade so I could be exempted from college math too. Obviously it worked or I would never have achieved a Ph.D.

You may wonder why I do not mention my mother as a conscious support. My mother holds a degree in pharmacology—but she is such an optimist that she could not give me the realistic—good and bad—strengths and weaknesses—kind of support I needed.

I was fortunate in marriage that my husband, Martin, listened to me when I told how my learning disability influenced who I was and what I could and could not do. As an example, Martin is an avid skier and our children were taught to ski early. He experienced early in our marriage that I cannot perceive contours when skiing. I nearly ran off a cliff—the slope looked so gentle. He recognized that skiing posed a real danger for me and never forced me to join in family skiing trips. He values my strengths and allows me to develop my potential to the maximum, while helping to create an environment which supports my creativity.

The person outside my family circle that had the greatest impact was my special education teacher. I spent three years with her in a class with several students who were mentally challenged and one girl—my buddy—who was paraplegic after polio. The great good fortune was that this teacher was trained by Maria Montessori in person before the war. She structured learning for me; she taught me adaptive compensatory strategies; but first and foremost she helped develop my awareness of myself as a learner and person, for better and worse. If one teacher can change a life, this teacher did it. When I was reintegrated in regular classes, I used her as a "consultant" whenever I had problems learning or coping. The ability she developed in me, to recognize when I needed consultative or collaborative help, has followed me through life.

Later in life, during high school, college, and the professional years, I have depended on the strengths that others can lend me and capitalized on the strengths I can lend them. I have had the good fortune of having found collaborators throughout my life. I have searched for collaborators consciously, recognizing that they were favorable social ecologies, and I have given generously to my collaborators. Successful collaborations have been my lifeline and remain so to this day.

Other Means for Adapting

Depending on favorable social ecologies and on others for support goes only so far. The rest of the way has to be forged by the individual with the learning disability. The model for success points this out and identified two features I relate strongly to. The first is learned creativity, that is, developing strategies, techniques and mechanisms that support and enhance performance. The second is goodness of fit, that is, identifying or establishing an environment that allows for success. In my case these two factors seem inextricably intertwined and I shall discuss them as one.

Learned creativity and searching for a goodness of fit can originate from inside the individual or can be initiated by outside forces and events. In my early school years I spent a lot of creative effort to develop ways in which to avoid or change situations which would expose my weaknesses. My first tactic was to show off what I could do when I was cornered. I would sing, tell a story, create a game, all to divert attention. I managed fairly well until I was faced with my special education teacher. She knew all my tricks and made me realize that avoidance would not make me succeed.

Another tactic I used in school was to memorize everything I heard. In that way I could pretend I could read or do math. My auditory memory became acute, but by the end of the second grade I could not keep it up any longer. And, of course, I used all the other creative tactics children with learning disabilities are known for. I shadowed others; cheated by looking; I hid behind others; I even "borrowed" work from children in a parallel class. I was a consummate operator and not too bad at lying either.

I needed confrontation to give up the less than adaptive tactics and develop strategies for succeeding. The first time I realized that there were strategies for succeeding was when my teacher told me that reading was a guessing game; that I could predict words, phrases, and even sentences; that I could sight read lots of words; that I only needed to sound out the first letter to get the right word in a context; that I did not need to read out loud to understand; that I could skim read, once I knew what information I was looking for and how the author presented it. She opened a Pandora's box that has not yet been exhausted.

My teacher also spent time to elicit, listen to, and modify options and strategies for real-life problem solving and decision making. I had a very real problem in making realistic decisions. I would go with intuition or impulse and often failed sorely, especially in the social domain. My teacher and parents collaborated in helping me talk through social problems, decisions, and outcomes. Nonetheless,

I am still weak in that area. Unfortunately, everyone had less success in teaching me strategies for math, algebra, and geometry.

The strategies I was taught worked well for me. As a result they formed a basis for developing strategies for more complex problem areas such as statistics, symbolic logic, and the like. I am aware that as an adult I have internalized scripts and higher level abstract schemata (mental models) that help me compare, contrast, and problem solve. I am especially aware of how the situational scripts and schematic representations of the world around me help me negotiate my way in space. This is because visual–spatial perception, orientation, and recollection remain areas where I fall apart if I get anxious, hurried, or in any other way emotionally involved.

It is not enough to develop scripts, schemata, and strategies. There is realistic need for using support systems and mechanisms to increase the chances of success. I learned in my special education class that teamwork pays if you have a disability. I teamed up with my classmate with paraplegia. I was her motor system and she was my visual–perceptual system. Together we felt whole and very competent—as an aside my teammate is now a researcher in pediatrics. As an adolescent and adult I have continued team building for better performance. I learned quickly what it requires to be an effective teammate. You must have insight into your strengths and weaknesses, knowledge of what you can give and what you are looking to get, and ability to cast off any trace of jealousy or greed. I am still working on being a better teammate.

There is also a need to use any available equipment or media to compensate for weaknesses and enhance performance in areas of strengths. In school I was allowed to use multiplication, log, and other appropriate math and statistics tables. The limitation was always that I could use the compensatory means only if I understood the conceptual bases for their use. This requirement for understanding has helped me perform in areas I would never have dreamed of—among them formal test design and experimentation, which are now part of my regular work.

In junior high and high school I was allowed to use a typewriter for written work and exams. Later the computer became my long-term, silent teammate. It spells for me; it takes handwriting away as tormentor; it allows me to edit easily; it is nonjudgmental. My husband, a computernik, has made sure I always have the best in computers relative to my needs and abilities as a computer operator. My son, another computernik, has also provided support in this area. In short, I learned early to spare no costs to obtain the tools that would allow me to fly.

The goodness of fit I am experiencing as an adult has been forged by circumstances outside of me as well as by choices I made along the way. Most of the time I have had professional experiences. My recurring problem was always that I have no sense of time. Appointments were the plague. Once I was with someone, I concentrated on that person and the issues at hand. As a result I was late for meetings, committees, trains, and planes until I had a secretary who organized my time and my work space as well.

As an adult professional, I ventured outside my limits. I tried my hand at chairing a department. The goals I set for the program were reached, but I found I was only good at and satisfied with the acts of conceptualizing and hated managing day-to-day activities. You could say I did not have the personality for it. You could also say that as long as my strengths were tapped and my social weaknesses were not challenged I could succeed.

Internal Decisions

So far I have focused on the observable. Yet many unobservable factors have contributed to my professional success. Even as a child I was curious and had a great desire to lean. That desire was stymied in the early school years when I fell further and further behind in reading, writing, and math. The desire was rekindled once my special education teacher made me an active participant in the processes of learning. Curiosity and desire to create have followed me throughout my adult career. I remember a day in 1975 when I told a colleague I was "pregnant with book"—I was so full of ideas about language-learning disabilities that I needed to write to get it out in the open.

I have also always had a strong goal orientation. I designed a complex spy game when I was eight. My friends and I played the game for close to a year. I told my special education classmates that one day I would teach adults to work with children like us. They laughed, but I kept the goal in mind. When I decided I was pregnant with book I knew the process would require goal setting and long-term persistence. I also knew there might be setbacks, and yet I dared to gamble on my ability to reach the goal. In my life it seems that challenges are renewed, new goals are set, and my inner cheerleader voice keeps telling me to go on. However, my desire and goal-oriented attitudes could not have done it alone. I recognize that reframing my disabilities, that is, changing the perspective of the disability to obtain a more effective approach, has always been the central process that kept me going in spite of all odds.

The process of reframing one's disability requires conscious efforts to make the best out of a bad situation. I have had lots of experiences with that, and they embrace more than my learning disability. When I was ten—in 1945—I was diagnosed with tuberculosis. I spent 6 months in isolation and the next 6 months in fresh air with other seriously ill people. I saw others die and observed that death was often presaged by the patients' attitudes. I saw a young woman decide to die and subsequently regress into death. Of course, not everyone who fought survived. However, among survivors was the attitude that you can change how you feel about your illness and what you do to combat it. Personally, I reframed the experience. During my time in isolation I decided to develop my storytelling abilities. I wrote stories and plays in my mind—none reached paper because everything I was in contact with was burned. I developed a large and varied set of characters for my stories and plays with paper dolls. I set a daily schedule for my aloneness and kept to it. I tried to be in control within the limitations set for me.

In the late teens I was diagnosed to have manic-depression. It came on top of the learning disability and I thought my life should be over—I did attempt suicide. Once I decided on life, however, I started to reframe that disability too. I learned all I could about it. I took advantage of the slightly hypomanic periods to generate ideas for my next ventures—some were crazy, of course, but many have been realized. I also learned that my periods of depression were helped by reading and preparing myself to implement my ideas. I did this in spite of the fact that I was very creative at hiding my mental disorder.

Obviously I have reframed my learning disability. I see now that my desire to explore language-learning disabilities came from reframing my own learning disability. I am in a way proud to have a learning disability. I have reframed negative images of the condition into positive ones. I see persons with learning disabilities as having immense potential—maybe not in the traditional mold, but in a different mold. I have reframed the stigma and negative images that go with manic-depression into positives. This has allowed me to become a very candid and effective advocate for persons with mental health problems. I have accepted that I will always live with a learning disability and remain a consumer of mental health services. All I can say is "So what"—if you don't like the person I am, there are plenty others you can associate with who are "normal."

A Remarkable Parallel

Stanley J. Antonoff, D.D.S.

Stanley J. Antonoff, D.D.S., has practiced dentistry for more than 35 years. Having received both his B.A. and D.D.S. degrees from New York University, he is currently a clinical professor and director of the learning disability program at the NYU Dental Center and maintains a private dental practice in Manhattan. He has written textbooks, articles, and lectured around the world. In addition to his professional affiliations as a fellow of the International College of Dentistry, the American College of Dentistry, the Greater New York Academy of Prosthodontics, and a member of the American Dental Association, Dr. Antonoff is also a past board member of the national Orton Dyslexia Society, a former president of the New York branch of the Orton Dyslexia Society, is currently active in dyslexia organizations in New York State, and speaks frequently at regional and national learning disabilities conferences. Married for more than 40 years and the father of five children, he enjoys tennis, golf, and dancing.

Researchers and interested individuals have sought the mechanisms that are instrumental for a person's success in the workplace with the hope that their identification could be taught to others to improve performance. But individuals behave differently to changing stimuli and conditions so every nuance cannot be factored into behavioral modification. At best, a few major factors might be identified that would help explain the greater success of one individual. Often, one or two central and powerful forces can be found in successful individuals. Motivation and perseverance are two frequently mentioned. Are these factors the result of a genetic predisposition or behaviorally learned? Fortunately, this question is not one that I need to answer.

Identifying successful persons and then trying to identify the reasons for their success is difficult to do and fraught with possible misinterpretations. Knowing this will ameliorate incorrect conclusions drawn along the way.

A Greek philosopher once noted that the world is filled with beautiful, magical things patiently waiting for our wits to grow sharper. The goal-oriented individual with dyslexia is aggressive in the pursuit of the world's rewards.

By the time I reached my 45th birthday I had accomplished what most people do not accomplish in a lifetime. I had been happily married almost 25 years, with five children and the rewards of financial success, an expensive home, and the other accoutrements of the American dream. Professionally, my dental practice was very successful. Promotions to full professor in a prominent dental school and completion of a research project were other ingredients of my success. My professional career involved membership, as a fellow, in several prestigious dental academies, coauthor of a dental textbook, and 10 articles published. Expertise in a dental speciality afforded me the opportunity to present over 35 lectures, both in the United States and abroad. This was accomplished without knowing of my dyslexia, a learning disability.

Upon reflection, I now realize that there were several reasons for my success. Primarily, it was the ability to compensate for difficulties that arose in both my professional and personal life. In addition, the ability to recognize when a mentor was necessary to achieve targeted goals was a factor that contributed to my achievements. A marriage to a kind, supportive, and understanding person was a great asset. Other factors were instrumental for success, namely, a career objective, the ability to identify where I wanted to go, and insight to visualize how to get there. Once these goals were defined, I worked hard to achieve them. Perseverance and motivation were close companions throughout my career. Fortunately, many people supported me, thus making my path easier and enriching. The selection of a profession in which I could excel was the most important step in my career, one that allowed me to utilize my talents. My particular capabilities were revealed early in my life. I was quite proficient in model building and demonstrated extraordinary hand dexterity. I could copy pictures and paintings with great skill. My interest in the health sciences, coupled with my skills and creativity, led me to dentistry.

Though an average student in college, I flourished in dental school where my dexterity and artistic sense allowed me to excel. My academic difficulties, due to my undiagnosed dyslexia, were compensated for by my outstanding performance in other areas of the dental curriculum. Assaults on my ego were a problem at school where I felt others were smarter than me. This was based on my inability to grasp the academic portion of the curriculum within the same time span as students without learning disabilities. My strategy was a simple axiom. If others could succeed, so could I. When facing a learning problem, I found a way of surmounting it. I was goal oriented and dedicated to success.

Support of friends was most important. At any stage in my academic career, when difficulty arose, I was fortunate to find an advisor for guidance. Once I received instruction, I repeated the process until I mastered the necessary skills to accomplish the task—strong evidence that perseverance, for me, was part of the chemistry for success.

I recognized early that the most important person to count on was myself. The responsibility for outcomes devolved upon me; otherwise I could not be certain if the task could or would be accomplished on time. In my professional career, I needed to control everything in which I was involved. It was difficult for me to delegate either authority or tasks; therefore, I needed more time to complete projects. Even at this time, I have not struck a dynamic equilibrium between delegation of authority and control. At times, I accepted projects that overreached my capacity, causing me to push myself. In this manner, motivation accompanied by perseverance helped me successfully complete my projects. I developed a reputation for reliability and always met promised deadlines, but at a cost. Unfortunately, at times when working with others I often found myself pushing harder because they lacked the work ethic that was my standard. To this day, I prefer doing things alone in order to maintain control. This is not always possible considering the number of projects with which I am involved.

When reflecting on my accomplishments and the steps necessary to achieve my goals I find a remarkable parallel with the model set forth in Chapter 7. I agree that the important determinants of success in the workplace, for persons with and without learning disabilities, are job maintenance, employment stability, career advancement, and the attainment of leadership roles and responsibilities. This is especially true when trying to identify and follow the levels of success attained by persons with learning disabilities. Should there be a different standard because of their disabling condition? Should the level of achievement be given greater importance because of the obstacles that persons with learning disabilities had to overcome? Chapter 7 clearly indicated that there are different levels of success even though the disabling conditions may essentially be the same. Success at any level, regardless of disability, is dependent on motivation, persistence, self-confidence, and the strength and force of character. This is well documented in the beginning of the chapter.

I feel the protocol for the research is well conceived. The sample selection, instrumentation, and interview process and training were more than adequate to obtain a larger amount of data. Further, I believe the data analysis leads inevitably to the conclusions set forth.

Perhaps Chapter 7 would be clearer if the definition of success were more specific. There are many levels of success. Indeed, the middle strata of persons interviewed might have been considered more successful than the upper strata if the measurements included the obstacles they had to overcome. They may have come from a dysfunctional family setting or their disability might have been more severe. Each of these possibilities alone, and certainly in combination, might have measured for greater success even though they achieved at a lower level. The level of success must be measured by the obstacles that were overcome. The definition of success in this investigation would have been better served if it included not only the severity of the individuals' learning disabilities but any other factors about their severity (i.e., poverty, dysfunctional family, etc.) that affected their life.

The definition of success also plays a role in the measurement of outcomes that the authors seek. It is arduous enough to develop a vehicle that measures outcomes. Without appropriate definitions, limitations and expectations relative to other criteria are extremely difficult to determine. It appears that the models for success were derived from the non–learning disabled arena. Perhaps a specific set of criteria for success for persons with learning disabilities should have been developed from that population and not from the non–LD population. This is essential, for there is a direct relationship between success and the severity of the disability. While the severity of the disability may impede one individual's ability to succeed, it may be the impetus to drive another person to great success.

The researchers have identified the factors that appear to lead to success if used appropriately. These factors (i.e., adaptability, coping mechanisms, appropriate fit between abilities and environment, support of other and planned experiences, coupled with a strong desire to succeed and goal orientation) would appear to lead to success for individuals without learning disabilities as well. Success is developmental, in that one builds upon each block of achievement until the edifice is complete.

In my opinion, the authors have established that it is important that the person with a learning disability have the same traits as the person without disabilities, namely, desire and goal orientation, in order to achieve success. The only difference is that the person with a learning disability must undergo reframing, which is the confrontation of the various challenges presented by the learning disability.

"Reframing" is perhaps the most difficult position to restructure. Needless energy is wasted on what I call the "Why me?" syndrome. Why do I have this problem? Why must I face so many difficulties presented by this problem? In my position, as director of the Learning Disability Program for students in a professional school, I have found that those students who have the "Why me?" syndrome usually fare the worst because they waste so much energy. Those who say "OK, this is what I have, now I understand some of my problems, how do I deal with it in the future" fare the best. They accept their status, and this creates understanding and hope. Desire and motivation alone are not always enough to create success. The research corroborates that reframing or acceptance of the problem is a necessary ingredient.

Reframing is a hard task; it is difficult to interpret the experiences involved with learning disabilities in a positive way. The ability to confront the various problems encountered with learning disabilities and overcome them is extremely challenging. Consider all the problems encountered with behavioral modification. The inability to reframe coupled with the great anxiety found in the workplace makes success difficult for the individuals with learning disabilities.

Another problem encountered by the person with learning disabilities is the inability to find support or a mentor in the workplace. Though persons with learning disabilities take longer to learn, once the skills are acquired they perform as well or better than their counterparts without disabilities. In the beginning, they frequently fall behind and are placed at a disadvantage because of their initial slowness. At this time mentors or support persons would be extremely helpful, but they are usually unavailable in the workplace, often involved in their own careers or impervious to the needs of the person with a learning disability. There is no question that many individuals with learning disabilities have become successful because of the intervention of an interested party. Most important is the concept of control. Unless self-employed it is extremely difficult to exercise control, especially if you are trying to improve your position in a large organization. Success in these institutions relies on the ability to work with others. This implies lack of control or at the very least a minimal exercise of control. If control is essential for the success of a person with a learning disability, then working for a large corporation may hamper that success.

It appears that the authors have identified the ingredients necessary for an adult with a learning disability to be successful. This is desirable, for it reveals the traits that a person with a learning disability must possess to achieve success. I believe, however, that it has limited usefulness as far as predictability is concerned. There are too many variables involved to determine whether a person with a learning disability will be successful in later life. It would be more important to identify younger persons with learning disabilities who have the aforesaid traits and nurture them thus maximizing their potential for success. I firmly believe that a society that does not provide the resources to help the young person with a learning disability achieve and reach his or her potential will suffer from self-inflicted wounds.

A Personal Response to the Model of Success

Coller Ochsner, M.D.

A third-generation physician, Coller Ochsner was born March 25, 1954, in Washington, D.C., during the time her father was doing his medical training. The second child of six children, she grew up primarily in New Orleans, the home of her parents. Her paternal grandfather founded Ochsner Foundation Hospital in New Orleans, an internationally known medical institution. Dr. Ochsner trained at Tulane Medical School, interned at Ochsner Foundation Hospital, and did her res-

idency followed by a fellowship at Tulane. She currently runs her own private practice in dermatology and allergy in the New Orleans area where she continues to reside. She is single and lives with three dogs and a cat. "I have a real passion for animals, and I heavily support the Louisiana S.P.C.A. I love the outdoors, and I love adventure. One thing I can say—I'm never bored."

Control

I do want to be in control of my life. Because this in itself is kind of all consuming, I don't feel the need to control others' lives. Thus I think I'm happier. Although now I'm not as ashamed of my learning disability as I was as a child, I still have some internal fears or obstacles or reminders of my problem. I've just begun to accept my limits. I'm an overachiever, if it's only to protect my learning disabilities. So I work 100 times harder at the times I can do so. Maybe it's a way of overcoming my embarrassment. I don't just cover up my problems; I excel.

As a child my poor skills, my learning disability, had too much control of me. Via the help of my mother when I was a child, she would tell me over and over again when I became a doctor I would not have to spell, write papers, and be in all those situations that were so painfully embarrassing as a child. Thus once I saw a light at the end of the tunnel no obstacle would be able to stop me from achieving that level. I knew the problem would not go away, but I did learn to believe that I could overcome it. I sought out situations where my skills that were faulty would not be needed as much. So the problem was less of a problem. The problem would not be the thing to control me. Instead, I would control it.

Internal Decisions

Desire

The hurdles are a bigger challenge for those with a learning disability. But hindsight makes me say that I'm stronger now than I would have been if I had less of a challenge. I feel that if I didn't have years of failures I would never have been as successful. In spite of my knowing that I was not "retarded," I still failed. That was the push to realizing that some other path needed to be taken and more work needed to be done. So at a very young age I started training myself in a way to succeed that has helped my entire life.

You see, if you have it easy when you are young, if you don't have to work hard but everything comes your way, you really don't have much of a reason to develop a strong work ethic. Why should you be a fighter if you never have to fight? Then when you're older, it's hard to change those habits. And when you are faced with a challenge you would have a much more difficult time in trying to overcome it. But since I was forced as a child to constantly learn to try new ways and to keep trying, never giving up, it is now a natural way with me. It's not that I don't ever get tired, but the tiredness doesn't last long and I don't get too discouraged. I just rest and know in my heart there's always a new day, a new chance, and a new way to overcome the problem.

In Chapter 7 I know that was me who said, "Just tell me I can't do it and I'll do it," because that's still me. I sometimes think that I am who I am because of my learning disability. As a child I knew that I was not stupid, yet that's how I looked to others. And that made me determined to prove I wasn't. I agree with the person who said that determination is three fourths of the battle. Failure was many times the incredible fuel because I was going to have to make sure it would never happen again. And once I got on a roll of being successful and accomplishing things, it felt good. And I wanted to keep feeling good. Now in my life I know that if I really want something I can do it or get it. All it takes is the work. So to me, first it's the desire and the degree of desire that determine the amount of work you will put in. Whatever I do I try to do to the best of my ability.

I'm lucky. I happen to be a worker so it might be a little easier for me since I am happiest when I'm working or achieving. It doesn't matter if it's medical work or yard work; I love to accomplish.

With all the determination and desire to accomplish I still need positive reinforcement. So I have learned to give it to myself. My mother gave me a lot. When it came to reading or writing in my school work she basically was my own tutor and supported me as a young child. As a young adult she did not cripple me. She said you work and make the money you need to get a tutor if you need it. Knowing that my writing and reading skills were so poor I did exactly that and paid for my own tutor from high school and up.

Another way I gave myself positive reinforcement was I would do things and accomplish things that did not require my LD skills. And I would do them well to prove to me and others I could do and just not do, but do anything wonderfully. I guess I thought this would outweigh my problems with my LD. It sure helped my ego.

I like when someone said that they didn't care how long it would take to get toward their goals. I realized that I love accomplishing but it is the process of it that is now so exciting because I can be proud of myself regularly day by day instead of just at the end of the total accomplishment.

I do question if desire can be taught. It might be able to be discovered in one's self via help. But I think you or I have a basic degree of desire. One might be happy just dreaming about it, while others need to attain it. But I still feel there is a basic *deep* down desire that is part of a particular person.

Goal Orientation

Each milestone that I accomplished had a snowball effect. Even though I couldn't read, by memorizing books I made it through the early grades in school. In high school and college, I had tutoring. Just making it through school gave me confidence that I could make it. When I got to medical school I was put to the test. This was my biggest success because I saw that even with the top people I could still do it. The more confidence I got, the stronger I attacked the next challenge.

Reframing

The learning disability made me very much look into myself. I feel that I'm very lucky because at a young part of my life it made me appreciate hard work. I don't know if I was emotional and the frustration over my learning disabilities brought out my emotions more, or if the fact that I had learning disabilities made me more emotional to release the frustrations. Either way I'm very emotional. I'm sure the learning disabilities gave me a deeper character. I care more. I cry easily. I cry for anything that has a disability. At the same time, I probably wouldn't enjoy life the way I do if it weren't for the learning disabilities.

External Manifestations

Persistence

This goes without saying. It must be.

Goodness of Fit

I feel that the more you love what you are doing and surround yourself as much as possible with an environment that is enjoyable and supportive and with control you can afford to spend your time accelerating with your strengths. I love being a doctor. It's a good mesh between my strengths and my need to help people. Medicine was familiar because of my family background. My father (a prominent physician) was my role model. And I believed I could excel in this area. You said it best—with enthusiasm and in an environment that permitted these adults to shine using their strengths—how can you not excel? I have learned to accept help and to accept constructive criticism, something I resisted as a child.

Learned Creativity

I have always used special strategies (learned creativity) to help me compensate and succeed. As I said, I memorized books in elementary school so it would look like I could read them. In college, I selected courses ahead of time that required the least amount of writing. I graduated magna cum laude. I tell myself the more I have to do today, the less I'll have to do tomorrow. I wake up very early in the morning (4 a.m.). That's when I do my studying or difficult things I have to work on. I save my evenings for exercise, and that gets rid of a lot of my frustration. Even my bad handwriting can work for me as a protective strategy. First, it's acceptable for a doctor. And when I can't spell a word, I purposely use messy handwriting.

Social Ecologies

I believe the amount of desire can be increased by external support and may even be decreased by external influence. With any disability if you don't have the right support, I think it's tough; you can go so many ways. I was able to get over my learning disability because I had a lot of support. For example, I had lots of positive reinforcement as a child that I could do it. Because I knew that my parents loved me and believed in me so much, I just couldn't let them down. I felt this was very important in my early years!

About Chapter 7—I think it's wonderful. I can't really alter or add much, but I feel you dissected the situation incredibly.

A Qualified Response

Paul Grossman, J.D.

For the past 20 years Paul Grossman has worked as a civil rights attorney for a federal agency where he supervises a legal team. He previously worked as legal counselor for the Oakland Police Department. He is a specialist in the area of discrimination law and has written about discrimination as it applies to disabilities in a number of professional publications. In addition to his responsibilities as a civil rights attorney, he currently teaches courses on disability and the law at the Hastings Law School in the San Francisco Bay area. He also has developed a reputation in the learning disabilities field through his frequent presentations at regional and national learning disabilities conferences. A native of Chicago, Mr. Grossman studied at Oxford University and is a graduate of the University of Wisconsin School of Law where he was accepted in the law honor society. He is married with one son.

Quest for Control

The organizing principle of the model of success, as I understand it, is that successful adults with learning disabilities (SALD) are highly motivated to obtain control over their lives. This thesis is stated in the strongest of terms. "One overriding theme characterized all efforts geared towards success. The driving factor underlying success for all participants was the quest to gain control over one's life." There are certainly ways in which I see this characteristic in my own life.[1] I also observe, however, an equally powerful continuing desire to accept defeat gracefully and to develop the skill to limit the pain that comes with inevitable disappointment. I take pride in the fact that I divorced with dignity and have maintained a friendship with my former spouse. Now I am working to accept the fact that in a reorganized bureaucracy, all managers will merely be team players with no special authority beyond the merit of their skills and ideas. In my workshops, I urge everyone to heed Martin Buber's admonition that we must know and accept the difference between what we can achieve and what we cannot.

"Fire in the belly" to succeed is a phenomenon I have observed in many individuals with learning disabilities on the road to success; the inability to know how to regulate the fire is a phenomenon I have observed in many such individuals on the road to ruin. The quest to control our lives derives from the desire to limit the opportunity to experience once again the excruciating humiliation that comes when we are betrayed by our brains. There are no words for what young children feel when their parents are called to school because they cannot read aloud in class or the humiliation of not knowing left from right in a junior high school dance class or the embarrassment of being unable to recall the order of the months necessary to complete an astronomy project with one's lab partner in high school. Particularly when one is young and does not know his or her own limits, the manifestations of a learning disability will come at unpredictable moments. They come not as foreseeable blows for which one may stiffen up stoically or duck, but as unexpected whacks on the back of the head.

Imagine a child reaching high school without regular bladder control. What will be the effect on his or her character when the telltale signs of incontinence appear on his or her slacks or dress for all to see? No doubt, an initial organizing principle for many such persons will be to avoid embarrassment at all costs. Perhaps a few such persons will decide that the only way to make sure they are no longer embarrassed is to become president of a corporation so they can have an office with a private washroom or to gain so much wealth, power, or respect that no one would dare laugh at them. But, what if such persons only make it to the office of the vice-president? What if after becoming president, the board of directors decides to save

---

[1]It is certainly not by accident that in college I repeatedly ran for political office. On the micro level, I simply could not stomach the infantilization that was entailed in dress codes, "lights-out" rules, and attempts to regulate my sex life. The heart of my successful "grass roots" political organization was ending domination of student government by fraternities and sororities that readily acceded to in loco parentis. On the macro level, like many of my classmates, I wanted to participate in the great debate about the right of the government to send us to Vietnam for a war we feared was inhumane and without any redeeming geopolitical value. (In those days, mere student organizations often organized around national and international political issues.) Similarly, as an adult, I campaigned hard and worked extraordinary hours to achieve the position of the head attorney in my office. There can be no doubt that one of the motivating factors was to have the authority to adapt the working environment to take advantage of my strengths and help me accommodate my weaknesses.

money and the president's office must be downsized by eliminating the washroom? What then describes the successful person? It is not fire in the belly. It is balance! It is the person who uses the pain of humiliation to drive him or herself to the president's office but perspective to realize that the solution to his or her problems may lie in the ability to realize that an embarrassing wet spot is not the essence of his or her merit as an executive. By the time the person who lacks bladder control makes it to president, it is inevitable that he or she knows a diplomatic way to comment on a telltale spot upon his or her clothing. One achieves as much psychological peace from knowing how to deal with embarrassment as from believing he controls his environment so much that no one will ever again notice his impairments.

In my opinion, the SALD is most likely to be described as someone with a lot of drive and a lot of ability to accept limitations. One characteristic is not a subset of the other, but an equally important balancing element. I think it is precisely because SALDs are driven to achieve balance that they are so good at reframing, looking for a career that fits, and developing support systems in the workplace. Persons of pure desire will resist reframing because it is the pain of being LD that stokes the fire in the belly. Thus they will resist reframing in order to preserve drive. The unbalanced desire to succeed will lead to setting career goals that cannot be achieved, not a good fit between career and abilities. The unbalanced quest (or will to succeed) can easily blind an individual with a learning disability to the self-limitations that necessitate looking for support at work.

Internal Decisions

Desire to Excel

Above I have explained my view of the roots to the desire to excel: pain avoidance. I can only add that at nearly 50 years of age, the desire has come into balance but has not diminished. My colleagues at work observe that if I have not placed a new challenge in my path, I will look for one. No doubt this explains why I am working to establish myself in a second career.

Goal Setting

My wife complains that I worry too much about the future. I am already setting up for a career change that can't occur for at least seven years. I love to spend time pouring over my small investment portfolio, planning for the next shift in the economy and my retirement. In my view, this is an aspect of balance. On the one hand, since I know that I am slower to accomplish tasks than most people, I am always looking to "get the drop" on my colleagues. If I know a memorandum on a particular topic will be requested in a month, why not start on it now? That way

I am sure to have it done on time. On the other hand, formal goal setting allows me to seriously consider whether I am working on a goal I can achieve. It is hard to back away from a prospective goal, but it is even harder to deal with the pain of realizing I have wasted energy on an unachievable goal. There are very few goals in life that I have deeply cared about that I have not attained, albeit these achievements may have been at an extraordinary cost. But, those very few critical goals I have worked on persistently and not achieved remain stuck in my mind as a source of unresolvable disappointment.

Reframing

I have reframed my experience with learning disabilities to such an extent that I am convinced it has given me much more in life that it has cost me. My learning disability is the source of my perspicacity, my drive, my commitment to civil rights, my insight into discrimination, the "female" side of my personality, my patience, and what gives me the sense of being distinguished as an individual from most "normal" (ordinary) people in a mass society. In my *pro bono* inspirational series I postulate what it would be like to discover my new son has a learning disability. I conclude by saying that I may actually prefer that he has such an impairment; guiding him through the experience, helping him to draw strength from it, bonding with him through it—I project all of these as very positive experiences.

External Manifestations—Adaptability

Persistence

Persistence is the great equalizer available to all persons with learning disabilities. While the "competition" watches football, we can study, research, write, etc. The only person who can take persistence away from us is ourselves. We are rewarded for persistence so often that it's an easy lesson to internalize for life. Right after getting out of law school I passed the bar of one state. But 15 years later, I decided to take on the most difficult bar examination in the country. Most applicants who don't pass this exam the first or second time never pass. In part, they are psyched out. In my case, I simply understood I needed more time to study and get the hang of writing a bar question. After two failures, no panic, I creamed it the third time. Now I tell my students, "I passed the bar the first time I studied for it."

My "summer vacation" this year was spent doing legal research and my Sundays are spent on "homework," just as they were 30 years ago. When my friends ask me if I had a good weekend, I always respond in terms of how much I got accomplished, not where I went or what movie I saw. If I didn't accomplish much I may feel depressed. If I was productive, I will feel quite buoyant.

Goodness of Fit

There can be no doubt that a great deal of my professional success derives from compatibility between the responsibilities of my job and my strengths. I am required to use my analytical skills deeply, frequently, and rapidly. Succinct, insightful, oral communications are the order of the day. Few assignments entail extensive reading and writing. Those that do, though time pressured, still entail longer time lines than is standard for the legal profession. It is truly rare that I don't at least have an afternoon and an evening to get a written assignment done—often, there may be an entire weekend "to catch up." Once again, there is an opportunity for persistence to pay off.

I do not have a good sense of whether I intuitively sought out and maintained a job that "fits" or whether this is merely a matter of good luck. One obvious point, however, is that, having found a job into which I fit, I have been very reluctant to change to another job or put my current job at risk.

Learned Creativity

In my *pro bono* lecture, I like to explain that there are many forms of intelligence. For example, Agatha Christie, who could not spell or read very well, expressed her great intelligence in terms of creativity.

There is also something I refer to as "LD intelligence." I sincerely believe that "LD intelligence" is as legitimate, useful, and productive as any other form of intelligence. In my lecture, I like to exemplify this point by telling the story of how I built a table, despite the fact that I cannot read plans. First, I assembled the top. Second, I attached legs of approximately equal length to the table top. Next I took the table to exactly where I expected to use it. The floors of this room are not perfectly level. But this was not a problem. I placed the table in the intended location and in small increments took a little off each leg until it was dead level. Unlike most of the furniture in my house, it remained rock steady through the quake.

My most important "learned creativity" was the strategy I adopted to enhance my reading skills. I call this adaptation using my "logic chip." I developed the chip because I have strong analytical skills but weak reading skills. With the chip engaged, immediately after I read a sentence, I automatically (subconsciously) ask myself the question, "If the sentence says what I think it says, was what the author wrote logical?" If the answer is "no," I reread the sentence as many times as is necessary for a new meaning to come to me. I rescan the sentence continuously until it passes the logic chip's test for quality control. As soon as a sentence passes the test, I proceed to the next one and so on. I sincerely believe that going to law school had a lot to do with developing the chip. And in this sense, I dissent with those "experts" who suggest that a learning disability can never be remediated through persistently practicing those skills which are weakest.

Social Ecologies

In my lecture, I frequently tell parents and educators that honing the social skills of students with learning disabilities may be as important to ensuring their success as adults as any other strategy that can be adopted. Since it is certain that we will need help in the workplace, it is important to learn how to be the kind of person people will want to help. We should not be preparing students to know how to look helpless. Rather we should be teaching them to be clear about what they can offer to others in the workplace, so that people want to help them. It may also be about developing their capacity for humor, team spirit, and gratitude. In my opinion, it is an error to teach students with learning disabilities how to have the strength of character to buck a fashion trend. Rather we should be teaching them to have the skill to observe what it takes to fit into a given environment.

Of all the attributes of success identified in the chapter, this is the one most likely to be affected by technology. In addition to preparing students to get along with others, we should be teaching them how to achieve independence through technology. The first time I used a spell checker, I celebrated the experience by writing a 12-page love letter. Why not? I had just gained a new degree of self-confidence and competence. In my opinion, one of the most constructive things anyone can do to prepare individuals with learning disabilities for success is teach them how to master a word processor, a home accounting package, a calendaring/time maintenance program, and an automated telephone dialing system.

A Final Question

I have thought a lot about who would benefit most from the observations contained in your article. Why not everyone? Have you described the essence of the successful individual with a learning disability or have you described the essence of success?

• •

Reflections on the Reactions

The four reactions to our model for vocational success for adults with learning disabilities clearly substantiate the key factors we identified as related to success. These four participants indicated that our description of the significant variables associated with their success captured the essence of the process they experienced. All the reactors discussed the importance of the internal decisions and external manifestations contained in the model. Although some slight modifications of the model may be in order based on the reactions of the four successful adults, it is obvious that our model withstood the rigorous critique of those whose lives we have tried to depict.

Thus, while leaving intact the basic model depicting the process of vocational success for adults with learning disabilities, comments from the four reactors suggest some areas for clarification or change of emphasis within the model. Specifically, we believe that the four reactions imply the need for a broader statement on the definitions of success and control, further emphasis on the importance of relying on oneself to achieve success, a somewhat paradoxical need for emphasizing the importance of support, and some discussion on the potential impact of technology on success.

The issue of how to conceptualize success was one with which we struggled. As discussed in Chapter 2, we defined success in a particular way with the clear understanding that our interpretation was subjective and that others were equally plausible. Thus, the comments of one of our reactors regarding concerns about the definition of success we used are well founded. There are, as Antonoff tells us, many levels of success, and another definition might have altered whom we defined as highly or moderately successful. Success is "in the eyes of the beholder," though we believe that our definition does capture a sense of the concept widely shared in our culture.

Concerning the issue of control, one reactor felt that the model overly emphasizes control as a primary factor. In fact, this individual suggested that control should be treated equally with the other factors we identified. Interestingly, however, this same reactor went on to talk about the factors in the model in ways that substantiate that control is, indeed, the overriding variable in the mix. Grossman tells us that successful adults with learning disabilities are survivors in a world where full control may not be achieved. Our point is just that—that the quest for control keys the success apparatus, not necessarily having full control. In our terms, his quoting of Buber, that one must know and accept the difference between what one can achieve and what one cannot, is a form of control for many people. Psychological peace for the adult with learning disabilities, Grossman tells us, comes from knowing how to deal with embarrassment. That is control in our terms. Perhaps our concept of control encompasses aspects of reframing, a factor that all four acknowledge. Thus, we submit that the concept of control we are establishing must include the idea of gaining a handle on one's life in order to move ahead. This may imply different specific scenarios for each individual, but control of one's life remains paramount.

All the reactors discussed the necessity of learning to rely on themselves to succeed. While several of the elements of the model imply a strong need for self-reliance, this is not a separate category, but rather one that transcends several of the key variables. One relies on herself or himself for desire, for setting goals, for reframing, for perseverance, for goodness of fit, for coping mechanisms, and for taking advantage of supportive opportunities. Thus, one reactor learned to give positive reinforcement to herself. Another explained, "I recognized early that the most important person to count on was myself." Another concluded, "depending on favorable ecologies and on others for support only goes so far. The rest has to be forged by the individual with the learning disability."

Interestingly, while emphasizing the need to rely on oneself, the reactors also emphasized the importance of support. These are not hypocritical attitudes since the successful person recognizes the opportunities for support and takes advantage of them. The reactors talked of supportive parents, cousins, spouses, teachers, and others who were significant in their development. The importance of what we called social ecologies, therefore, what one reactor referred to as "the intervention of an interested party," must be underscored again as a key for success for those with learning disabilities.

Finally, the potential for technology as a supportive mechanism was suggested by several of the reactors. We probably didn't highlight this enough in the development of the factors associated with the model. One reactor talked about teaching youngsters with learning disabilities how to achieve independence through technology. Another explained the need "to use any available equipment or media to compensate for weaknesses and enhance performance in areas of strength." Such comments emphasize the possible impetus that technology may be for aiding persons with learning disabilities in the quest for success. Perhaps because many of those we interviewed achieved success before the recent explosion of user-friendly and sophisticated technological advances, this issue of utilizing available technology was not emphasized as much as it might have been. The comments of the reactors suggest that technology may be the catalyst for success in several of the factors identified in our model.

The positive reactions to the model of all four of these four participants lend credibility to the conclusions we reached. Success, though difficult to achieve, is clearly attainable with the proper initiative, hard work, creativity, and support. One reactor told us that "I am who I am because of the learning disability." Attaining success was possible because certain individuals who had learning disabilities followed a pattern we described in the model.

Critical Incidents: Stops, Starts, and Turning Points

Chapter 9

In Chapter 7 we discussed a "model of employment success" based on the commonalities in the process that the adults in our study used to accomplish their significant achievements. The components of this model illustrate a complex and dynamic interaction that contributes to success in adults with learning disabilities. Yet within the data collected for the study is an intriguing set of other events that may have contributed to success "despite the odds." Although these data are smaller in the context of the larger work, they are not necessarily insignificant in the powerful effects of complementing the model on vocational success. In this chapter we examine critical incidents in the lives of our participants. These events have shaped thoughts, choices, and actions leading to goal setting and risk-taking behaviors over their life span.

Folded into this somewhat "magical experience" of critical incidents are derived meanings, that is, interpretations as to present and future implications or effects of the critical incident experience. Derived meanings do not necessarily emerge immediately, but they can occur at any time and may be promulgated by anyone, from a loved one to an esteemed supervisor to a complete stranger (Gerber, Reiff, & Ginsberg, 1994). They provide clarity on strengths and weaknesses, consolidate issues regarding self-reliance and support systems, and fuel motivational systems.

The Critical Incident Technique

The critical incident technique developed by Flanagan (1954, 1962) is a systematic procedure that collects direct statements from individuals in order "to solve practical problems and to develop broad psychological principles" (p. 327). Flanagan has defined a critical incident as a human event that is observable and complete enough in itself for inferences and predictions to be made about the people involved. It also has as its main assumption that "if an individual can recall and fully describe an incident, one can be reasonably sure that this event had an effect on that observer (individual)" (Maker, 1978, p. 8). In other words, if we remember a particular event vividly, it is probably important to us at some level.

Maker (1978), who studied eminent scientists with disabilities, has listed the advantages of the critical incident technique: Incidents judged to be significant by the participant are studied further; specific details of critical events are given; the person being interviewed is required to specify reasons for identifying the incident; and individuals give their view of causes and effects of critical events. In a methodological sense, the technique is advantageous because it is open ended and qualitative in nature. Also, it has been refined over numerous years with a diversity of research populations.

The main disadvantage of the technique is a total reliance on the participant's recall. Flanagan (1954, 1962) would counter this disadvantage by asserting that an incident that is not recalled in a retrospective interview probably should not be considered a critical incident anyway. However, this view needs to be considered with respect to the length of retrospective. For example, a lifetime retrospective potentially can contain far more years than a retrospective on an employment experience. From the perspective of the interviewer, the open-ended format of the critical incident technique (which was listed earlier as an advantage) can be a disadvantage when interviewer probes influence the direction and the content of the participant's response. This potential methodological flaw is typically mitigated by interviewer training as well as independent methodological audits of interviews.

The critical incident technique has enjoyed widespread use with many different research populations. In the area of disabilities, the technique has been used to study nurses working in residential institutions for persons with mental retardation (Larsen, 1975), and to evaluate the in-service needs of staff members working in selected institutions for individuals with disabilities (Fleming, 1967).

In addition, the critical incident technique has been used to study instructional techniques in special education settings. It has been used to study effective classroom procedures that can be used with students who have mental disabilities (Rothberg, 1968), to investigate specific roles of special education faculty members (Ingram, 1974), and to determine the competencies needed to direct special education centers (Blackhurst, Wright, & Ingram, 1974).

Overview of the Data Trends in Critical Incidents

The highly successful adults with learning disabilities in our study recollected critical incidents in childhood, adolescence, and adulthood. Most adults recounted numerous critical incidents, and the average was approximately three.

Only one participant did not share a critical incident experience. The critical incidents took place in educational environments, career settings, and social situations. Table 9.1 presents a quantitative analysis (by developmental stage and setting) of critical incidents reported in the interviews. That is, the recollected critical incidents are categorized in terms of when they happened (childhood, adolescence, or adulthood) and where they happened (school, career, or social).

The majority of critical incidents took place during adulthood and in educational environments. A surprise in the analysis of the interviews was the high number of positive critical experiences relative to the negative critical incidents shared by the adults with learning disabilities. One possible explanation for the recollection of critical incidents in adulthood stems from the fact that those interviewed most readily remembered significant events that occurred closer to their perceived successes. Negative experiences from the past did not emerge to a large degree amidst the happier times that success brought. However, this finding does not negate the pain, struggle, and consternation experienced in the daily trials and tribulations of being learning disabled throughout the years as is shown in the examples presented in the following section.

A Wide Array of Critical Incidents

The adults in our study related a diversity of critical incidents in their lives. Many different themes and subthemes emerged from their words. All are instructive of how critical incidents can change ways of thinking, reverse directions, or help set goals to accomplish. One prominent theme that emerged from the interviews was how participants thought about their learning disability differently as a result of a critical incident. In earlier years of development there were incidents such as these:

> I was diagnosed as educationally handicapped (learning disabled). I was told that I was smart, but it took longer to do things. I knew that I could do it, but that I wouldn't enjoy it.

> The first critical incident is when they found out I could not read. The letters did not make sense to me, and they said I was dyslexic. At the transition of second and third grade they put me in a group of mentally retarded children. The teacher was trained by Maria Montessori. She used the Montessori method. She saw that I had problems with organization, concentration, and so on. She did the program in all areas for three years with me. She thoroughly enjoyed it because I made so much progress. The mentally retarded students did not make that progress. It was a critical incident in her life and mine.

Table 9.1
Critical Incidents of Adults with Learning Disabilities
by Developmental Stage and Setting

	Education		Career		Social		Total	
	n	%	n	%	n	%	n	%
Childhood	16	14	—	—	5	5	21	19
Adolescence	16	14	1	1	4	4	21	19
Adulthood	22	20	25	23	22	20	69	62
Total	54	49	26	24	31	28	111	100

n = 111.

In the adult years examples of critical incidents included these:

> I read the article "Hidden Handicap" in the February 1986 *Psychology Today*. I thought of it as "Paul on the Road to Damascus." Up to that point I thought LD was only dyslexia which I did not have. . . . As a result I became involved with ACLD [Association of Children with Learning Disabilities] and began to learn to come to grips with my learning disability.

> Before I went to graduate school I thought I could not "hack it." I thought I was just stupid and not aware of my learning disabilities. My husband's partner who was a graduate of Harvard said that he had problems with school. He said I was bright, and he had the same problems with spelling and writing, but he also could understand concepts. Because he told me that, I decided to try graduate school. I compared myself to my husband. He is left-brained and brilliant, like a computer. He can give all of the facts. I always thought his kind of thinking was the difference between being smart and being dumb. I never thought of myself as being bright and able to do those kinds of things.

Another set of critical incidents centered on strategies or actions that were devised as a result of certain realizations about the strengths and limitations of having a learning disability. For some of our participants, these incidents provide building blocks to develop learned creativity.

> I saw my friends mastering skills that I couldn't grasp or apply. I found out that I could do what they did by using "by-pass" techniques.

> I found out that people use only 15 percent of their brain's capacity. It affected me in that I thought I might be stupid, but if I could use a greater fraction of my brain power, I could succeed and that is what I set out to do.

> I learned that it was okay to get by and that you don't have to get straight A's, but it's okay not to fail. Just stay in between.

I realized that something was wrong, but I didn't know what. I was afraid that someone was going to find out that I really didn't know what I was doing. I developed systems to fool people. Those systems actually helped me to learn a different way.

I knew something was wrong, though I didn't know exactly what. I started to develop in my mind that I needed to find what I could do well and then stick to it. . . . When I found out I could sell groceries and make a living at it, I decided that I was going to do it the rest of my life. Though in high school I had thought about architecture and had been offered a full college football scholarship to an out-of-town university, I chose to stay in the grocery business. I kept reverting back to what I knew I could do.

Another set of critical incident quotations illustrates how significant events changed the perception of self and provided a springboard for positive results. In essence, the positive self-attributions of the participants were a catalyst for interactions that fueled feelings of positive regard and a gradual move toward successful experiences. In terms of the success model, these incidents facilitated the reframing process.

I was identified with achievers, peers who were academically oriented. I was accepted by them despite my learning problems.

The turnaround for me happened in a community college where I was diagnosed and tutored. It changed my self-esteem for then I became much happier and people saw the difference.

I computerized an auto parts operation in California to import parts to Hawaii at the age of 19. The Ford Motor Company became interested in it. I really amazed myself. I said to myself I am unusual, and I can outdistance others, even though I don't know why.

Closely related to the preceding theme is the realization of positive aspects about self. A recognition of important assets was helpful in generating the move to greater success. Critical events in this area had a similar effect to those quoted in the previous grouping.

Early in life I realized that I was a good person because I had strength in my personality and popularity. I had lots of friends.

I did things because I wanted to. For example, when my VW broke down, and I had no money to pay for repairs, I figured out how to take the engine apart and rebuild it. I've learned by doing and have been fixing cars ever since. (Quotation from a female neurologist.)

In stat class I had a problem, and I spent a week and a half pondering it. Suddenly, I got this "bolt" and answered it. Wrote it all up and handed it in. Only got a B. I surprised myself that I could see through it. But the ability to see through it got me interested in graduate school statistics. My professor hadn't seen the beauty that I saw in it, but it didn't bother me.

Social ecologies was another area where it was common to find critical incidents in the adults that we interviewed. Family support was important, particularly during the childhood years. However, two of the most frequently cited areas of critical incidents were the influence of mentors and being exposed to or being put in a new set of social interactions.

My father [a physician] was a major influence in my life. He has somewhat of a reading problem, and he studies every night. I would ask him, "Didn't you learn it all?" He would say you never learn it all, you can never be sure of what you learn. I thought I could be happy if I could do that because he seemed very happy.

I remember being ticked-off at my mother because she said I could do anything I wanted to if I made my made up to do it. I thought that's not true. Now, I know she was right.

I was motivated by my mother who wouldn't let me quit. I would have quit if she hadn't been there to keep me going. She died when I was in high school and her death stimulated me to make sure I didn't let myself go. It forced me to do things on my own.

During school-age years, mentors in the form of teachers had an impact on self-esteem and even in some causes pointed toward a career early on.

I always have had developmental dyspraxia. Can't balance, can't ride a bike, etc. I was a horror in gym. I was expelled from gym in junior high. I had to sit in the corner and watch because I had several accidents. A new teacher saw me and said, "It's now over, Elisabeth. You have a mouth and a brain, and you are going to help me teach this class." And she literally taught me how to teach gym without being able to do it at all. Her attitude was that the main thing was that I was involved. I had a talent that she observed, and she was going to bring it about. She in a way determined my desire to go into human services and teaching because I realized teaching was something I really could do.

In junior high my ceramics instructor said if I can make an object, you'll get an A. In high school, in metal shop the instructor asked me to help with a project (despite being a girl). That evolved into working with him during his lunch hour on metal casting. He suggested that I go to the art center.

Later on while in higher education some of the adults with learning disabilities were influenced by their professors.

I had a professor who believed in me. He was my buddy!

I had a Ph.D. professor who "took me under his wing." The first paper I wrote he threw at me. At the end (of my program) we coauthored a book together.

I was having a difficult time in dental school and was energized by a professor who was my support and role model. He said, "Hang tough, hang in there. You do what you have to do, and I'll run defense for you." And he did.

Still later on in the careers of some of our participants mentors played a key role in their professional development.

I was employed in a district attorney's office and had a chance to serve under Mario Marolla. I learned some of his craft and skill in political management.

I was very attached to my mentors—Mr. Donohue and Mr. Abramowitz. Mr. Abramowitz taught me about life and how to live and how to give.

Being placed in another social setting and/or environment was a source of profound change for a number of the participants. Their perspective changed because their environment changed. Emanating from their new social ecology were different thoughts and feelings about the world stemming from different interactions and experiences in their daily lives.

Being Catholic and going to Catholic schools with rather rigid discipline and rules and regulations, I was willing to accept authority and that helped me move forward. It propelled me, instilling in me the drive to accomplish.

I changed schools, had smaller classes and more friends.

About age 14 I went to camp and was named camper of the year. I was on an emotional high and I remember as a result of it the most dynamite looking female was willing to go out with me—even after camp.

Numerous critical incident responses identify marriage as a critical experience. Several participants simply responded "meeting my wife," "meeting my husband and being opened to a new world of nurturing friends," and "meeting my wife and getting married after breaking up with my girlfriend and having a hard time for several years." Another critical incident quotation was even more emphatic:

If I had not met my wife or somebody like her, I might have turned out to be a bum because I would just as soon do nothing. She is the one that motivated me educationally.

It is possible to track a strand of critical incidents where success fueled the motivation to attain more success. One of the participants spoke of the satisfaction of winning a science fair in elementary school and setting his sights on working in a scientific field. Other critical incidents validated the feeling "I have arrived!" in spite of being learning disabled. Examples were "my first published book," "being a partner in a dental office," and "becoming a navy commander." Another participant said, "My first job out of college I was in management training at Sears, and I ended up in the wig department. I had the highest sales in wigs in Indiana."

After settling into their careers later in life, our participants continued to experience critical incidents. Many of these events played significant roles in furthering their vocational success.

> I was commissioned to do a postsecondary study by ACLD [Association of Children with Learning Disabilities] in 1970.

> At IBM I was moved to regional staff in two years which was unheard of to move that quickly. Then I was recognized by IBM as an "innovator." Then I was nominated by IBM to the President's Commission on Executive Exchange [commission which included 25 executives representing the top companies in the United States].

> I was discovering things that paleontologists had not found before such as the first baby dinosaurs in the world and the first nest of baby dinosaur eggs in the Western Hemisphere. Then I was awarded a MacArthur Fellowship [commonly known as the genius award]. I received an honorary doctorate from the University of Montana. That was odd because I mostly got D's when I went there. I was expelled seven times for having less than 2.0.

A number of our participants set their vocational goals as a result of a critical incident. It is noteworthy that these events are dispersed throughout the life span; consistent with an adult developmental perspective, critical incidents may have the power to catalyze profound change at any point in life.

> In junior high I went to my counselor because of abuse at home. The counselor did not help, and I left the office thinking, "I can do better than you did." I knew then that was my field.

> I was quite young and so depressed and afraid of the world. Therapy through remediation brought me to realize that it is okay to be dyslexic—to be different. It changed my life and from that point on I knew that I wanted to be a therapist. I had a goal. Before I even knew about visualization and any of that I could see myself doing therapy and giving lectures. All that came true. I really believe that I was making my own world by thinking about it and visualizing it. I was ready to leap on to the opportunities that were there, and I wasn't afraid.

I met a 17-year-old who introduced me to photography. I then went to school in Vienna. When I got off the train the professor who headed the program "had a very calming effect." When I was in college I met a photographer for "the first time." One year later I went to the National Press Club. I didn't even know what questions to ask.

I worked for a dentist for a few years. He told me that I was one of the best people he has worked with as far as picking up things quickly. He said I had great potential as a dentist. As his office grew I ended up managing his whole office. I then decided that I could work for myself.

Included in the critical incident quotations were some that described "bad" moments. However, the adults worked through these moments and ultimately turned "a sow's ear into a silk purse" through direct thought or action.

I can remember very well the first time my parents were asked to come to my grammar school when I was in second grade because I couldn't read. Afterwards, my parents told me to try harder. I remember crying and feeling bad. I felt I had let my father, in particular, down. This was a critical event in that it made me want to ultimately succeed academically.

I remember getting an F in college. I was told I was getting an F because I plagiarized in English Literature. I had so much trouble that I just took chunks of text from books, and then put the books in the bibliography. It started my thinking that I was not going to make it through school. After that I really applied myself.

My algebra teacher embarrassed me in front of the class and that gave me resolve to succeed.

My family told me that they never expected me to succeed. When I first started college my mother wrote a nasty letter that spurred me to succeed despite her. Therefore, throughout my life you just tell me that I can't do something, and I'll prove you wrong. As long as it's something I want.

Still other critical incidents had the tone of the preceding statements. More specifically, they exemplify the reframing that made a difference in the lives of the adults with learning disabilities we interviewed.

I remember one of my failures. I got talked into selling dictionaries between my freshman and sophomore years. No, it was between my sophomore and junior years for the Southwestern Corporation. They sent me down to train in Nashville, Tennessee, and I was selling dictionaries up in Minnesota. The big thing that they were pushing was that if you quit then you are quitting forever. Even though I had physically quit selling them it took me a week to accept the fact that I was going to quit. They put pressure on me with the fact that if you quit once, you will always quit. That was the hardest thing for me to deal with. Maybe with other people it didn't, but for me to acknowledge the fact that I was up against something that I couldn't beat was very hard for me. I think frankly that it was good for me realizing that there were some things I am just going to have to give up on. There is no way I can win, and recognize which battles are important enough to fight and which ones you just let slide by.

I was younger and going through my own problems. I rebelled against the "flakiness" of my two hippie-like siblings. I modeled myself after my conservative sister. I needed more structure in my life.

My solitary judgment is important. I decided judgment of myself always meant more that anyone else's evaluation and that's still true. I don't care what others want of me. I'm not interested in pleasing that stereotype.

I took a statistics course in my master's program, and I had to go back and learn calculus. And I remember the first time I took an exam I totally blanked out. I remembered if you close your eyes and count to ten and take several deep breaths and open up your eyes you would be fine and it wasn't. I failed, I mean miserably. Then it was an uphill battle I had to face.

A number of assorted quotations illustrate a pronounced anger stemming from experiences from being learning disabled. Whereas anger may be an underpinning to some of the examples cited earlier, these quotations explicitly impart the visceral nature of the anger dimension in these adults. We know that anger can be debilitating. But these adults turned their anger into motivation or desire to succeed.

My social studies teacher told me I wouldn't succeed. That made me mad.

I experienced some success and that helped my self-esteem. I said, "Screw you guys," and I got mad. I said, "I'm not going to let you do this to me."

When the woman who had given me five years of wonderful tutoring/therapy left the United States, she referred me to an ex-teacher who was tutoring. One day we were talking, and I mentioned going to a certain university, and she laughed because I couldn't read or write. I remember saying to myself, "Fuck you. I'll show you you bitch." This pushed me in that direction because I had gotten from my parents and my therapist for years that you could get anything you want. I believed this so much that when this came up, it sort of motivated me to show her up.

Critical incidents had a significant impact on an overall reevaluation of one's life for some adults in the study. The incidents most typically occur in the adult years. In some instances, as the following example illustrates, such self-actualization may occur earlier, building a bridge from adolescence to adulthood:

> After the first three semesters of college I was hospitalized with mononucleosis. I had had a seizure and was very sick. I had three weeks in the hospital just to think, and I decided that there was a limit to how hard I can push myself. There were some things I had to accept that I wasn't going to be able to do. I also understood that social skills were more important than I thought them to be. Previously, I thought book work was the most important. I learned that a lot more people cared about me than I thought. When I came out of the hospital I became active in student government and ran for president of a dorm association. There was a high rate of suicide in our dorm. I was able to articulate kids' anger and put together a campaign organization. I also saw how people use social contacts to further their own interests—and I don't mean in a negative way—the point being that you can't do it on your own. This was a very important lesson. I never saw myself as courageous, but strangely enough, the greater the adversity the better. I performed then and still do to this day in emergency situations.

Some of our participants indicated that being given a break made a big difference on the road to success. All of these critical incidents were connected to higher education.

> Yale [University] was willing to allow me to take honor's courses, not do well in them, but foster a good feeling of self-respect. They understood I had other strengths and they wanted me to learn.

> Critical to my success was the ability to accomplish grad courses without negotiation. That was my ultimate success.

> In the state of Wisconsin if you take a certain curriculum and rank high enough in your [law] class, you don't have to take the bar exam. That was a big break for me. To practice in the northern district of California you must take the California State bar exam. It took me three times to pass it.

Finally, apparently serendipitous events had tremendous influence on the lives of some participants. These kinds of incidents are largely inexplicable. Nevertheless, such occurrences deserve recognition in any discourse on critical incidents, success, and learning disabilities.

> A stranger on a bus told me that I looked like I was going places. He advised me to mind my own business and keep going, and I'll get it done.

> **There are more things in heaven and earth, Horatio,**
> **Than are dreamt of in your philosophy.**
> —*Hamlet*, Act I, Scene 5

It is difficult to say precisely what will be a critical event and what will not. At face value some events seem explosive, heart-rendering, or even silly. Critical incidents have much more room for introspection and interpretation on a retrospective basis. Their predictive qualities have little value in a scientific sense. Yet at the time they occur they are energizing and are destined to incur long lasting and profound effects.

The impact of any event over the course of a lifetime or even over a day can have very different consequences. Werner (1993) points out that life events are critical turning points (critical incidents) in whether an individual is likely to overcome or succumb to challenging circumstances. Richmond and Beardslee (1988) have observed, "No matter what the risk or the number of social stressors, somewhat surprisingly, some children are spared of their effects" (p. 162). This observation can be extended beyond childhood into adolescence and adulthood when critical incidents are woven into the lives of successful adults with learning disabilities. We are reminded by Rutter (1987) that self-concept can change even in adulthood. Moreover, it was in adulthood where the participants of our study realized the far reaches of their success.

Critical events are tied into such basic psychological concepts as motivation, self-attribution, reinforcement, and self-concept. But there are also less-than-exact explanations of critical incidents that can be seemingly magical and mystical in nature. These explanations are often linked with a person's inner life, personal philosophy, or spiritual nature, either individually or in combination. Some critical events foster anger at the system, or at a teacher or loved one. Others are precipitated by love, support, and encouragement. But why do some incidents become critical and have a lasting impact while others do not? We do know that positive reinforcement at important times gives "an extra boost." And the effects of that action are the foundation for resilience. In the parlance of the literature on risk and resilience it can be an important "protective factor."

The likelihood that a comment, interaction, or event will become a critical incident depends on its derived meaning. Both the retrospections of the participants of this study and previous discussions (Gerber, Reiff, & Ginsberg, 1994) suggest that critical incidents happen all along the life span and in a variety of environments. Critical incidents have been described as a "wild card" or as unpredictable. Despite these rather mercurial descriptions their impact can be great. When trying to explain the human experience or even in examining the "formula" for success, we look for cause and effect. In the case of the critical incidents it is not that easy. Yet simply because we do not fully understand a phenomenon, we cannot dismiss the power of its effects.

Part IV

Implications
for Practice

Turning the Model into a Teaching Tool

Chapter 10

Perspectives on Pedagogy

Thus far, we have focused largely on how adults with learning disabilities have achieved success. The model of vocational success has many implications for decison making and actions relative to the world of work. It may be thought of as a map for finding the road to success. This road can, and *should*, originate in childhood and during the school-age years. We feel that the methods used by these adults to achieve have direct curricular and instructional implications. The model is composed of alterable variables, that is, processes that can be facilitated by the right combination of circumstances. For most of these adults, these fortuitous combinations resulted from highly individual circumstances, reflecting both force of will and idiosyncratic factors including a healthy dose of good fortune.

Does Teaching Make a Difference?

Only a few individuals will be likely to find this providential alignment on their own. Our participants do indeed demonstrate that it is possible. But for other persons with learning disabilities, who will not find the path to success on their own, could some kind of map or blueprint at least point them in the right direction? We believe the way we educate students with learning disabilities can have a powerful effect on what will happen in adulthood. Moreover, the methods that other adults with learning disabilities have used to become successful represent an unarguably empirical source for pedagogical philosophy and practices. After all, much of what and how we teach is based more on assumptions about skills needed in adulthood rather than on empirical research or observable outcomes. Teaching approaches for students with learning disabilities have often relied on dubious etiological theories, unsupported claims that basic psychological processes can be remediated, and a reduction of time devoted to direct academic instruction (Hammill & Larson, 1978). Few of us would argue that our methods for teaching students with learning disabilities have been dramatically successful.

The situation may be improving, with record numbers of students with disabilities entering 2- and 4-year postsecondary institutions (Dalke & Schmitt, 1987; Rose, 1991; Vogel, 1987). Somewhat surprisingly, however, many successful college students with learning disabilities see little relation between their success and the educational services, special and otherwise, that they have received (Reiff & Gerber, 1991). Moreover, the world beyond school has not been particularly favorable to individuals with learning disabilities, who continue to drop out of school at high rates (Wagner, 1989), face greater unemployment and underemployment than the general population (Wagner, 1989), and express dissatisfaction with both personal and occupational outcomes (Okolo & Sitlington, 1988; Reiff & Gerber, 1991).

Part of the historic difficulty in finding adequate teaching strategies may stem from the heterogeneity of persons with learning disabilities. In trying to respond to the needs of students with learning disabilities in general, approaches have either reflected a specific theoretical orientation about learning or have centered on addressing specific learning styles or needs. Yet researchers generally concur that several psychological processes are simultaneously involved in most learning activities (Lerner, 1993).

At best, any circumscribed approach can only meet the needs of some students with learning disabilities. There simply is no such thing as a "typical" child, adolescent, or adult with learning disabilities. Instead, we may increase the likelihood of facilitating successful transitions to adulthood by adapting generic strategies that have a successful track record to meet individual needs. At the same time, these strategies must have particular relevance to children and youth who do not learn easily in the educational system, perhaps the one commonality of persons with learning disabilities. Yet the adults in our study, who usually did not do well with "traditional" learning, did become active, involved, and independent learners who learned how to learn.

What makes the learning process different for persons with learning disabilities? By definition, being labeled as a student with learning disabilities results from not performing to potential or, in a sense, not living up to expectations. Most professionals in the learning disabilities field embrace a well-supported belief that, with the "right" kinds of educational interventions, particularly compensatory and bypass strategies, students with learning disabilities can improve their performance. Additionally, most teachers have found that students with learning disabilities tend not to develop broad repertoires of such strategies on their own. Rather, a collaborative effort on the part of teachers, parents, and influential others can provide direct support to help such skills. Finally, students with learning disabilities who do succeed, no matter how effective their compensation techniques, usually have to work harder and longer than their nondisabled peers to achieve the same results. Strategies that have worked, that helped persons who had difficulty learning to exceed expectations, lie at the heart of our model of success.

New Wine for an Old Bottle

The Old Bottle

Teachers, parents, mentors, and others can increase the likelihood that children and youth with learning disabilities will find adulthood satisfying. Part of the reason for believing that we can and should make a difference lies simply in the essential role that education plays for anyone. In the introduction to *The Book of Virtues* (1993), former Secretary of Education William J. Bennett writes: "Aristotle wrote that good habits formed at youth make all the difference" (p. 11). The struggle to educate youths with learning disabilities has been to discover habits that individuals who learn and think in different and unusual ways can use to level the playing field. The stories of 71 adults with learning disabilities have revealed at least some of those habits. In this chapter, we invite the reader to consider the "teachability" of those habits.

As is so often the case with wisdom that has guided us for thousands of years, contemporary research offers an empirical basis for such a value system. In Benjamin Bloom's landmark work (1980, 1982) to delineate the alterable variables associated with successful outcomes of gifted and talented individuals, he and his associates concluded that, in addition to innate qualities, critical learning experiences shaped successful outcomes. However, conventional education did not tend to play a pivotal role. Instead, more individual influences of parents, mentors (often a special teacher), and eventually master teachers inspired a sense of self-worth, created and sustained the will to work hard, and instilled a belief in the possibility of attaining success.

The influence that teachers exert can have either profound negative or positive impacts. As one college student with learning disabilities has reflected, "I'd tell my best teacher, 'Thank you for taking the time to get me where I am. I wouldn't be in college right now.' I'd tell my worst teacher to get another job" (as quoted by Brobeck, 1990, p. 11). Joyce Brobeck, a resource room teacher for middle school adolescents with learning disabilities, has often wondered if her efforts at teaching are worth it, if she can really make a difference in the lives of her students. But she has not given up. One of the forces that drive this teacher comes from her interviews with successful adults with learning disabilities. One college graduate with a successful career in social work told her, "If more teachers had been aware of my learning disabilities and behaviors, things could have been so much better" (as quoted by Brobeck, 1990, p. 11). Such assertions have convinced Brobeck that teachers can make life better for students with learning disabilities: "I have obtained strong evidence that the difference I make is that one spark that illuminates for students the idea that they are OK, that they can make it in life and their efforts do pay off. . . . I must not give up, not if I really want to make a difference in the lives of these children. . . . A little compassion and understanding from others can go a long way in promoting a positive sense of self-worth" (Brobeck, 1990, p. 11).

We do have some evidence of educational processes that appear to lead to successful outcomes in persons with learning disabilities. In research done by Adelman and Vogel (1990), successful college graduates with learning disabilities indicated that they developed generic compensatory strategies that worked in both school and work. They elaborated that the specialized college learning support program in which they participated promoted the self-awareness and insight critical to the development of effective compensations. Successful adult outcomes are also related to support received in the earlier years of education. Young adults with learning disabilities who have made a comfortable transition to independent living, attained secure and satisfying occupations, and cultivated a wide variety of interests have cited supportive family backgrounds, the cooperation of their families and school personnel, early diagnosis, appropriate support services, and effective remediation efforts as contributing to their success (Gerber & Reiff, 1991; Rogan & Hartman, 1990; Wambsgans, 1990). Kokaska and Skolnik (1986) examined adults with learning disabilities in professions such as teaching, skilled labor, and service industries. These adults attributed their success to choosing a career commensurate with personal strengths and style, improving their interpersonal skills, being willing to work harder and longer than others, and being honest with themselves in terms of the impact of their learning disabilities.

The New Wine

These studies and observations provide evidence that educational experiences can increase the likelihood that students with learning disabilities will make a transition to successful adulthood. Yet we are not aware of an approach to teaching based on a systemic assessment of the success process. The difference is significant. The model of employment success delineates an interactive system of specific alterable variables that can be taught and learned. In addition, the extent to which our participants made use of these factors often proved to distinguish the highly successful adults from the moderately successful ones.

We propose to use observable outcomes of success as the source of a teaching model. The commonalities of how the adults in our study became successful, as depicted in the model of vocational success, suggest that a combination of predictable and systematic events enhances the likelihood of significant achievement. These predictable and systematic events recurred throughout the sample in spite of the obvious differences among these individuals.

It should also be obvious that replicating the internal decision making and the external manifestations of the model will not guarantee success. Other factors are involved, such as character, cognition, and coincidence, which may not be readily alterable. Following the blueprint of the model can assist in finding the right direction on the road to success, but how and where one travels the road will be largely an individual matter. On the other hand, persons with disabilities who do not have some kind of plan for success are likely to be doomed to failure. In *Speaking for Themselves* (Gerber & Reiff, 1991), a striking commonality of the marginally adjusted adult group was their utter, albeit inadvertent, disregard for any kind of systematic process for improving their stations in life. They had dreams but few ideas about how to realize them.

We need to go beyond offering a handful or hodgepodge of good ideas. Instead, the following proposal about educating students with learning disabilities presents an integrated and unified approach to curriculum and instruction. A pedagogical focus on success rather than failure, on what persons with learning disabilities can do rather than on what they cannot, represents both the underlying philosophy as well as the curricular and instructional method. This approach clearly echoes the contemporary notion of empowerment. As a society, we have begun to embrace the right of traditionally disenfranchised constituencies to take control of their lives. This same spirit lies at the heart of the success model. We begin our discussion of turning the model into a teaching tool by examining the issue of control.

A "Model" Classroom

Taking Control

The adults in our study became successful by taking control of their lives. Being "in control" is vital to our sense of well-being. Conversely, when we say that we, or things, are "out of control," we usually do not feel that we are being successful, nor do we have the ability to marshal our resources to achieve. Our participants frequently defined success as having control of their lives. Remarks such as "In my case, I define success by doing what I enjoy doing," "being able to do what I want to do when I want to do it," "a person who has gotten his life together," "a constant controller," or "success is somebody who can control their life and circumstances" clearly demonstrate the connection between control and success.

When an individual has learning disabilities, the issue is often acute. For many of our participants, the experience of having learning disabilities, particularly in the school-age years, represented a loss of control. Because they learned differently, they were not in control and therefore not able to measure up to the expectations one would have of children and youth of normal or above normal intelligence. In many ways, the learning disabilities took over control, leaving the child feeling helpless, frustrated, "stupid," and alone. Small wonder that "external locus of control" and "learned helplessness" continue to stand out as characteristics of many students with learning disabilities.

How do we help children with learning disabilities regain control, particularly when they often find themselves in environments sending them messages that they are out of control? The first step to regaining control is to control oneself. Self-discipline is the basis for our ability to control the course of our lives and development. As Bennett (1993) reminds the reader, self-discipline means making a disciple of oneself, becoming one's own teacher, trainer, coach, mentor, and disciplinarian. Teachers and parents have, of course, habitually wondered how to encourage children and students to be self-disciplined. Obviously, modeling self-discipline and inculcating it as a family and classroom value should undergird any attempt to teach self-discipline. Holding children and youth accountable for their own actions helps to make self-discipline a part of everyday life. In the case of children and youth with learning disabilities, being organized and having consistent routines do not come easily, yet these two qualities lie at the heart of self-discipline and control. Consequently, we may begin to understand the urgency of one participant's advice to parents of children and youth with learning disabilities: "Help them organize their lives. . . . There's no reason why they can't do the same thing every day. Use the carrot to get them to be more responsible."

Another issue central to control lies in being prepared, both to face expected as well as unexpected situations. Sometimes, we write off this phenomenon as luck, as being in the right place at the right time. But good luck seems to fall most often to people who have consciously and doggedly prepared themselves to be in the right place and time. People make their own luck; this is the outcome of control. One of our participants began his interview by quoting the noted industrialist and philanthropist, Armand Hammer: "The harder I work, the luckier I get."

This type of preparation also is inexorably connected to the abilities to anticipate, predict, and plan. Some of us, who have a "natural" ability to "think on our feet," may not always need to rely on a great deal of preparation. A small number of individuals even eschew meticulous planning, because they feel their learning-style strength revolves around responding spontaneously, improvising, and, to no small measure, living on the edge. When faced with an unknown or novel set of circumstances, they do not necessarily feel out of control; rather, they *seize* control from chaos. But for persons with learning disabilities who cannot process information effectively in immediate or spontaneous situations, being prepared takes on added importance.

Many of the adults in our study consistently utilized a high degree of preparation to face any possible problem. They simply could not afford to be caught off guard, and put forth extraordinary effort to predict all likely outcomes in any situation. One of our participants offered this advice to gain control: "Learning disabled people need to be taught strategies to anticipate problems." Teachers and parents can begin this process by emphasizing activities that involve making reasonable predictions of possible outcomes and then using these predictions to formulate advance plans of action.

Strategies for Developing Control

Role playing and simulation activities offer students with learning disabilities opportunities to practice this process, often in relation to pragmatic and relevant issues. For example, many of us have had the nightmarish experience of studying hard for an exam or test, only to open up a test with questions on topics that we seemed to have overlooked. (In fact, this does seem to be a recurring kind of anxiety dream that plagues many of us years after we have finished our schooling.) The anxiety stems from feeling out of control. Yet many of us would know what to do. We would use some method to calm down. We would find ways to express what we had learned, even if we did not answer the question directly. We would look for cues in the content of the question itself. In the case of some types of essay questions, we might even use our first paragraph to redefine or reinvent the question to fit our expertise. In any case, we would not leave the test blank. We would find some way to gain an advantage, to take control. For students with learning disabilities, who often do not internalize such strategies based on experiential or incidental learning, part of preparing for an exam may involve discussing exactly this kind of situation. In this way, teachers and parents would explicitly elicit strategies that help students stay in control.

In day-to-day school life, students with learning disabilities can learn to prepare for the seemingly unexpected by thinking about what to expect. Such strategies actually allow for making "bad" decisions—something we all do. Instead, the student learns to focus on what can be done to ameliorate the situation. For example, students, no matter how conscientious, may wait until the last minute to do homework or may even miss the deadline for an assignment. Recognizing that such "mistakes" are part of life, teachers and parents can ask students to consider how to deal with consequences of procrastination by using strategies such as talking and negotiating with the teacher, using cues in class discussions to appear prepared, etc.

Students with learning disabilities also face the same societal and peer pressures as all other students, yet we know they can be even more vulnerable to these pressures. Consequently, explicit training to prepare them to react sensibly is essential. An example that has particular relevance for youth of today is dealing with drugs and alcohol. The slogan "Just say no!" may empower some students, but it is likely to be somewhat hollow and meaningless to others. Instead, we need to ask students with learning disabilities to consider how they may find themselves unintentionally involved with drugs or alcohol, the possible consequences, and what kinds of strategies they can use to say no and stay "in control" of the situation. In many ways, we are simply asking students to increase their awareness of the relation between cause and effect, a relation that students with learning disabilities notoriously overlook. An emphasis on gaining control implicitly requires that students think about the consequences of their actions. Consequently, teaching strategies for control may also encourage a greater sense of individual accountability. As students with learning disabilities learn that much of the seemingly chaotic life around them is, in fact, predictable, they will build both confidence and the strategies that are inexorably linked with success in adulthood.

The following outline summarizes specific strategies for developing control:

I. Utilize role playing.

   A. Students act out a particular conflict or crisis situation in order to determine or brainstorm an effective outcome.

   B. Teachers may wish to use Goldstein's prosocial skills training program (Goldstein, 1988): (1) Define the problem, (2) role-play, (3) get feedback, (4) generalize.

II. Develop test-taking strategies.

   A. Students need to predict what is likely to be on a test. Encourage students to develop and answer questions they think will appear.

   B. Develop strategies to cope with facing unexpected test questions. Do not leave answers blank. On essay questions in particular, students are likely to receive some credit if they show they know something, even if it is not the specific answer.

III. Find and use opportunities to develop an awareness of cause and effect.

Internal Decisions

Desire

Finding the pathways to success begins with desire—the desire to succeed. One can have all the ability in the world, but if the spark to achieve is absent, talent means little. For the adults in our study, desire was not an ephemeral abstraction. Rather, it was a central, internalized, gut reaction that defined their self-image. It was real and tangible, a fire in the belly. Many of these adults were plainly angry. Growing up, they had been told repeatedly what they could not or should not do. Some needed to redefine themselves as capable and dynamic individuals, not only for themselves but for the world at large. "I'll show them I'm not an idiot," became a rallying cry, an affirmation that would dictate the course of all their actions. The adults in our study transformed pain and hurt into something productive. They made their anger work for them. In many cases, this process exacted an emotional toll, an anger that not only pushed them to achieve but that also permeated their psyche. Some were—and still are—mad at the world.

Anger can be powerful motivation, but it can also be turned inward and become self-destructive. As we consider ways to instill the desire to succeed in children and students, do we want to employ strategies that tap into anger? If we unleash a certain amount of anger, how do we direct it toward a positive outcome that empowers rather than incapacitates? And even if anger fuels the fire to succeed, do we want to produce individuals who continue to be mad at the world?

Individuals who possess solid self-esteem, a sense of purpose, and a belief in themselves are more likely to respond to challenges in a healthy and positive manner. We may routinely witness the proactive channeling of anger in competitive athletics. We do not want to suggest that teachers and parents emulate coaches who intimidate and terrorize in a Machiavellian manner. On the other hand, an effective coach, the kind we would label as a true motivator, is not afraid to challenge players, to demand their best, to make them accountable, but only after instilling in them a belief that they are winners. Successful coaches employ such varied methods as team songs, drills that through repetition internalize skills and success, positive self-talk, and visualization of successful outcomes—all with the intent to forge an inner core of belief in oneself. When we internalize a confidence that we are winners, we have fashioned a fundamental building block not only of the desire to succeed, but of the attainment of success itself.

Anger can become an active response to a challenge and the will to win becomes stronger when athletes or students believe in themselves (Cammer,

1977). Perhaps if we expected students to get excited about academic achievement, we would observe more enthusiasm. Scholars as eminent as Benjamin Bloom have wondered what would happen if students exhibited the same intensity for final exams as for the final football game (Bloom & Sosniak, 1981).

As we recognize that students will respond to challenges when they have confidence in themselves, we may create a new context for understanding the desire to succeed. Within the framework of Maslow's hierarchy of needs or motives model (Maslow, 1954), an upper level motive, such as this desire, develops only after more basic needs have been met. Adult figures who are supportive, work that is demanding but reasonable, and learning tasks that are worthwhile may all help children and youth feel safe, secure, accepted, competent, and effective (Woolfolk, 1990). Unfortunately, students with learning disabilities, particularly those in inclusive classrooms, may not encounter this ideal learning environment. They are the students who are more likely to make mistakes, whose attempts at learning are often met with an exasperated roll of the eyes or possibly even a rebuke that they are not trying or paying enough attention—little wonder that many choose not to participate, to become invisible. The desire to learn and achieve evaporates along with their self-confidence.

We can build a psychologically safe class environment by allowing mistakes to become opportunities for learning. Mistakes are part of the problem-solving process and a powerful tool for learning. If we can refrain from becoming irritated with children's initial failures and let them pursue a natural course of their own learning, they will be more likely to develop a high need for achievement (McClelland & Pilon, 1983). In this way, we maximize the opportunities for success. The results of our study reinforce the conventional wisdom that nothing whets the appetite for success like the taste of it.

We would also do well to remember that children and youth perceive success differently than do adults. Typically, adults seem to be consumed by the final product, where winning and losing are synonymous with success and failure. Children and youth tend to see success as a process of trying one's best and making improvements (Weiss, 1989). Consequently, if teachers and parents "reinforce and encourage effort and improvement much more than product measures, such as points scored or place earned" (Weiss, 1989, p. 195), they can instill a belief in the possibility of winning, an ethic of "work orientation" (Helmreich & Spence, 1978), a desire to succeed. Furthermore, teachers and parents give *themselves* opportunities to see and validate success in students with learning disabilities, a mutually beneficial process.

Another way to bear witness to the success of persons with learning disabilities is through the use of role models. Our study offers ample proof that there are many adults with learning disabilities who have achieved at least some degree of success. Moreover, we do not need to search for role models from the pages of history nor from sports and entertainment. As much as alluding to such figures may be comforting, students with learning disabilities need to become aware of adults who have found success in careers that offer more realistic possibilities. The adults in our study chose careers such as business, education, human services, medicine—areas that are accessible to many others with learning disabilities. Most importantly, such role models can help students develop a realistic appreciation of what it takes to succeed.

Our experience indicates that many successful adults with learning disabilities want to share their stories. A significant number of our participants concluded their interviews by stating that they were glad to have taken time out of busy schedules to help others with learning disabilities. Teachers and parents should be aware of the tremendous resource potential represented by adults with learning disabilities in local communities. These individuals have a credibility that those of us without learning disabilities lack. They are survivors; they have exceeded expectations; and they offer living proof that success is possible. If children and youth with learning disabilities are exposed to such models early and often, their desire for success is likely to be whetted. Invite adults with learning disabilities to your class, or even your home. As teachers and parents we tell children and youth that no one can do it alone. We need to follow our own advice. And if our children and students see that we value the input of adults with learning disabilities, they will receive an implicit affirmation of their own worth. The following are specific strategies for encouraging desire:

I. Implement cooperative learning activities.

  A. Students brainstorm strengths and abilities of each group member.

  B. Groups prepare presentations about famous persons with disabilities.

II. Invite successful adults with learning disabilities to the classroom. They may become more effective role models than celebrities.

III. Reward desire and effort. Emphasize the process rather than just the product.

IV. Provide opportunities for success. Nothing whets the appetite for success like the taste of it.

V. Do not be afraid to challenge, but instill a belief that the child is a winner.

Goal Orientation

Our participants generally did not inadvertently stumble onto the road to success. They knew where they wanted to go and they devised a way to get there.

Some of our children and youth are so defeated that they simply do not seem to have aspirations. But they probably do have dreams. Others may have fantastic goals. But that's the problem—the goals are more entwined with fantasy than reality. Still others may have developed perfectly reasonable ambitions, yet they do not have any step-by-step notion of how to move toward them.

The challenge to teachers and parents is formidable. We need to listen to our children and youth, discover, share, and nurture their dreams. We must help them define and refine their dreams into a realistic context, neither underestimating their potential nor leading them on a quixotic quest that is doomed to fail. As Teddy Roosevelt counseled, "Reach for the stars but keep your feet on the ground." Finally, as workable and achievable goals are developed, we have to devise a systematic plan of attack that breaks down the goals into a series of discrete objectives, each an accomplishment that steadily culminates toward a higher purpose. Even Don Quixote might find this agenda intimidating.

Another quality that we want to instill in children and students with learning disabilities is risk taking. People do not achieve their goals, or even pursue them, if they are afraid of failing. One adult in our study opined, "When the disabled have the courage to fail, they have the courage to try again." Few of us are right 100% of the time. Goals that are worth achieving generally do not come easily. They also represent a foray into unknown territory.

Fortunately, and perhaps ironically, many children and students with learning disabilities may have some advantages with the goal setting process, especially if they receive some guidance along the way. Most students with learning disabilities do know something about failing. Simply showing up day after day at school represents an admirable willingness to take risks. Of course, some learn to shy away from anything new, a trait teachers often term *learned helplessness*. One of the adults in our study combats learned helplessness through his readiness to admit that he may not know much, but "I'm not afraid to learn whatever I need to learn." In fact, most of those children and youth are not as helpless as they seem. Teachers and parents can remind them that they face and meet new challenges everyday at school. Focusing on what children and youth can do rather than what they cannot do provides a strong foundation for building the self-esteem required for taking risks.

We can encourage children to be risk takers by increasing our tolerance for errors. Taking risks invariably involves making mistakes. Further, most great discoveries occur only after a long series of setbacks. If we label such setbacks as failures, we doom ourselves to falling short of our goals. But if momentary reversals become opportunities for learning about new ways to reach a solution, risk taking ultimately pays off. Wasserman (1989) believes that we can build classrooms where risk taking and making mistakes are valued as integral to the learning process: "Think of the excitement of a classroom that functions as a learning laboratory in which error is examined clinically, critically and wisely, without the emotional baggage of negative judgment encumbering it. Think of how children and youth may be encouraged to take risks and raise provocative questions, absent of the fear of 'making a mistake' or 'getting it wrong'" (p. 234).

An effective goal setting orientation can evolve from helping students with learning disabilities develop goals that are specific, moderately difficult, and likely to be reached in the near future (Woolfolk, 1990). Of course, such a systematic approach does not come naturally to many students with learning disabilities. Children and youth with learning disabilities often do not predict outcomes in a logical and systematic fashion (Reiff & Gerber, 1990). On the other hand, students with learning disabilities may improve their reading comprehension when they receive specific instruction in how to make logical predictions (Palincsar & Brown, 1984). Teachers and parents can model and use systematic approaches to train children and youth to plan and organize more effectively.

Task analysis is probably the most commonly used method for breaking down a goal into a series of sequential, hierarchical, or developmental steps, each of which is attainable. Applying this goal setting process to classroom teaching in general utilizes Bloom's (1968) theory of mastery learning and may be particularly useful for students with learning disabilities. The teacher analyzes a given curriculum and breaks it down into a series of specific task objectives. Criteria for achievement of each task are explicit, and the students do not move on until they master each step. Students may develop a more realistic notion of how to structure goals. Instead of overwhelming themselves with goals that are complex, distant, and seemingly unattainable, students and children with learning disabilities can set themselves up for success one step at a time.

Using task analysis to make goals attainable is not limited to the classroom. In everyday living, we should encourage children and youth to view a variety of activities as goals that can be more readily accomplished by breaking them down into smaller, more manageable individual tasks. Cooking, cleaning, shopping, and so on can prove too much for some individuals with learning disabilities if they do not have a plan. Once the activity becomes a series of tasks, often monitored through some sort of checklist, these children and youth can be just as successful as anyone else. In the process, they may come to believe that they are capable and competent of meeting new challenges.

Effective goal setting takes on added importance as adolescents and young adults with learning disabilities begin to formulate transition plans, either from secondary education to career or from secondary education to postsecondary education. Unfortunately, a number of students with learning disabilities, especially those in restrictive settings, may lack awareness about the world beyond school. They tend to make uninformed, capricious, and unrealistic career choices (Reiff, Evans, & Anderson, 1989). We recommend the use of instruments such as the *Myers-Briggs Personality Inventory* (Myers & McCaulley, 1985) and *The Self-Directed Search* (Holland, 1985) to facilitate realistic goal orientation. These types of assessments help individuals understand respective strengths and weaknesses, likes and dislikes, and other important variables in determining career paths. In addition to self-assessment, students with learning disabilities need exposure to ongoing career education, beginning as early as elementary school. Self-insight becomes much more valuable when it is coupled with an informed understanding of what happens after schooling ends.

Finally, adolescents and young adults with learning disabilities have the potential to be more focused in their career planning and goal setting than many of their peers. We probably all remember any number of young adults who, in spite of obvious talents, have spent much time wandering from one job or career to another. They often express angst about trying to "find" themselves. In some ways, they have the luxury of seemingly aimless exploration because they are capable in many different areas.

Individuals with learning disabilities are not as likely to have this luxury. This may be a blessing in disguise. Many of our participants found they did not waste any time investigating a multitude of options. They knew certain directions simply were not sensible. Instead, they turned toward an area of strength and pursued it without second guessing themselves. They were goal oriented because they had to be. As one of the adults in our study reflected, "It [learning disability] has greatly impacted my success by narrowing my field, not as a limitation, but as giving direction. It has pointed me to something I can do very well." Outlined below are specific strategies for fostering goal orientation.

I. Create a goal-oriented system of classroom management. The teacher uses a level system where students earn a hierarchy of privileges for demonstrating increasing levels of appropriate behaviors.

II. Apply the concept of task analysis to the goal setting process.

A. Analyze teaching units in terms of a sequence of component tasks; students should master each before proceeding.

B. Students can break down each task into a series of steps, each of which is attainable.

III. Help students choose reasonable and logical goals that take into account both individual strengths as well as weaknesses. Use IEPs and other planning tools to share goals and the steps needed to attain them.

IV. For career goals, use instruments such as *The Self-Directed Search* (Holland, 1985) to explore possible career directions and to analyze the variables used in determining career paths.

Reframing

We have already discussed the process of reframing in some detail. It merits special attention because it represents the component of the success model most unique to persons with learning disabilities. Other models of success, such as Covey's (1990) *The Seven Habits of Highly Effective People*, do not refer to the necessity of recognizing, accepting, and understanding the implications of learning differently. These success models are not aimed at people who have a significant yet invisible disability. In fact, coming to grips with a disability that is not always apparent and is sometimes viewed with skepticism presents a special set of challenges. Reframing is a complex, ongoing process. It is also intensely personal, necessarily subjective, and largely unpredictable. Nevertheless, this process of internal exploration need not be mystifying. We can trace its theoretical foundation to Maslow's (1954) notion of self-actualization. Moreover, it may represent a distinct type of intelligence, what Gardner (1983) terms *intrapersonal intelligence*. The individual *learns* to develop a plan of action to deal with the world based on deep and purposeful knowledge and understanding of self and on an accurate assessment of strengths as well as weaknesses. Teachers and parents can make use of such theoretical frameworks and offer support and direction to their children and youth with learning disabilities as they embark on this lifelong journey of self-discovery.

We must begin this journey with the realization that it will not be easy and may be downright painful at times. Writing in the *Journal of Learning Disabilities*, Margaret Stolowitz, an adult with learning disabilities and attention deficit disorder, relates the pain of ultimately reframing the learning disabilities experience into something positive overall: "Because of this quest for self-identity and personal satisfaction, I have grown in many ways. It has not been easy and remains a hard path to follow. Yet, if I can finally live up to what I am truly capable of, then it might almost have been worth the emotional pain and continued struggle" (Stolowitz, 1995, p. 4).

On the other hand, an unwillingness to undertake the struggle of self-discovery inherent to reframing is likely to lead to deleterious consequences. Denial of learning disabilities, the antithesis of reframing the learning disabilities experience, represents a maladaptive coping strategy. In an in-depth, ethnographic study of 14 adults with learning disabilities, Shessel (1995) found that denial of learning disabilities in some of the participants led to "not focusing on the 'real' problems," "fighting with others," "poor health, even hospitalization," "disassociation," and "use of drugs" (pp. 140–141). Therefore, as teachers and parents we have a critical responsibility to prevent denial and to facilitate the process of reframing in children and youth with learning disabilities.

Many adults in our study stressed that reframing the learning disabilities experience began with recognition. As KM explained in Chapter 2, "I'm just finding out. I'm starting to realize the coping skills or the strategies. I find as I listen to other people I'm starting to learn myself how to deal with it. The beginning is just to recognize it." Yet "just to recognize it" may overwhelm and discourage some children and youth. Most students do not react positively to finding out they are "different."

How do we help children and youth recognize their learning differences without damaging their self-concept? In Maslow's (1954) theory of facilitating self-actualization, this process can only commence when basic psychological needs have been met. Teachers and parents can facilitate this process by structuring environments where children and youth feel safe and secure about themselves. In this way, they will learn to become more accountable in learning and overall social development. Recognition of differences should not act as a crutch or excuse for failure but may provide a catalyst for exploring new and different ways to learn and succeed. Vogel, Hruby, and Adelman (1993) suggest that the initial evaluation of learning disabilities offers an advantageous time to foster constructive dialogue.

Constructive and systematic approaches to recognizing that learning disabilities exist will foster acceptance of oneself. This process involves an ongoing confrontation of an initially cold reality: "I am different." Acceptance is crucial, because it is the starting point for developing a deeper and more productive understanding of one's self, of one's strengths and weaknesses. Although trying to accept the reality of learning disabilities often poses some discomfort, the process can offer a positive resolution.

Effective reframing of the learning disabilities experience culminates in using one's understanding of personal strengths and weaknesses to plan proactively. It facilitates the development of strategies that maximize personal attributes and minimize the limitations of the learning disabilities. One participant reframed the experience of having learning disabilities into an integrated and comfortable wholeness: "You must learn where your weaknesses are and how to avoid them or compensate. I have learned to accept who I am, what I can do, what I cannot do, who I should not try to be, and who I should try to be."

Developing adaptive attitudes and strategies rooted in self-acceptance and self-understanding suggests Gardner's (1983) construct of intrapersonal intelligence. Armstrong (1994) defines intrapersonal intelligence as "self-knowledge and the ability to act adaptively on the basis of that knowledge. This intelligence includes having an accurate picture of oneself (one's strengths and limitations); awareness of inner moods, intentions, motivations, temperaments, and desires; and the capacity for self-discipline, self-understanding, and self-esteem" (p. 3). Armstrong recommends that students can develop intrapersonal strengths through activities such as meditative and reflective thinking, personal counseling, developing special hobbies, goal setting, assessing strengths and weaknesses, working on one's own, and maintaining a personal diary. Teachers can develop curricular approaches that help students achieve a heightened awareness of intrapersonal intelligence. Teaching activities such as individualized instruction, independent study, options in course of study, and self-esteem building where students connect academic content to their personal lives will contribute to this effort. Moreover, teachers can integrate such approaches within the content of almost any curriculum. As an example, Armstrong (1994) presents a lesson focusing on understanding and using punctuation marks. Part of the instruction asks students to create their own, personally relevant sentences using each of the punctuation marks. This is obviously not a radical departure from standard practices; instead, it simply integrates an opportunity to involve personal reflection as part of a typical language arts task.

Another useful connection between reframing and intrapersonal intelligence comes from Armstrong's (1994) thoughts on classroom management. Armstrong emphasizes a clear and simple philosophy: Children and youth need to take charge of their own behavior. Too often, we hear the term *learned helplessness* used in the same breath as learning disabilities. Certainly, many students do not effectively come to terms with their learning disabilities. They may be the "deniers," and, in doing so, deny their own accountability for their failure or success. We associate such behaviors with an external locus of control, a mind-set of helplessness and vulnerability. On the other hand, an essential component of the reframing process lies in accountability. A proactive outlook, in which systematic planning is based on self-understanding, represents a significant internal locus of control and essentially dismisses the tendency to make excuses for oneself.

Classroom (and home) management can provide opportunities for developing the accountability inherent in successful reframing. Students should be responsible for making their own classroom (and home rules); they can learn to go to nonpunitive "time-out" areas voluntarily when they need to gain control; they can live up to behavior contracts (Armstrong, 1994). As teachers and parents, many of us have been inadvertently guilty of making special allowances for our children and youth because they have learning disabilities. We should be willing to confront excuses and learned helplessness not as adversaries, but as facilitators who can take advantage of these situations to develop recognition, acceptance, and understanding of learning disabilities without buying into pity or commiseration. We can begin this process by acting as role models. Teachers and parents who are honest and accepting of themselves, who are forthright about being less than perfect, demonstrate that all people have limitations but can succeed in spite of those limitations.

We need to enhance the self-confidence of children and youth with learning disabilities. Confidence-building experiences such as Outward Bound challenge individuals to confront and acknowledge personal experiences in order to perform above previously held expectations. Peer support groups also offer children and youth a safe environment to recognize, accept, and understand their learning disabilities. We have found that support groups for college students with learning disabilities have provided a therapeutic forum for discussing personal issues with the peer group most likely to understand and help, that is, other students with learning disabilities (Reiff, 1993). Successful college students with learning disabilities understand themselves and their learning styles and put this knowledge into a plan of action (Adelman & Vogel, 1990; Reiff, 1993; Vogel et al., 1993). By observing that successful students know the value of being prepared, discover personally effective ways to study, and accept the fact that they have to work harder and longer than their roommates and friends, other students find that they are not alone in their struggles and fears and may learn new ways to cope and plan. Finally, the one-to-one interaction of counseling services may play an integral role in guiding children and youth to reframe the experience of learning disabilities into a positive and effective perspective on dealing with life.

In many cases, successful reframing results in an entirely new perspective, in which learning disabilities evolve from anathema to gift. In the previous section on goal orientation, we have already heard a participant say, "It [learning disability] has greatly impacted my success by narrowing my field, not as a limitation, but as giving direction. It has pointed me to something I can do very well" or "The biggest advantage is that once you realize you can't do all these things, you become good at finding alternative solutions and making the most of what you have." A vice president at an academic institution found this "gift" in her learning disabilities. Her motivation and productivity surpass the norm because things do not come easily. The fact that she has always had to work harder than others has become the foundation of her achievements. She reflects, "You're different, you're unique, and you can succeed at a level far superior to what a normal person can do. Because a normal person takes it for granted. You will be able to think, to function, to succeed at a level a normal person could never even reach for." If we can help our children and youth to reframe their learning disabilities in this manner, they will exceed expectations. The following outline summarizes specific strategies for promoting reframing:

I. Facilitate personal assessments.

   A. Students complete self-analysis of strengths and weaknesses.

   B. Individual students transform "I can't" statements to "I can" statements.

II. Make students accountable for their actions.

    A. Involve students in monitoring and enforcing their own behavioral management systems.

    B. Use individual behavior contracts.

III. Encourage students to participate in confidence-building experiences.

    A. Incorporate activities and programs traditionally used in various walks of education and business such as Outward Bound.

    B. Work with students to develop and pursue special hobbies.

IV. Develop peer support groups.

 V. Utilize school counseling services.

VI. Build intrapersonal intelligence. Integrate meditative and reflective activities into curriculum.

External Manifestations

Persistence

If success comes to people who work hard, it also comes to people with learning disabilities who work harder. In many ways, the "gift" just described may be termed *persistence*. Most of the adults in our study developed extraordinary levels of tenacity and resilience because they realized they had little choice, at least if they wanted to survive in school. Working long and hard was not something that they chose to do only in extreme circumstances; it was a way of life, nurtured in childhood or adolescence. This habit of survival was transformed into a pattern for success in the adult world. Why was this trait so effective? "There is always a place for someone who wants to work hard because most people in the world do not want to work at all," remarked one of our participants.

Persons with learning disabilities can learn to be persistent. An emphasis at school and at home on imparting this behavior can give students with learning disabilities a tremendous advantage over their peers. One of the adults in the study stated, "I have learned persistence and am surprised by the number of people who lack persistence." We would certainly love to be able teach all children and youth to work harder and longer, to face adversity willingly, and to rebound from any failure with a renewed sense of resolve to succeed. Yet when we picture many students with learning disabilities, we often see children and youth who give up more quickly than their peers. Some of this difficulty undoubtedly stems from feelings of insecurity and a sense of defeat. We have already discussed some strategies to bolster self-esteem and will offer additional ones in this section. However, as teachers and parents, we may be unwittingly discouraging children and youth with learning disabilities from putting forth maximum effort. For a number of years, special educators in particular have talked about assuring success, sometimes no matter what. It is possible to hear special education supervisors direct remarks such as "there will be no special education students who will fail" to teachers. Such sentiments may be grounded in well-intentioned policy to protect students from the ravages of chronic failure. Ironically, we may be denying students exactly those experiences that can lead to increased levels of persistence. One participant sounded this warning by commenting, "The worst thing is just to pass a child. People need to fail to become successful. Having to work harder to do something that is easy for someone else is no excuse for getting by easily."

"Failure plays a major role in being successful," proclaimed another adult with learning disabilities. No one who has ever become successful has avoided failure. In fact, many of the adults in our study credited a significant portion of their success to failure, or at least in learning how to deal with failure. After all, do any of us really learn and grow without making mistakes along the way? "You learn more from your failures than from your success if you don't let it paralyze you," counseled one of our participants.

Failure can teach us at least two important lessons. First, we can learn not to give up. The more we are willing to bounce back, to pick ourselves up after we've been knocked down, the better we will be able to respond to the realities of the workplace and perhaps life in general. It is exceedingly hard if not impossible to develop this strength unless we are tested by the act of failing. Second, failure can give us new, and otherwise unseen, insights into solutions that might eventually work. In many ways, this describes the scientific process. Hypotheses are revised, refined, and ultimately verified through new knowledge that comes only from finding one's earlier hypotheses to be mistaken. Consider how many more times Edison was wrong before he was right! Eby and Smutny (1989), in their work on gifted and talented individuals, refer to a higher order level of creativity as "creative processes." They describe this phenomenon as finding new ways to think about things after initial approaches do not work. A number of participants pointed out that their friends in school, to whom everything came easily, were not prepared to cope with the frustrations of the adult world.

We add a caveat to the "no pain, no gain" school of thought. When children and youth with learning disabilities face adversity, they need support. Parents and teachers must walk a fine line between allowing children to fend for themselves and protecting them from overwhelming and catastrophic failure. The foundation for building the strength to cope lies in recognizing and reinforcing the strengths that children and youth with learning disabilities already possess.

We will be more willing to persist when we believe in ourselves. One adult in the study, who is a renowned psychologist, shared this advice for parents of children and youth with learning disabilities: "Tell your child he is good, whole, and don't make a game of comparison. Look for individual gifts and greatness as well as the things they struggle with. It's OK to struggle. It can make them better individuals. They'll hurt, but it's going to be OK, and you'll be there to provide support."

Teachers and parents can help children and youth with learning disabilities learn not only the value but the behaviors and habits of persistence. Persistence is desire turned into action. Consequently, activities we have discussed that promote building the desire to succeed provide an essential foundation for developing persistence. Moreover, activities that reward persistence, regardless of outcome, help children and youth realize that working hard pays off. At the same time, we need to help children and youth with learning disabilities choose goals where effort is likely to produce a positive outcome. The traditional curriculum has tended to emphasize performance goals. These goals involve an external judgment of success based on standards that are often incongruent with the way students with learning disabilities learn and perform. In the typical classroom environment, these standards may put the student with learning disabilities at a distinct disadvantage. On the other hand, Bandura (1986) contends that individuals tend to persist in their efforts until standards are met when goals reflect self-efficacy. Consequently, teachers and parents should help children and youth with learning disabilities select performance goals consistent with their own sense of personal competence.

Furthermore, in contrast to performance goals, learning goals, which center on personal improvement, tend to inspire greater effort (Dweck, 1986). These kinds of goals impart a heightened sense of control to children and youth with learning disabilities. The focus is on personal improvement as opposed to an invariant standard. Children and youth can measure their own progress. Nevertheless, many students with learning disabilities are amazingly adept at ignoring or denying any kind of success. It is vital that parents and teachers focus on even incremental change and point out and reinforce personal improvement. Emphasizing progress and making connections between past efforts, maintaining individual portfolios with examples of good work, and returning work with specific suggestions for revisions to improve grades communicate to students that they do succeed when they persist (Woolfolk, 1990).

We must remind students and children with learning disabilities that there is no shame in failing as long as they keep trying. Students need to know that persistence pays off. Yet most of us do not have the patience of Job. It is often difficult to work with children and youth with learning disabilities as they struggle without becoming frustrated ourselves or doing the work for them. Computers may rescue us from our own imperfections while providing a stimulating and structured learning environment. As the following advertisement from the *Whole Earth Software Catalog* suggests, computers have infinite patience and will not give up teaching children and youth with learning disabilities to be persistent:

> Programs offer learning substance in an adventure format. . . . Computers don't get frustrated, don't roll their eyes while you take a slow time coming up with the wrong answer to something. . . . Mistakes are trivial to a computer! Fact is, they do the best possible thing for learners—they reward mistakes. So go ahead, make them—steer by them—steering successfully is the reward. (Brand, 1984)

The following strategies help build persistence:

    I. Devise activities that reward and reinforce persistence.

        A. Mastery learning approaches embrace this concept in demanding effort, in spite of initial shortcomings, until the task is mastered.

        B. Develop goals that are obtainable and center on personal improvement.

        C. Allow students to fail, as long as they can try again.

   II. Devise activities that require the use of "creative processes."

  III. Offer extra options to complete a requirement.

  IV. Use behavior modification methods as a relatively easy means for reinforcing determination and persistence in a systematic manner.

Goodness of Fit

The more children and youth with learning disabilities understand the meaning of their individual strengths and weaknesses, the more they can apply the concept of goodness of fit to their activities. Equally important, they need to factor in their personal likes and dislikes. Successful persons tend to enjoy what they do. Therefore, knowing oneself is integral to determining goodness of fit. In this sense, reframing drives goodness of fit. A plan of action means choosing environments that are supportive.

    The successful adults in our study used their understanding of their strengths and weaknesses to choose and create such environments. They determined the extent to which they could adapt to their environment and the extent to which they could adapt the environment to their needs. As they negotiated the road to success, they also learned when to bail out and start anew, sometimes by charting new career directions altogether. This last component, the flexibility to change, has particular meaning for persons with learning disabilities. They may not make the optimal choice the first time out. As with our discussions on desire and persistence, there is nothing wrong with being wrong, as long as one moves on. In many cases, individuals with learning disabilities will discover and understand goodness of fit only after experiencing a poor fit. Teachers and parents need to help children and youth understand when the fit is poor, why it is poor, and what they can do about it.

In speaking with less-than-successful adults, we have noticed that they may be unaware of goodness of fit, or are at least slow to recognize the implications. A memorable interview took place with a young man who had specific problems with visual–spatial relations, including difficulty reading maps and letter reversals or inversions. He obtained a job as a delivery truck driver. Needless to say, he often was late or did not find his destinations. Perhaps the most remarkable problem occurred when he was supposed to drive through Reserve, Louisiana, to make a delivery. When he reached the outskirts, he read the sign as "Reverse," backed up his truck, and never entered the town. He did not devise ways to adapt to the demands of the job, nor did he find ways to adapt the job to his needs. Unfortunately, he seemed to make little connection between being fired and his specific deficits (Gerber & Reiff, 1991).

Creating goodness of fit does not necessitate restricting oneself to environments that only require one's strengths, as long as there are ways to adapt or change the environment. Another young man with learning disabilities found work as an electrician. He was skilled with the electrical work and was particularly adept at analyzing visual schematics. However, he had significant reading and spelling problems. When it came time to order parts, he found it almost impossible to fill out an invoice to send to his supervisor. He adapted his environment by working out a numerical code for the parts with his supervisor: Instead of writing out the name, he simply wrote a number. This relatively simple change circumvented a major difficulty. By being aware of his own weaknesses and taking a proactive stance, this young man created goodness of fit (Gerber & Reiff, 1991).

Some individuals with learning disabilities even find that what were considered weaknesses in some environments become strengths in others. One participant who had chronic difficulties with visual reversals always found reading to be very hard. Academics were a constant struggle. By the time he was in college, he realized his grades were not good enough to achieve his lifelong dream of attending medical school. Instead of giving up, he modified his dream, applied and was accepted to dental school. This turned out to be a fortuitous choice. When the students began working with dental mirrors, most were thoroughly disoriented. For our participant, his propensity for reversals proved to be an advantage; the mirror presented no problems. In the environment of dentistry, the world had straightened out (Gerber & Reiff, 1991).

Children and youth with learning disabilities do not necessarily have a great many opportunities to exercise such choice, particularly at school. They usually cannot control what subjects they will take. They do not choose their teachers. The classroom environment often does not maximize their strengths and minimize their weaknesses.

Parents, however, are in a position to help their children and youth learn about and explore how to utilize goodness of fit. Supporting children and youth as they develop hobbies and interests, pointing them to things they can do well, and creating opportunities where they can experience success will emphasize that certain types of environments present favorable conditions. At the same time, we need to be honest in helping children and youth understand that they are likely to experience difficulties in some areas due to their learning disabilities. We do not want to send a message to give up or not to try. We do need to communicate, however, that goals must be realistic. Choosing environments that complement strengths and allow compensation for weaknesses plays a critical role in achieving goals.

Some parents are in the fortunate position to be able to choose the best educational environment for their children and youth with learning disabilities. An increasing number of private schools specifically designed to meet the needs of students with learning disabilities may offer an effective alternative to the public educational system. We do not wish to take a position on the most appropriate educational placement; it is always a case-by-case process. However, we can state that a number of studies credit successful outcomes of adults with learning disabilities at least partially to specially designed alternative programs (Gerber & Reiff, 1991; Vogel et al., 1993).

Teachers can devise specific classroom activities to promote an understanding of goodness of fit. For example, it is not uncommon to assign a large-scale research project at the later elementary grades. (Do you remember doing a report on your town or state in third or fourth grade?) As they begin their work and at various stages throughout, students can fill out checklists regarding their strengths, weaknesses, likes, dislikes, what will work for them, what will not, what help they will need from the teacher or other students, what they can do on their own, and so on. They can learn to make choices to create an environment conducive to success. Role playing in the classroom presents another opportunity to explore goodness of fit. Instead of assigning roles for a given simulation, the teacher allows the students to choose. A discussion then ensues about why a given role is a good match or not with the particular student's strengths and weaknesses. Finally, simulations and role-play, usually for older students, can focus on specific employment situations. As an example, a student with significant reading and spelling problems might role-play a waiter. This simulation would allow students to discuss the ramifications of those problems in such an environment and to suggest ways to modify the environment to be more friendly (e.g., some sort of coding system when taking orders). Of course, such activities should not be limited to focusing on potential problems that students with learning disabilities are likely to encounter. Teachers should make an effort to point out things that students do well and demonstrate the advantages of working within one's areas of strength.

In general, the classroom should provide a model of how goodness of fit allows for the greatest development of potential. Effective teachers build classrooms that maximize strengths, accommodate weaknesses, and promote a genuine concern in one's own learning process. Approaches utilizing theories such as Gardner's (1983) construct of multiple intelligences may increase opportunities for students with learning disabilities to experience successful learning. Assessment that accurately identifies strengths as well as weaknesses, a broad repertoire of instructional strategies, and the ability to respond to diverse learning styles will make the classroom a "good fit" for students with learning disabilities.

As students become older, additional opportunities for understanding goodness of fit abound. As we mentioned in our discussion of goal orientation, the use of career and personality inventories may assist students in developing a sense of the types of environments likely to be "friendly." Career education will help adolescents with learning disabilities discover likes and dislikes, make informed decisions about career opportunities, and select employment that will optimize their chances for success. For students with learning disabilities pursuing postsecondary education, parents and teachers can help with selecting institutions. Many postsecondary institutions offer support services to students with learning disabilities. Services should match the needs of the individual student, not only academically, but socially, emotionally, and recreationally as well. Once the student has entered postsecondary education, goodness of fit requires attention to course selection and choice of major.

From the type of classroom in which a child is placed to the career path an adult develops, goodness of fit may play a critical role in ultimate success or failure. The individual with learning disabilities plays an active role in determining how good the fit is, not only in choosing an environment but in responding to it. The outline below summarizes specific strategies for helping students understand goodness of fit.

    I. Encourage children and youth to investigate personal interests. Use preference inventories where students determine preferences in areas such as music, food, recreation, hobbies, concerts, menus, camps etc.

   II. Begin career awareness experiences early in education and build on them progressively and systematically.

III. Use simulation activities to help students increase understanding of goodness of fit.

    A. Help children understand positive and negative consequences of choices involving topics from course selection to employment opportunities.

    B. Poor choices should be an opportunity for learning.

IV. Design assessments that identify strengths as well as weaknesses.

  V. Make the classroom an environment that provides goodness of fit for diverse learning styles.

In the next section, we discuss ways to develop responses based on the unique needs of persons with learning disabilities. We term this behavior *learned creativity*.

Learned Creativity

Learned creativity has helped successful adults with learning disabilities cope with academic, vocational, social, and daily living demands. An awareness and understanding of one's particular learning style and strengths and weaknesses may lead to the development of a repertoire of personal and unique strategies. Our participants learned to compensate for their deficient areas and utilize their special abilities. Learned creativity is more likely to lead to successful outcomes when connected to reframing and goodness of fit.

In some cases, they found that, in the right circumstances, they could reinvent themselves by turning apparent weaknesses into strengths. One adult in our study explained it this way:

> I think I do things in a very creative way. Everybody else was going through the maze, and somehow I couldn't get through that maze. I was too fat or too skinny or something. If I was going to get to the finish line, I had to find another way. And in that process I ended up going through parts of the maze that nobody had ever seen. Looking at that whole experience of being in a maze from a larger picture, I think I turned the lemon into lemonade, in that it's not easy for me to do the things I do, but I've made the struggle.

Writing in the *The Rebus Institute Report*, Jeffrey Roloff (1994), an adult with attention deficit disorder, has learned to harness and utilize his impulsive thought processes. He has discovered

> a technique called "Mind Mapping" or "Power Writing" that is an incredibly powerful tool for capturing the chaos of multidirectional thoughts when I need

to write a letter or plan something. This allows me to grab the thoughts as they fly by, and follow the many thought threads, and jump back and forth between ideas, without losing any of them. For me this has changed the process of writing simple letters from a dreadful task that used to take a long time, to a skill that I am much faster at and am proud of. This does not seem to appeal to everyone, but I find this so liberating and empowering that I would gladly give presentations on this. (p. 2)

A number of other participants experienced great frustration in school because they were rarely able to arrive at correct answers on their first attempt. They had difficulty with convergent thinking, but they excelled at divergent thinking, partially because they had to come up with many different answers in order to keep up in school. One adult explained how he had transformed his inability to get it right the first time into an asset in the business world: "I never look at a problem the way a traditional person looks at it, like a textbook looks at it, or like a professor describes it. I always see that problem in about ten different ways because I've always had to use different problem solving methods in my life."

The term *learned creativity* clearly implies that we can teach individuals with learning disabilities to respond to demands in unique, personal, effective, and occasionally clever ways. We do not yet know a great deal about teaching creative coping skills per se, but we do know something about teaching creativity. Frederikson (1984) provides several maxims for promoting creativity in students that may undergird our specific concern about students with learning disabilities: (a) Accept and encourage divergent thinking, (b) tolerate dissent, (c) encourage students to trust their own judgment, (d) emphasize that everyone is capable of creativity in some form, and (e) be a stimulus for creative thinking.

Divergent thinking and unusual approaches to problem solving are useful in many areas of the real world. Many students with learning disabilities possess these traits. Teachers can encourage the development of such skills by evaluating the purposes of the tasks they ask students to perform, and, when appropriate, being more open to creative and unexpected ways of responding. Teachers have long used the approach of brainstorming (Osborne, 1963) to facilitate the use of divergent thinking. The classroom will foster learned creativity as one idea triggers another.

Brainstorming sometimes gives students with learning disabilities a more accessible forum to demonstrate their problem-solving abilities. For example, the teacher presents a math problem such as determining the best shopping buy, calculating probabilities, or developing a theorem. Students give their individual ideas about the best way to solve it. They may then see that a number of different approaches will work. Their collective ideas may offer solutions that draw on a number of different good ideas. While not all learning activities are geared toward divergent strategies, some teachers may limit students with learning disabilities unintentionally. Several participants remembered failing at math, not because of an inability to get the right answer, but because they did not do it the teacher's way.

Evaluating the purpose of different types of learning tasks may lead to a broader perspective of how students show that they've learned something and are capable. Activities that have numerous options for completion (such as a project that can be turned in not only as a written report, but as a video, dramatization, etc.) allow individual students to develop and use approaches that work best for them. If original and personally effective ways of solving problems result in positive reinforcement, children and youth with learning disabilities will learn to utilize their creative abilities, to focus on what they can do rather than what they cannot, and to inculcate a work ethic that is more likely to have successful outcomes.

Research has indicated that successful college students with learning disabilities use creative strategies to deal with academic demands (Vogel et al., 1993). In our experience with college students with learning disabilities, we have observed a myriad of special approaches that others can easily learn and personalize. Students who have difficulty listening and writing commonly use tape recorders in classes, particularly lectures. Successful students go beyond merely turning on the tape recorder, sitting back, and perhaps listening to the tape sometime later. Instead, they have found it is essential to be involved actively in the class. For many, this means writing down at least some sketchy notes. In fact, Suritsky and Hughes (1991) contend that the use of note takers may be detrimental to some students with learning disabilities, who may have less incentive to focus their attention effectively, a difficult task even when they are actively engaged. Writing down something tends to force the student to pay attention and process information. Some students make the tape recording an integral part of their note-taking strategies by jotting down the tape counter number whenever material is particularly important. In this way, they focus their attention on discerning relevant from irrelevant information. Additionally, they may not need to replay the entire tape, only those spots that they have noted.

There are a number of ways to use the recording itself. The "counters" may literally transcribe the critical moments of the class. Other students take notes during the class in the form of questions and then use the tape to fill in the answers. Others take relatively comprehensive notes and use the recording to fill in blanks, listen to the class again while simultaneously reading their notes, or both. Specific strategies for note taking are teachable and adaptable to individual learning styles. Parents, teachers, and service providers should consider helping students with learned disabilities develop personalized approaches to note taking as well as other study behaviors.

Specialized methods of time management and organization can play a critical role in school and college as well as employment. For some individuals, learning disabilities directly interfere with the ability to be organized. They need specific compensatory strategies. Others may have adequate or excellent organizational abilities, so they develop advanced skills to compensate for other areas of weakness. Still others have the ability to be organized but cannot rely on typical aids. For example, as we mentioned in Chapter 7, one of our participants, a successful attorney, found that identifying clients' files through written names was inefficient; reading the name was difficult and did not create an association with the person. Instead, he attached the client's photograph to each file folder, a much faster and deeper means of recognition.

In working with college students with learning disabilities, service providers place great emphasis on teaching time management and organization. Schooling through high school usually provides a great deal of structure, making the freedom of college life an abrupt transition. A major component of learned creativity in college lies in planning how to be a successful student. Successful students typically use daily, weekly, and monthly planners. Times are blocked out for classes, other activities, and especially studying. Effective planning incorporates setting goals for each class, determining what kind of study-time commitment the goal requires, and balancing different time commitments. Routine study habits—regular times, regular places, regular study routines—are a key ingredient to overall planning and organization.

Younger students with learning disabilities can learn to make use of organizational strategies. Parents can help children organize their chores and responsibilities around the house. Checklists, schedules, bright visual calendars on the refrigerator, routine study habits, and so on all facilitate development and internalization of organizational strategies. At the same time, children and youth need to experience the consequences of how they organize themselves. Attention to encouraging students to develop their own approaches will ease the transition to the often unstructured world of adulthood.

The range and types of learned creativity are virtually unbounded. No one teacher or parent can possibly anticipate all individual differences and adaptations as well as the kinds of situations requiring strategic responses. On the other hand, we have a resource of strategies in children and students with learning disabilities. When students with learning disabilities interact in a structured group discussion, they often share their tricks and tools of the trade. They learn from each other, gaining insight into coping with situations most relevant to them. Adolescents and young adults with learning disabilities frequently participate in support groups, an excellent forum for asking "What works for you?" Picking up ideas from peers begins the process of creating effective compensatory skills. Teachers and parents will play a vital role by talking with children and students, helping them connect their self-understanding with their coping behaviors. The following are specific strategies for developing learned creativity:

  I. Promote creativity and divergent thinking at every opportunity. Use brainstorming activities (e.g., how many different ways can we answer a math problem?)

 II. Utilize group sharing activities as a means to pass on strategies that work from one child to another.

III. Select activities that have numerous options for completion.

 IV. Teach a variety of specific study strategies.

  V. Develop individual planning guides.

Social Ecologies

In interview after interview, successful adults with learning disabilities credited many of their accomplishments to supportive and useful interpersonal relationships. As teachers and parents, we want to provide these kinds of relationships. We want our children and youth to learn to build their own favorable social ecologies.

Most of the adults in our study felt that a supportive parent or parents provided the core foundation for success. At critical junctures of development, when it seemed "everything" was hopeless and no one cared or understood, only a parent with unconditional love and faith kept our participants from giving up. One participant had this direct advice concerning parenting skills:

> Sit with your child and go through problems from the beginning of their education and go through the tasks. It's part of being intimate with your child. . . . The most important thing is building your child's soul for individual gifts and greatness as well as the things they'll struggle with. . . . When it goes beyond what you know you can be helpful with, call for help. Inspire others to help this person. Make the system responsive to the child.

All parents want their children to grow up to be independent, self-assured adults. Parents of children with learning disabilities share this desire. They may have greater cause to worry about the pitfalls their children and youth are likely to encounter along the way. No one is in a position to soften every hard edge of our child's environment. And, as we have stated before, we believe children and youth grow and become more resolute by facing adversity. Rather than try to protect their children from all hardships, parents can help their children through these pitfalls. Parents should act as advocates for their children, adults who offer unconditional faith and support. This role initiates the building of a favorable social ecology. Children and youth with learning disabilities need and respect adults who believe in them. One participant remembered the critical role his mother played in counteracting the negative forces in a childhood with learning disabilities. "My mother never gave up on me. She would never ask how many I got right on the test, only how many I finished. . . . She explained that it never hurt to keep trying. She just refused to believe all those people who called me a dummy or retard."

Parents can do more than "never give up" and "refuse to believe all those people." They can provide children with tools to fight back. Fournier (1992) contends that children and youth with learning disabilities can learn to "turn the meaning upside down," when they are exposed to negative comments. A parent can work with a child to reinterpret "The teacher says I did it wrong" as "The teacher wants me to ask questions." "Did not complete" becomes "Find ways to learn how to finish." "You spelled four out of ten words incorrectly" just as readily means "You spelled six out of ten words correctly." As students with learning disabilities learn to see themselves in a more positive light, they develop an essential building block of effective self-advocacy, a key to creating a favorable social ecology.

In Shessel's (1995) study of 14 adults with learning disabilities, several had well-developed methods to turn negative meanings into positive ones. Shessel views this element of the reframing process as a kind of cognitive dissonance. Most persons with learning disabilities experience a variance between how they view themselves (e.g., functional) and how others view them (e.g., dysfunctional). The individual can resolve the cognitive dissonance by choosing *either* perspective. It is often easier and faster to reduce dissonance by fulfilling others' expectations. Yet many persons with learning disabilities devote much energy to fighting negative messages. The process can culminate in a positive self-affirmation through reframing the learning disabilities experience. In this sense, teaching children and youth to reinterpret the negative provides a part of the social ecology that may facilitate the reframing process. In turn, successful reframing will help individuals with learning disabilities construct social ecologies that best respond to their needs.

Parents play an important role in the choice between seeing oneself as capable or incapable. They need to supply plenty of self-worth affirmation so that their children have some ammunition to fight back negative comments. Children and youth who experience success and receive positive feedback from their environment are additionally prepared to maintain self-esteem in the face of adversity. Parents may also need to employ some kind of counseling to help deal with these issues. Counseling, when appropriate, is a useful component of a favorable social ecology.

The classroom should also serve as a favorable social ecology in the overall environment of students with learning disabilities. If learning is fun, if students feel comfortable taking risks, if individual accountability is clear and consistent, and if individual differences are embraced, the classroom offers the opportunities to maximize positive self-development. In recent years, many educators have touted cooperative learning as a vehicle to realize these goals. Evidence suggests that cooperative learning approaches promote achievement, positive self-esteem, psychological adjustment, and acceptance of individual differences (Putnam, 1993).

Implementing effective cooperative methods has particular relevance for students with learning disabilities. Most students with learning disabilities in public schools attend inclusive classrooms most or all of the school day. The philosophies of inclusive education and cooperative learning share the same goals, namely, to create learning environments where students support each other and accept individual differences (Johnson & Johnson, 1993). Consequently, we may imagine that cooperative learning stands to be the method of choice in the majority of today's classrooms.

Simply throwing students together in small groups, however, will not automatically result in positive social outcomes. Many educators agree that successful cooperative groups depend on positive interdependence, individual accountability, cooperative skills, face-to-face interaction, student reflection and goal setting, heterogeneous grouping, and equal opportunities for success (Putnam, 1993). To achieve these conditions, Johnson, Johnson, and Holubec (1987) recommend an eight-step lesson-planning method: (a) correlate instructional objectives with IEP objectives, (b) group students heterogeneously, (c) arrange group spaces to facilitate face-to-face interaction, (d) design goals that encourage interdependent participation of all students, (e) make expectations and criteria for success explicit, (f) use direct observation, (g) intervene when necessary, and (h) assess both academic and social skills.

Cooperative group activities utilize assessment of group performance on group goals. Students naturally tend to act more as a team when they work toward common goals. This situation may offer support specifically to students with learning disabilities who often are not part of the "team," whatever it may be. Nevertheless, individual accountability is a central tenet. Proponents of cooperative learning argue that individual evaluation should be based on intrapersonal growth; that is, individual improvement should be the primary basis of evaluation. At a minimum, this system rewards desire and persistence. It offers greater possibilities for success for students who really are trying to learn and achieve, and is less likely to reward students who simply do not try.

As they embark in the transition to independent adulthood, older students are preparing to have much more control in creating their own social ecologies. They need to have skills in interdependency, which cooperative learning promotes. Individuals with learning disabilities learn that they are more likely to be successful when they utilize the support they need. The sophisticated and complex systems of almost any career path are quickly making the use of external human resources an essential job requirement. The worker, supervisor, or executive who can do it all alone has almost faded into oblivion. A focus for students with learning disabilities on interdependency may give them an edge in the future business world.

Support groups provide an environment that encourages interdependent behaviors. Students learn from each other. Every student has something to contribute, from sharing study tips to disclosing anxiety. For many students, simply finding out that they are not alone, that other students have the same experiences, provides an essential measure of safety and security.

Support groups take on an additional role of facilitating other components of the model. When students learn successful survival strategies from other students, they enlarge their repertoire of learned creativity. Support groups for college students with learning disabilities often include discussions about instructors or courses that are "LD friendly." In this way, students may apply a goodness of fit principle to their course selection. A support group may be a place where one student's persistence inspires another. An effective support group potentially acts as a microcosm of the whole notion of a favorable social ecology—and favorable social ecologies may represent the heart of the whole model of success. The list below summarizes specific strategies for creating favorable social ecologies:

I. Utilize reciprocal teaching.

II. Implement cooperative learning experiences.

III. Offer support groups.

IV. Work with parents and significant others in the child's life to develop expectations that are realistic, neither too low nor too high.

V. Refer students to counseling when appropriate.

VI. Be an advocate for children and youths with learning disabilities.

The suggestions and activities based on the model of success presented in this chapter are far from inclusive. We strongly encourage parents and teachers to develop their own activities using ideas presented in this chapter.

Conclusions

A colleague, Isabel Shessel, recently wrote a dissertation based on in-depth interviews and follow-up interviews with a diverse group of 14 adults with learning disabilities (Shessel, 1995). She found that her participants employed, in one form or another, the components of the model of success to cope with their lives. Some were quite successful and well adapted; others were struggling, in some cases bordering on a dysfunctional existence. We asked if she had determined a significant variable that accounted for these different outcomes. She responded emphatically that attitude played the single most decisive role. The participants who had better outlooks on life were more successful. In addition, almost all of her participants stressed the importance of having some kind of support, of feeling loved and cared for, that is, of having a positive social ecology.

Favorable social ecologies promote emotional health. Perhaps this is the key to the relation of social ecologies to the rest of the model. The attitudes, habits, and behaviors that figure into successful outcomes are more likely to be learned and effectively utilized when persons with learning disabilities have a strong and secure emotional foundation. Desire to succeed certainly is stronger if one believes one can succeed. As we have previously discussed, students are more likely to take the risks associated with goal orientation in emotionally secure and safe classrooms. Reframing, with the ultimate goal of gaining a positive perspective and internal locus of control, requires emotional health and confidence. Not giving up on oneself, the embodiment of persistence and resiliency, surely emanates from inner faith. Individuals with learning disabilities will employ goodness of fit when they believe that positive outcomes are possible. And finally, one can have the most impressive learned creativity imaginable, but it may serve little purpose without a proactive and purposeful attitude.

In fact, when we picture a person with learning disabilities who has embraced, learned, and utilized the different attitudes, habits, and behaviors of the model of success, we see somebody with a "can do" attitude. In other words, utilizing the model helps the individual gain control; the more control one has, the better one's outlook will be. In this sense, the model is perpetually interactive. The feeling of self-confidence that it inspires may turn out to be the decisive factor, the driving force that ultimately accounts for success.

We also believe that, in spite of the power of positive attitude, attitude without skills and strategies may not be sufficient to overcome the obstacles of a learning disability. How many children and youth with learning disabilities start out with a strong self-concept only to be gradually worn down and destroyed by repeated failures? We would be disingenuous to suggest that developing skills and strategies will guarantee unlimited success. But for most children and youth with learning disabilities to be on a level playing field with other children and youth, they do need special ways to meet and respond to the demands of school and life. As they start to hold their own, they will be able to inculcate the belief and faith that we already have in them. Parents and teachers must help children and youth with learning disabilities develop and build this combination of behavioral strategies, affective skills, and emotional strengths. With this kind of education, individuals with learning disabilities may even exceed expectations.

Self-Advocacy in the Era of the Americans with Disabilities Act

Chapter 11

Putting the basic tenets of the model of employment success into action will not automatically lead to positive vocational outcomes. If adults with learning disabilities are to realize their full potential in the workplace, they need to master the complex skills of self-advocacy. Self-advocacy truly empowers the person with learning disabilities in job finding, at the point of job entry, and along the path of job advancement to the attainment of leadership roles. Thus the process of self-advocacy, when done effectively, allows the system to be responsive to the individual. It lets the individual with learning disabilities "put his or her best foot forward" without letting the disability get in the way of achievement.

Individuals with learning disabilities experience two very different cultures apropos to their learning disability. First is the culture of the school. Second is the culture of the world of work, whether in the public sector or in business and industry. During their school-age years, students with learning disabilities generally experience some degree of understanding and acceptance vis-à-vis their disability. The degree of understanding and acceptance is dependent on numerous factors. Schools have been involved with students with disabilities at least since the enactment of P.L. 94-142 in 1975. Special and general education teachers and other helping professionals have become "system advocates" through their efforts to ensure a free and appropriate education. They have been the architects of individual education programs and service delivery models to "normalize" the school experience for individuals with disabilities. In addition, parents have served as advocates either in an informal role or through their rights outlined in the processes and procedures of mandatory special education laws. All in all, numerous individuals intervene on behalf of children and youth with learning disabilities. Dane (1990) sums up this kind of advocacy by calling it the *protected experience* of childhood.

Protected experience takes on different forms and meanings. Some of its interventions are positive, some negative. In a positive sense advocacy has resulted in an evolution of change and educational reform. In effect, it has played the role of watchdog to ensure the maintenance of individual rights. On the negative side advocacy is usually undertaken by parents and other interested parties on behalf of students. This can result in maladaptive behavior such as increased dependence, learned helplessness, feelings of omnipotence, etc. Ultimately, young adults may self-advocate but take on the attitude of "You have to take care of me."

In direct contrast to this protected experience is the culture of the world of work. In employment environments individuals with learning disabilities must become self-advocates. No longer do they have system advocates to lay out their path or sort through the issues related to their disability. Moreover, they are in a social system that is generally barely knowledgeable about the issues of disability, yet compliance with the relatively new Americans with Disabilities Act (ADA) is mandated throughout the land. In addition, it is not uncommon for employers to believe that learning disabilities and mental disabilities are synonymous. Some employers are thrown by the invisibility of the learning disability and have a difficult time acknowledging its validity. Individuals with learning disabilities typically are told "You look normal and seem normal when you work. What do you mean you need special considerations?" In this type of interaction self-advocacy is of the utmost importance.

Gerber (1992b) studied the private sector workplace at the beginning of the ADA era from two perspectives: the employer and the employee with learning disabilities. His findings have implications for self-advocacy and individuals with learning disabilities. From the employer perspective Gerber found the following:

1. Companies are interested in the concept of diversity in the workplace, which includes employees with learning disabilities.

2. Business and industry are committed to the maximum productivity of all of their employees and are willing to modify their training procedures for their employees with learning disabilities.

3. The mission of companies is productivity stemming from effectiveness and efficiency. They wish to be good corporate citizens but are mindful that they are not running a social service agency.

4. Businesses are planning for full compliance with the ADA through an assortment of activities. At the same time, they are naturally concerned and worried about their ability to comply with the sweeping scope of the act's provisions. Consequently, they are seeking to develop processes and procedures to protect themselves as well.

From the perspective of the employee with learning disabilities, Gerber found the following:

1. Individuals with learning disabilities compete with a nondisabled labor pool. The ADA "levels the playing field" but is not an affirmative action program.

2. Job-getting skills are very important and issues such as self-disclosure in the context of the ADA must be thought through.

3. The term *learning disabilities* has a variety of meanings to the lay public and a great deal of misinformation abounds.

4. Managers and supervisors are not very knowledgeable about all of the implications of learning disabilities and individuals with learning disabilities need to be their own self-advocates.

A specific context is necessary to appreciate and understand these findings. First, under the ADA individuals with learning disabilities must be "qualified" by having the "essential functions" needed to do their job. Only after these two principles have been established does the concept of "reasonable accommodation" become operational. Second, even though the ADA prohibits discrimination, self-disclosure of learning disabilities is a sensitive issue. In essence, does the individual want to be known as having a learning disability? Could disclosure have negative repercussions, civil rights not withstanding? Third, Reiff and deFur (1992) have identified a number of pervasive "myths" about learning disabilities. These "myths" may help us understand the reticence of many adults with learning disabilities to "go public":

1. Learning disabilities are only a school-based problem.

2. Students with learning disabilities graduate at the same rate as students without disabilities.

3. Comprehensive transition services are not necessary for adolescents and young adults with learning disabilities.

4. Adults with learning disabilities do not have difficulties seeking or maintaining employment.

The Need for Self-Advocacy Skills

In the current vernacular, self-advocacy translates into consumer empowerment. This empowerment allows an individual with learning disabilities to gain control of his or her own destiny and pull it out of the grasp of external (human service) agencies. The philosophy of empowerment has fundamentally shifted the focus of disability policy in this country and is the underpinning of the ADA. West, Mast, Cosel, and Cosel (1992) have observed that "the desired outcomes of this transfer of power to consumers are increased independence, greater motivation to participate and succeed, and more dignity for the consumer" (p. 378). However, self-advocacy, although acknowledged as an important skill, particularly for adult adjustment, oftentimes is given only "lip service" in the latter years of schooling and in planning for the transition process. Sometimes it simply is not viewed as an "exit skill" or "lifelong skill" much to the detriment of young adults with learning disabilities.

Although the focus of this discussion is employment, we need to remember that self-advocacy supersedes it in importance. The process of self-advocacy extends to all facets of one's life. Employment is one of those important facets, but it is linked with other quality of life issues such as independent living, community adjustment, and postsecondary education and training.

Reasonable Accommodation and the Model of Success

The model for employment success is closely tied to the principle of reasonable accommodation, which is a basic right under the ADA. Reasonable accommodation is part of Title 1 of the act. It is defined as "a modification or adjustment in a job role, the work environment, or the way things usually are done that enables a qualified individual with a disability to enjoy an equal employment opportunity" (U.S. Equal Opportunity Commission [USEOC], 1992, p. III-2). The ADA mandates reasonable accommodations in three aspects of employment:

1. To ensure equal opportunity in the application process;

2. To enable a qualified individual with a disability to perform the essential functions of a job; and

3. To enable an employee with a disability to enjoy equal benefits and privileges of employment (USEOC, 1992, p. III-2).

Item 1 necessitates the need for self-advocacy as it applies to self-disclosure of having a learning disability whether at job entry or after being on the job. (*Note:* Self-disclosure of a learning disability is the prerogative of a person who is learning disabled. If one is to obtain rights mandated by the ADA, self-disclosure is necessary.) Key to success in the workplace is item 2, job modification or adjustment, because it addresses the conditions that a person with learning disabilities depends on to do his or her job. It is here that the theme of external manifestations or adaptability from the model comes into play. Adaptability refers to adapting to the work environment or adapting the work environment to a person with learning disabilities—in essence, reasonable accommodation. Item 3 necessitates the ongoing process of self-advocacy in order to ensure that each element of the employment process and related employment practices is fair and equitable for individuals with learning disabilities.

Elements of the Model and Reasonable Accommodation

A number of elements from the model of success have a direct bearing on self-advocacy: reframing, from internal decisions; and goodness of fit and learned creativity, from the external manifestations (adaptability) theme. When they are combined with a broader set of knowledge and skills needed for self-advocacy such as understanding of rights, communication strategies, and knowledge of the service delivery system (the employment system) (West et al., 1992), they become very empowering to individuals with learning disabilities.

The process of reframing, often thought of as the "trigger mechanism" of the model, allows individuals with learning disabilities to understand from their experience what a learning disability is and is not. Moreover, they are more apt to maintain a personal inventory of strengths and weaknesses and a good general understanding of how these strengths and weaknesses affect their ability to function in various environments. This introspective quality provides the foundation for adaptability. A successful reframing process may lead to an acceptance of one's own learning disability that can transfer to the acceptance of an employer, supervisor, or work colleague.

Reframing leads directly to the concepts of goodness of fit and learned creativity. The self-knowledge from reframing drives the best fit when it comes to employment. That fit aligns the capabilities of the individual with learning disabilities and the requirements of the job. The element of learned creativity provides the wherewithal for negotiated reasonable accommodations. Jobs that fit just right are infrequent. Inevitably, the issue of reasonable accommodation will emerge. When it does arise, a creative problem-solving opportunity exists, which leads to the notion of how to tailor the work situation to the individual with learning disabilities.

We have found that creativity to provide the best fit was one of the important factors in not only succeeding in a specific job, but it was also key to the process of job advancement. Many times the onus was put on the individuals with learning disabilities to explain the problem that called for reasonable accommodation. Oftentimes, they were left to solve the problem by themselves.

However, in a few cases, employers collaborated on finding a workable solution. Usually this collaboration occurred in higher education settings with such reasonable accommodations as computers and graduate assistance and in business through the use of personal secretaries and executive assistants.

Self-Advocacy Via the Model of Success

As previously mentioned, the model of success can be used in part as a tool for self-advocacy. The process of self-advocacy must be intermixed with the model in order for individuals with learning disabilities to realize their true potential in the workplace. Persons with learning disabilities will maximize their opportunities by having a full understanding of their rights under the ADA. The ADA protects persons with learning disabilities in all aspects of the employment process including application, testing, hiring, assignments, performance assessment, disciplinary actions, training, promotion, medical examinations, layoff/recall, termination, compensation, leave, and benefits. In addition, adults with learning disabilities should have a full understanding of the chief legal concepts of the employment section of the ADA including being "qualified," being able to perform "essential functions," and when it is necessary to request "reasonable accommodations." In addition, all individuals with learning disabilities must expect and be able to have the self-knowledge to answer the following questions when they explain their disability and/or express their needs to employers (Gerber, Reiff & Ginsberg, 1996):

1. What exactly is your disability?

2. What does learning disability or dyslexia mean?

3. What kinds of modifications do you need in your work environment?

4. What reasonable accommodations do you need? Why/how do you see them as reasonable?

5. How can you best be efficient?

6. Will your learning disability interfere with your productivity?

7. If we need to train you how do you learn best?

8. Can you work well on a team?

9. Can you be given a lead role in a work group?

10. Why should I hire you when I can hire another person who is not disabled? Aren't I taking a risk?

Most important, the ADA does not require an employer to approach a person to ask whether he or she has a disability or needs a reasonable accommodation. Two publications from the USEOC, one from the employee perspective (1991) and one from the employer perspective (1992), place the responsibility on individuals with disabilities to initiate remedial measures on their own behalf under the ADA. The precepts of self-advocacy are consistent with that posture. Empowerment and self-advocacy carry responsibility and accountability. Persons with learning disabilities will not be truly empowered if they have to depend on others to advocate for them.

Participants in Our Study and Self-Advocacy

The participants in our study could not have reached their levels of success without having an instinctive or intuitive knack for self-advocacy. Yet the interviews gave no indication that any of our participants had received formal self-advocacy training. Through trial and error they were able to advocate for themselves in a way that improved their employment situation. Naturally, the more successful they became the easier it was to advocate for themselves.

In most instances the process of self-advocacy was not highly distinguishable in interactions with employers. Self-advocacy often was incremental in nature and often quite subtle in intent—a comment here and a suggestion there. Sometimes it was confluent with a better way to accomplish something or a more efficient way to perform a task. Above all, the participants in our study were successful in self-advocacy because they had either developed credibility or put forth a positive attitude or both. They had developed social ecologies where trying new ideas was possible. In that atmosphere many, if not all, things were credible. They used the elements of the external manifestations (adaptability) part of our model to their fullest advantage and were often rewarded for their efforts.

Because of the design of this study, all individuals had reached their high levels of success prior to the ADA era. (The data were collected in the project years 1988 to 1990.) However, some of the participants we studied probably profited from the provisions of Sections 502, 503, and 504 of the Rehabilitation Act of 1973 that affected public sector employment as well as organizations and agencies that received federal contracts and grants. But the protections that are now common practice and taken for granted to some extent were generally nonexistent in the workplace then. This fact alone magnifies the accomplishments of the participants of our study. It also provides a scenario of optimism for those individuals who are looking for work, working, or aspiring to advance to higher job levels.

Thoughts and Advice from Adults with Learning Disabilities

W hen we decided to use a qualitative approach to investigating successful adults with learning disabilities, we hoped that the rich, ethnographic nature of our information would yield a wide array of descriptive data. We wanted not only to study the process by which these adults had become successful, we also wanted to get to know these individuals as people. Success is undoubtedly related to personological variables. Thus, the more we could learn about these adults as people, the more insightful we could be about their path to success. We also wanted to gain a larger perspective, to see the world of successful adults with learning disabilities through their eyes.

We approached our participants with the recognition that they are the real experts on the subject of learning disabilities. They could provide us with invaluable information to help us understand our primary questions. Throughout this book we have presented our analysis of the data we chose to collect. It seems equally fitting and altogether proper that this book should not be devoted only to our assumptions and agendas; the firsthand experts should have the right to express their perceptions, unadulterated by someone else's interpretations.

In this spirit we concluded each interview by soliciting these extraordinary persons for their advice and suggestions on parenting, teaching, employment and employability, and finally to other persons with learning disabilities. These successful adults with learning disabilities, who graciously shared their time, reflections, and often private thoughts and feelings, speak for themselves in this chapter. Each viewpoint is the product of unique circumstances. In some cases, the advice and suggestions may be too idiosyncratic to have immediate meaning. But in others, we may find wisdom and relevance to our own lives through the personal experience of another human being.

All of us can learn something from adults with learning disabilities. When we embrace them as colleagues in our search to understand why people learn and behave differently, we empower ourselves not only in our research but in our humanity. We are simply utilizing our best resource. We hope we are also forming a partnership.

Parenting

Do any of us share an identical view on parenting? Do we even parent each of our children in the same way? To some extent, any approach to parenting is defined by the dynamic interaction of the individual parent and individual child. Yet we are confident that there are commonalities of effective parenting. We usually begin with love, followed by a long list of characteristics such as warmth, security, consistency, discipline, support—to name but a few. Parenting a child with learning disabilities is not qualitatively different. Our participants do remind us that the mix of these characteristics may have to be carefully considered. We may have to be more consistent; we may have to be more understanding; we definitely will have to be "more" of something to be the best parent to a child with special needs.

Nonetheless, many of our participants focus primarily on perhaps the most elemental, essential, and universal aspects of parenting. All children, and maybe particularly those with learning disabilities, must know that they are loved and supported, that their parents believe in them and have faith in them:

Give children love. Try to find the child's strengths and interests, and don't pressure the child. Don't spread the child too thin. Stick to a couple of interests or activities.

Give unconditional love and acceptance.

Parents must continue to have faith in their kids. They should have unrestricted faith.

Support your kids. Give them every bit of confidence you can give them. They are different, and they need to know that's OK. Give them the proof that they are different, not just lip service. Also show them proof of their strong points. Give them the tools to deal with their weak areas because they're always going to be weak.

Stick with them and support them. Find their good, not their bad. . . . Never give up hope.

Support your kids. Give them every bit of confidence you can give them. They are different and they need to know that that's OK. . . . Let them do the things that they are good at without forcing skills that will never be mastered no matter how long you spend on them. If you stifle their creativity, then you've damaged them for life.

Value the child as they are and look at their strengths and always compliment, compliment, compliment.

Understand what your child has; then you can deal with it by supporting, by helping him or her find success, their niche. Get them remediation, some kind of help. Get them good role models so they can see how other people do it. A child can learn from another successful child. Help them organize their lives. There is no reason why they can't do the same thing every day. Use the carrot to get them to be more responsible.

Give as much to your child as you possibly can in terms of encouragement, rewards, understanding and passion, in educational opportunities, in knowledge of the world . . . to push but not drown . . . to not lecture to the point of dictating.

Are these ideas about parenting children with learning disabilities different from parenting any other children? The commonalities certainly outweigh the differences. Offering unconditional support, nurturing strengths, setting realistic expectations—these approaches are likely to appear in any textbook on parenting.

Yet parents of children with learning disabilities do confront issues that other parents may not have to face. Although most of us do use the home to supplement teaching from school, we usually do not find ourselves under the pressure of trying to help a child who is constantly behind, frustrated, and often defeated. Several of our participants clearly caution parents not to let their anxieties or well-intentioned support usurp their primary role as parents. Where one role ends and another begins may present a special challenge to parents of children with learning disabilities.

Don't crack down on what you think is a behavior disorder. Most of the non-adaptive and abrasive behaviors can be related to the learning disability and/or to emotional reactions. The stricter you are, the more they'll rebel. Remember to be a mother first. Don't try to be the teacher. That doesn't mean you can't teach something but don't do it in the same way the classroom teachers do it. Your child is going to be confused in role models. Make sure to anticipate what kinds of problems your learning disabled child may have problems with later on, like dating, driving, college. You should be ahead of your child.

Several of our participants also encourage these parents to access professional support. Undoubtedly, professional resources, ranging from family counseling to individual tutoring, have been a saving grace to many families. Yet the decision to seek professional help is not an easy one for many parents. The cost, the stigma, the lack of guaranteed results, the loss of autonomy or control can create real dilemmas in certain circumstances.

Get professional help as much as you can afford. Use all the positive reinforcement you can give these kids. You shouldn't try to teach but get the kids involved in things other than academics. Always insist that they be involved in sports or some other hobby that is more suited to them so they can get satisfaction at something. Praise them in the academic things that they do well and don't be too hard on them for things that they are having difficulty with. Still expect a lot in spite of all that. Give them the motivation you can and help them with self-discipline.

No matter what the costs, send them to the best possible professional help, whether that is a school, a tutor, or whatever. If it is not where you live, move, quit your job and go where it is. Because, if you don't do something for that child to give him a chance, his life may be ruined.

Trust your kid. Stay with him. Stay with your own gut. Some of those behaviors are caused by that outside. You can tell it by when he started school and what happened to him from the time he started school out there from the time he was at home. What you see is what you've got to trust. Don't give up. Seek professional help and don't be intimidated by the institutions. Learn as much as you possibly can.

Finally, one participant from our study seems to pull together the multiple roles that parents of children with learning disabilities may be asked to play. This parent emphasizes the importance of introspection, of evaluating and understanding ourselves before we minister to our children:

Go to your child's classroom. Watch your child with his peers. Watch how he's being asked to learn. Look into your child's eyes. Do you see fear? Do you see excitement? Do you see recognition of what they're getting and what's happening? Observe what your child is going through in his world. Sit with your child and go through problems from the beginning of their education and go through tasks. It's part of being intimate with your child. It's not something separate. How your child learns is part of your love. Watch out for your own impatience. Relate what's going on. We've all experienced some pain. Help your child learn. Use your own tricks and learn some more. The most important thing is building your child's soul.

In one way or another, all the preceding suggestions revolve around a fundamental theme of offering unconditional support. Interestingly, support is one of the main external manifestations (i.e., favorable social ecologies) we discuss in the model developed in Chapter 7. Although support may include getting professional help or choosing the right school, almost all of these adults stress the need to listen, nurture, and help build the self-confidence of the child. The adults in our study remind us of a fundamental, if somewhat uncomfortable, reality: Parenting any child requires dedication, commitment, sacrifice, and perseverance; parenting a child with learning disabilities requires even more.

Teaching

In Chapter 10, we proposed approaches to teaching based on what we consider to be a highly empirical source of information, the means by which these individuals with learning disabilities achieved success. Nevertheless, our suggestions rested on our interpretations of what might prepare students with learning disabilities to succeed. In this section, we move one step closer to the source: the thoughts and advice of our participants. As we discussed in Chapter 3, their schooling particularly shaped their attitudes about how best to teach students with learning disabilities. In many cases, they reacted to the negative and unhappy experiences of their education; their overriding concern as adults is to prevent students with learning disabilities from being treated in the same manner. Most have moved beyond reactivity and formulated philosophies that incorporate what worked for them as well as what did not. Still others have become educators themselves. They have integrated their personal experiences with professional training.

In the era that most of our participants attended school, understanding of learning disabilities was often limited, ignored, or erroneous. Consequently, many of these adults stress the importance of educating teachers about learning disabilities. Certainly, many current teachers, particularly in special education, have received in-depth training to teach students with learning disabilities. The majority of general education teachers have received some training, yet most feel that their exposure was cursory and inadequate to prepare them for effectively educating students with such diverse learning needs (Evans & Reiff, 1989). The current push for inclusive education virtually guarantees that many students with learning disabilities will encounter teachers who do not have a broad background in this area. Consequently, the voices crying out against ignorance and neglect in the past take on special significance for the future.

> For God's sake, if you are a regular teacher, learn a little something about LD and be sensitive to the fact that you may have a student with LD.

> Train the teachers in elementary schools. They have all these programs now where LD kids can go to college. So what! Look at all these first and second graders. There is nobody at that level with the ability or the authority to pick out a learning disabled child.

> Get a better system of training for teachers to work with handicapped students.

> Teachers need to be taught special education as well as education. When they get their teacher's credentials they should take a special ed. class.

It is the teachers' responsibility to identify the problem. They have to educate themselves so that they know the problems.

In the contemporary public school system, teachers face an increasingly heterogeneous, pluralistic, and multicultural population of students with and without learning disabilities. Current teacher training attempts to expose teachers to this diversity of needs and stresses the importance of building a vast repertoire of strategies and approaches. It is clear, however, that no one teacher will be endowed with a solution for every problem. As with most facets of an increasingly complex society, it is not the teacher who knows it all who has the best chance to succeed, but the teacher who knows where to look for help. Thus, teacher training programs typically stress the importance of using human, material, and technological resources. In many ways, the experiences of our participants led them to anticipate this need. They do not necessarily blame their teachers for not knowing the best way to teach a student with learning disabilities, but they do expect that a good teacher will have enough integrity to ask for help when it is needed.

Please don't let your need to be in control [and] know everything stand in the way of helping a child. When it goes beyond what you know you can be helpful with, call for help. Inspire others to help this person. Make the system responsive to the child.

Learn as much as you can about the problems you face in the classroom, not just LD, but slow learners and others who are going to show up in your classes. Take extra courses, but also rely on the consultants around the school for methodology.

Be educated in what to look for. Find out where the help is. Be willing to stick out your neck and get the child the help he or she needs.

In special education we speak of the importance of formative assessment. Teachers need to learn as much as they can about individual students in order to develop approaches that best respond to their unique learning styles. Yet much of assessment has traditionally focused on the weaknesses and limitations of students with learning disabilities. Our participants do not dismiss the utility of discovering what a student cannot do, but they do emphasize the necessity of uncovering the strengths and abilities that enable all individuals to learn and succeed.

We need to find out not only how someone learns best but also what ways are most meaningful to them. . . . We need to help them grow in a direction that they can succeed and their interests will take them. . . . [We need to] find ways to support their education. . . . Education in this country is built upon somebody's definition of what everyone should learn. This is ridiculous. It does not work. We are all capable of learning and communicating. People can master within the limits of their IQ and perception, but all can master something. All can articulate and share. . . . The most important human quality is communication. . . . We communicate in different ways. Mine is not better or worse, but I resent the fact that I constantly have to prove myself and say that my way is OK, especially like spelling.

A very important aspect of teaching is learning from your pupils. As teachers we always have to be one step ahead of our pupils, but we have to learn from them, what they are interested in learning, [and] create a need for learning. You can't just give it to the students and say do it. Sometimes you have to teach them how to learn. . . . It may be the most important aspect of teaching. Don't have them spew back a few facts, but teach them how to deal with those facts . . . how to learn!

Pay attention to kids on the periphery, those with no place to go. Teachers need to stress strengths and find qualities that are special.

As we might expect, a number of comments centered on the importance of developing special, individualized techniques. Several of our participants recognized that innovative teaching may require initiative and a willingness to buck the system. "Be more assertive to modify the curriculum to provide more adequate instruction. Take risks and be willing to stand up to the administration. Try to crawl into the mind of the LD child," asserted one participant. Another offered a fairly specific approach, reminiscent of our discussion on goal orientation in Chapter 10: "Break instruction into small steps. Provide practice so that students become confident and the skills are eventually automized."

Most of our participants were not quite so prescriptive. Instead, they offer the essential precept of accommodating, adapting, and modifying curriculum and instruction to respond to individual needs. They stress the same characteristics that we reiterate in teacher training—the need to be flexible and creative. And such an approach is unlikely to evolve unless teachers trust their own intuition.

Be willing to change. Be flexible so the child can succeed.

Be creative, not so rigid. Teach creatively.

Try whatever works! Be creative.

Fly by the seat of your pants and do what you think is best.

Many of our participants remember the frustrations of being the square pegs in the round holes of the educational system. They were more wrong than right, yet few teachers were willing to analyze why they were having such problems and what the implications of those problems could be. Their self-esteem deteriorated; they withdrew, or they acted out, or they developed some sort of compensatory persona. Their advice to teachers focuses on recognizing, understanding, and responding to the affective and emotional needs of students with learning disabilities.

> [Teachers] need to realize how frustrated LD kids will get. Tell them they can do it, but it takes longer. Students need to be patted on the back.

> Listen to the kids. I'm amazed how few people truly listen to those kids. Errors are not just errors. Errors are predictable and related. When a student who is learning disabled makes an error, explore where he comes from. Listen to what this student has to contend with. Listen to me as a child who fell down the stairs because I cannot judge visually what the stair will look like. Explore with them why they fall, why they push, why they shove, why they lose their cool, because there's a reason. It's not random. Remember how important it is to provide emotional and behavioral support.

> I would like to have the teachers understand how a kid feels when he's not learning something. I think if that was understood, teachers would be a lot more understanding.

> Teachers need to teach not just basic skills but techniques to help the thinking process. Students need to get meaningful ideas, not just facts. An excitement about learning has to be developed. This will make the struggle less difficult.

> Be strong and patient. Keep the child on task. Realize it's going to take longer. Stay with the child. Don't give up; the child can make it. Just take a deep breath every now and then.

Many teachers treated our participants harshly, unfairly, even brutally. However, other participants were concerned that some of their teachers had been willing to allow learning disabilities to be an excuse for failure. We hear the term *learned helplessness* to describe students who have been taught to blame their learning disabilities for their shortcomings. Often, teachers lighten up on these students with the best of intentions. They want to protect them from frustration, they do not want them to feel bad about themselves, and so they try to protect them by making life a little easier. A number of the adults in our study were deeply concerned about teachers who are afraid to push students with learning disabilities to perform to their potential. They encourage teachers to have standards yet to be creative enough to see and nurture the inherent strengths that all students possess.

> Take care to find the line in each child between the disability and a simple "I don't have to do it if I don't want to" attitude. Push to the line, go one step over it, and then back off. Give the child back responsibility for himself.

Organize the world for each child in a loving, caring environment but teach him responsibility for his own actions.

Have your standards, your own system. Be aware of feelings. Be aware of long-term goals. Be aware of the big picture, not always so concerned with individual details. . . . Be creative and fair to the individual LD person, other students and yourself. Encourage different learning styles. Develop ways to measure this.

Employment and Employability

The impetus of this study stemmed from investigating how adults with learning disabilities achieved success in their employment. We discussed in Chapter 6 that success may be defined in many different ways. Because we focused on vocational achievement as the centerpiece of our examination, we asked our participants to offer advice to employers and employees. They themselves are employers and employees who have risen to the top. To paraphrase stockbroker E. F. Hutton's popular television commercial, when these adults speak, we'd better listen! They have hurdled obstacles that most of us cannot imagine; every day they face challenges that are mind-boggling. And, as we have seen, they have not only persevered, they have triumphed.

There are no absolute how to's in the workplace. There are, however, some helpful guidelines for do's and don'ts. The adults in our study obviously figured out their respective systems and parlayed that understanding into productive behavior. Along the way, they also realized and acted on the effect that their learning disabilities had on their careers. They became experts about learning disabilities and the world of work.

It is important to view suggestions in this area from two perspectives: employers and employees. The former view is quite unique for it is almost totally missing in the literature (c.f., Gerber, 1992b). We are able to bring this view to the reader because many of our participants have built businesses and continue to hire workers, rely on staff, and keep their eyes on the bottom line. The employee perspective is more traditional. What is unique, however, is that all the employees giving advice are individuals with learning disabilities who learned the lessons of employment one step at a time—from job entry to job advancement to the attainment of leadership positions in their respective work organizations.

The advice of our participants to employers shows a theme of hiring individuals with learning disabilities for jobs that fit their capabilities. This advice is consistent with the goodness of fit aspect identified in our model:

Find a place where LD people can fit. If a person is willing to put forth the effort, he deserves a chance to try in different areas.

Interview to see if you can match the situation to the talent. Place them in a job where you can optimize their strengths.

Keep them away from what they cannot do. You can hire an acute dyslexic, but not for a job requiring reading.

Match skills with the job. Don't set up that person for what he cannot do.

The employer should see the strengths during the interview process and should put the person with LD into a job that emphasizes their strengths. Push people's talents.

Realize that LDs have tremendous capabilities in many different areas. Be flexible in the types of job assignments.

Other advice to employers implores them to look beyond the label "learning disabilities" and see the positive attributes common to adults with learning disabilities in employment settings. Some of these adults with learning disabilities stressed learned creativity:

In general, they make very innovative, very hard-working people. Most of the studies I have read show them to be better employees. They are more intuitive or able to get around problems better—something that makes up for their deficits. So I say it's worth taking a chance on them.

I believe you would have a very creative, innovative group of people if you employ adults with learning disabilities. They would bring more insight and a new way of doing things to your business. It might show you some creative and innovative ways to enhance your business.

Other participants focused more on desire, drive, persistence, and determination:

They have been to the bottom and have the drive to do well.

The employer should realize that learning disabled people will be better employees than most people as long as employers understand what they can do. They tend to be more conscientious. They are on time and dependable. You just have to be careful not to put them in a job they cannot do. It may take longer for them to adjust to a task at hand, but once they do, they'll do a great job for you.

If I were in a skills field, such as machinery or mechanics or something of that nature, I'd hire any dyslexic I could find because they are so determined to do it right and prove to themselves they can do it. They could do a dynamite job for you if they made it that far.

The issue of compensating for a learning disability also emerges as a theme in advice to employers. Our participants are quick to point out that success in the workplace will be quite difficult without an employer who is open to compensatory strategies for successful performance. Although our data were collected before the implementation of the Americans with Disabilities Act, which mandates "reasonable accommodation," the advice from our participants foreshadowed this federal initiative for opening the workplace to persons with disabilities:

> Eventually LD people get to a point where their disability is overtaxed. Provide them with support or provide opportunities to use their talents to a maximum.

> Reach out and help them realize what their contributions can be. Help them discover how their personal style and skills can contribute to the organization.

> If disability is unrelated to the task but may come up, be clear about whether assistance will be available or if it doesn't matter.

> Have inservices and brochures . . . help educate them.

> Realize they may need some special guidelines like extra time spans to work at their own pace.

> Provide for reasonable accommodations.

Several participants specifically encourage employers to recognize and be aware of the implications of learning disabilities in the workplace, a logical prerequisite for providing support mechanisms. A responsive employer will need to understand the paradoxical manifestations that learning disabilities may present:

> You have to give LD people equal treatment. But that may also require extra patience sometimes.

> You have to be understanding. Competition can be hard. You have to understand that an LD person can look brutally stupid but actually be quite brilliant. He can look stupid at one point then carry the day on an important issue.

> Learn their strengths and forgive their weaknesses.

The straightforward recommendations of one participant, an extremely successful entrepreneur, capture the pervasive spirit of all of these suggestions (and perhaps the spirit of the ADA) in one succinct statement:

> You're not paying them to be learning disabled. If they are competent to do the job then they are competent. You should let them do it. And if it doesn't work, fire them. It's simple. And if they need special help you should give it

to them . . . whatever they need to be successful on the job. That's the best thing to tell employers—not to be frightened of learning disabled people, because they are not stupid. They just do things differently than other people. The job gets done.

Advice to employees with learning disabilities shows several important trends as well. Not surprisingly, our participants share an almost fanatical belief that success comes as a result of hard work, a prominent feature of the model of success. Simply put, nothing can replace a concerted and unrelenting effort to get the job done:

Start early in the morning and stay up late at night to get the job done. Set up checks and balances for yourself.

Take work home and stay after work. Work harder and do better and you will stay in business. Life is not fair so be thankful for the positive things you have.

Work harder than the average person and figure out what parts of the job you can do better than others and focus in on them. There are no shortcuts.

Work hard and try not to get (in) over your head because repeated failures make you anxious. . . . Start off slowly, and as you get confidence, you can tackle more difficult things.

There is no way around the fact that to be equally successful, you're going to have to work harder.

Whatever you do, just go for it! Don't worry about people who try to tell you that you can't do it. In order to get where you want to go sometimes you can't make it on the route you want to take. It's the same with anybody. So you have to accept the fact that you might have to start all over again. If you really want to do it that much, you are going to do it.

Take the hard work to be your friend. You will be able to think, to function, to succeed at a level a normal person could never reach for. When you are faced with adversaries, forgive them, for they know not what they do. Accept them and move forward. Don't give up!

These last two comments integrate the theme of reframing. These participants exhort persons with learning disabilities to go beyond the notion of simply accepting that hard work is necessary. They believe that success comes from internalizing a ferocious work ethic, living it, breathing it, becoming one with it. And herein lies the special gift that some persons are able to find within their learning disabilities.

Another cluster of comments focuses on the issue of finding a good fit between one's strengths and weaknesses and the type of career or work environment:

Realize your limitations. Know what you can do and you can't do. Interview for the job you can do. Accentuate your abilities and not your disabilities.

Don't go into a work situation in which you will have to perform in your area of disability. Your employer will think you are stupid, and you'll feel stupid. . . . Emphasize strengths and be dedicated.

Find out what kind of work you are suited for.

You can't worry about problems. Don't ignore them, but find something you like doing. If you work hard at it, you will succeed.

You have to find out exactly what your weak points are. Work to improve them completely. Be realistic. Don't choose a profession that stresses your weaknesses. You'll make yourself miserable. . . . Be honest with yourself.

In the model of success, we spoke of the importance of favorable social ecologies, of proactively developing and building interpersonal support systems. A willingness not only to get help when needed but to assert one's strengths represents a potentially powerful form of self-advocacy in the ADA-era workplace. A number of our participants express a similar perspective in sharing their insights about dealing with coworkers:

The less defensive you are, the more help you can get. The more support systems you can use, the more easily you will develop.

Make your fellow employees aware that there are certain areas that you are weak in, and you have other areas that you are dynamite in. Don't forget to tell them that it may take longer for you to catch on, but once you do, you'll have a great coworker.

Persons with Learning Disabilities

We ended each interview by asking the participants to give general advice to others with learning disabilities. As we have seen, our participants are a diverse lot; not unexpectedly, their responses are quite varied. Much of this advice is motivational in nature, some is introspective, and some is philosophical. None is cynical or pessimistic in tone.

Our participants are individuals who took control of their lives. Therefore, we would expect some of them to address the notion of self-destiny, often incorporating Shakespeare's credo, "To thine own self, be true." For persons with learning disabilities, such autonomy is inexorably connected to understanding one's disability and all its ramifications.

You need to find out who you are and you are not going to be in order to succeed. You need to look in the mirror and say, "OK, I can live with you, good and bad, I can live with you," maybe then you're on the road to success. You can't get other people to respect you or love you when you can't do the same to yourself.

Be yourself. Don't be false. Build on your strengths and push your weaknesses aside.

Look within . . . look for answers within yourself to solve problems.

Be all that you can be. Like yourself. Desire to be happy. The price one pays is worth the reward. And stand up and say, "I failed." So what! Don't worry about what everyone else thinks. It's so hard to climb out of it. You still have to. Because of those experiences, what a great asset you can be to others that hurt. If you can use dyslexia or LD to your advantage, use it. You can't blame anyone else for how you feel.

We control our disability. We don't have a wall. We can go as far as we want to or we can stop.

I'm the bumblebee they said wouldn't fly. I was successful because no one told me I wasn't.

Another participant shared his way of reframing his learning disabilities. In learning to deal with and overcome his disability, he gained a perspective that placed other life challenges on a smaller scale.

My son has some of the same problems and what I told him was that "this is not a curse. This is God's greatest gift to you, and I will tell you why. You are not going to think it is at times, because you are going to have to struggle just to stay alive, just to survive in this world. But once you have been able to accomplish that, then when things get rough, it is like everything you have to do." . . . So I think the one thing, if nothing else, the learning disabilities did for me is that it taught me how to work, it taught me not to get discouraged, and even though I read much slower than everyone else and things like this, I kept plugging away and I would eventually finish it. That it wasn't so important how fast I did it as long as I did it.

Reframing allows the individual to reinterpret the learning disabilities experience from something dysfunctional to something functional. The internal decision making is the catalyst for this metamorphosis, but learned creativity is the machine that produces results. A number of participants stress the importance of using self-knowledge to develop compensatory mechanisms and strategies.

Be a military strategist. Find out exactly where your weak points are and work to improve them or figure out ways around them.

Be flexible; learn. . . . Don't keep yourself on a track leading to disaster.

Recognize what your limitations are, strengths and weaknesses. Then *deal* with them.

Identify strengths and weaknesses at an early age so accommodations can be made.

Although the processes of self-acceptance and self-understanding are integral components of learning to move ahead, the willingness to seek and accept support when necessary, a major component of a favorable social ecology, also plays a pivotal role. Thus, a number of participants encourage others with learning disabilities to utilize support mechanisms and cultivate resources:

Get yourself to a specialist to help you figure out what is going on and to develop compensatory mechanisms.

Get a thorough evaluation to understand the disability.

Ask for help. Don't be afraid to admit that there are things you don't know. Use resources around you to try to be more aware of your strengths and weaknesses.

As we stated at the outset, this book celebrates the triumph of adults with learning disabilities despite overwhelming odds. We hope that these stories of success inspire other people who have learning disabilities. One of our participants seemed to anticipate the spirit of this effort, a fitting conclusion to these pieces of advice:

It is very important to show the child, as well as the parents, the success stories. I think there are a lot of people that have disabilities. I heard that Nelson Rockefeller couldn't read. We started talking about different people—someone said Winston Churchill had problems. I've heard that Einstein had problems too. I know in terms of a learning problem, maybe not learning disabilities, but Thomas Edison had difficulties. Gee whiz, that's a nice group of people to be with. And I think maybe it's high time that we give these families and we give these kids some solid role models to say, "Hey, you know, look at these people. They have it worse than you do and they went on to achieve."

These parting thoughts do not lend themselves to simple or discrete categories. They are often the most personal and intimate of all the responses in the interviews and consequently are largely individualistic, even idiosyncratic reflections. Yet a core commonality emerges. These adults with learning disabilities who have survived and, in many ways, overcome the trials and tribulations of their disabilities, have good, solid, uplifting advice to share with others. Undoubtedly, their positive frame of mind and their success are related. The more success they have experienced, the more positively they have been able to reframe their learning disabilities. Yet it is also obvious that a positive frame of mind, a core belief in one's self, lies at the root of much of their success. Or perhaps it would be more accurate to suggest that the two are so tightly inter-woven as to be inseparable. In this sense, the wisdom these adults have gained from living with a disability transcends advice specifically to others with learn-ing disabilities; their sagacious reflections speak volumes about simply making the most of life. That's advice we can all use!

> The day that we open the door to people with differences is the day that we all grow. LD is just a normal variation of learning. We need to respect the diversity of life. LD is a normal, healthy, wonderful variation of how people go about learning and communicating.

Epilogue

When we began our investigation of successful adults with learning disabilities, we had several clear goals. We expected we would add to the general knowledge base of employment outcomes of individuals with learning disabilities. We wanted to uncover, identify, and delineate the alterable variables related to the successful employment outcomes of our participants. We hoped to share perspectives evolving from a holistic, nonpathological research paradigm. We also knew that an open-ended, ethnographic research approach might take us in directions previously unimagined. After all, the possibilities of serendipitous discoveries represent a significant strength and compelling purpose of a qualitative design.

As this book comes to a close, it seems fitting to evaluate the extent to which we achieved our goals. Did our study of successful adults with learning disabilities enlarge the general knowledge base? Our research clearly has indicated that persons with learning disabilities can and do succeed in the workplace. Moreover, our investigation has led us to examine issues related to the employment and employability of individuals with learning disabilities in general, to tackle the complex question of what employment success means, to consider the instructional implications of successful outcomes, and to frame our findings within current social and political contexts. Thus, the stories of these 71 adults have contributed to our overall understanding of the impact of learning disabilities in adulthood, particularly in relation to employment.

There was a time in the field of learning disabilities when the issue of employment was found way down the "to do" priority list. So much needed attention—sorting out definitional issues, formulating appropriate assessment batteries, finding the undiagnosed children, and implementing a quality delivery system. The fruits of these efforts culminate in what happens to individuals with learning disabilities in adulthood. In a sense, employment becomes a significant marker of the effectiveness of those efforts, a mirror of who we are as a learning disability community, an insight into how we define our "inclusive" society. When people with learning disabilities do extraordinary things in the workplace, we are proud of them, and we are proud of ourselves. When individuals with learning disabilities do not succeed, then we must, at least in part, feel the pain and take the responsibility.

Beyond adding new knowledge, our ambition hinged on introducing a new theoretical perspective. We acknowledge that contemporary popular business literature is bursting with different ideas on how to become successful in the workplace. Nevertheless, most of these theories about the success process rely largely on opinion, conjecture, and informal observations. *Exceeding Expectations* stands apart because of its foundation in systematic research. Through a methodical analysis of the wealth of information from the interviews, we have uncovered common patterns among these adults and explained how they became successful. Discovering the key ingredients that drive success has taken us a step further in understanding factors of employment and the ultimate effects of education and training. And perhaps for the first time, a "model of success" is presented that has a true empirical basis.

Underpinning the entire model are the personal voices of the 71 participants. We submit that first-hand recollection of experience is often the most empirical and authoritative source of data. We have tried to blend scholarly discussions of contemporary issues with real-life observations. Consequently, the reader can use this context of actual events to evaluate theoretical issues about learning disabilities in adulthood.

The learning disability community is hungry for good news with a credible foundation. Through their numerous presentations and shorter publications, the authors have witnessed a passionate interest from adults with learning disabilities about the study. Moreover, many of these adults have related that the "model of success" accurately represented their experiences. The book has a clearly positive message: Not only is success possible for persons with learning disabilities, *they* have the power to enhance the likelihood of their success. The book's treatment of a large-scale study provides compelling evidence to support this message of self-empowerment.

We intended to develop this type of model. We could not foresee, however, all the vistas that would open up to us when we looked through the eyes of these adults with learning disabilities. We learned what it is like to grow up with learning disabilities from very personal, and often very moving, perspectives. We found that although the meaning of the term *learning disabilities* differed for many of the participants, unifying themes evolved in aggregate. We discovered that in addition to the predictable pathways to success depicted in our model, a less predictable set of circumstances or critical incidents played a vital role in the success process. We realized that simply listening to advice and suggestions from these individuals offered insights not only about the interactive or ecological nature of learning disabilities but about the nature of human relations in general.

As we learned something about how human beings relate to each other, we understood that we needed to broaden our concept of success. Success, like beauty, may be largely in the eye of the beholder. To some extent this axiom is true of the successful adults with learning disabilities in this book. Those who have reached high levels of employment success today are the highest profile people in the learning disability community. They are written about, they write about themselves, they speak at learning disabilities conferences, and they have become advocates for people of all ages who are learning disabled. In essence, they have replaced the names of Einstein, da Vinci, Edison, and Rockefeller as individuals who have made it in spite of the trials and tribulations of their disability. In their respective fields of endeavor and in their home communities, they have become exemplars and the source of inspiration to many.

We must be very careful in our judgment of success, however. Many persons with learning disabilities work just as hard to achieve without attaining the eminence of the successful adults in our study. These "other" individuals, a kind of "silent majority," quietly go about their business, making their own contributions in the workplace, community, and home. In this book, we have not heard their stories. Yet we rejoice in their "lesser triumphs."

In combination, all individuals with learning disabilities who succeed in the workplace have far reaching value to the entire culture of work. When they succeed they make it easier for the next person with learning disabilities to enter the workplace or advance in a business organization. When their remarkable stories are told, it inspires all those within their reach.

Perhaps our most meaningful serendipitous discovery was our sense of connectedness with our participants. We consciously chose not to reduce the human beings we interviewed to cases or data points. Instead of using a clinical artificiality to distance ourselves from our participants, the interview process gave us the opportunity to enter their lives. We could not help but admire the courage and the straightforward humanity it took to share intimacies. We began as strangers, but after the experience of profound self-revelation, we often ended as friends.

As we pored over the thousands of pages of transcripts of the interviews, as we searched to answer the questions we had constructed to drive the research project, we began to see beyond the learning disabilities. We saw the multidimensional textures of the lives of our participants. The words on the pages represented not merely an account of the impact of learning disabilities but living, breathing human beings. Did we lose our sense of scientific objectivity? We respond by asking "What is more objective or truthful than realizing that we are more alike than we are different?"

The core philosophy undergirding and driving our entire study makes this conclusion possible. In *Exceeding Expectations*, we have focused on success rather than failure, on what people can do rather than what they cannot, on abilities rather than deficits. We have highlighted the person with a disability rather than the disability. This perspective demands a human connection. In encouraging this connection, we invite the reader to make a difference in the lives of persons with learning disabilities. As we better understand the possibilities of success for individuals with learning disabilities, we may be able to contribute, at some level, to creating an environment responsive to the potential of these individuals. In this book, we have celebrated the successes of adults with learning disabilities who "made it." Now it is time, individually and collectively, to participate in facilitating the possibilities for success of adults with learning disabilities. They will not need to exceed expectations to become successful. We will expect them to succeed.

References

Aaron, P. G., Phillips, S., & Larsen, S. (1988). Specific reading disability in historically famous persons. *Journal of Learning Disabilities, 21*, 523–538.

Adelman, K. A., & Adelman, H. S. (1987). Rodin, Patton, Edison, Wilson, Einstein: Were they really learning disabled? *Journal of Learning Disabilities, 20*(5), 270–279.

Adelman, P. B., & Vogel, S. A. (1990). College graduates with learning disabilities—Employment attainment and career patterns. *Learning Disability Quarterly, 13*, 154–166.

Adults with learning disabilities. (1994, September/October). *LDA News Briefs*, 3–4.

Americans with Disabilities Act of 1990. 42 U.S.C. § 12101 *et seq.*

Anderson, R. (1995). *Getting ahead: Career skills that work for everyone.* New York: McGraw-Hill.

Armstrong, T. (1994). *Multiple intelligences in the classroom.* Alexandria, VA: ASCD Publications.

Atkinson, J. W., & Litwin, G. H. (1973). Achievement motive and test anxiety conceived as motive to approach success and motive to avoid failure. In D. C. McClelland & R. S. Steele (Eds.), *Human motivation: A book of readings* (pp. 145–163). Morristown, NJ: General Learning Press.

Baker, H. (1972). *Famous persons who have been handicapped: A critical analysis.* Paper presented at the Distinguished Lecture Series in Special Education and Rehabilitation, University of Southern California, Los Angeles, CA.

Bandler, R., & Grinder, J. (1982). *Reframing: Neuro-linguistic programming and the transformation of meaning.* Moab, UT: Real People Press.

Bandura, A. (1986). *Social foundations of thought and action.* Englewood Cliffs, NJ: Prentice Hall.

Baxter, N. (1986, Spring). New projections to 1995. *Occupational Outlook Quarterly, 30*(1), 31–34.

Bender, W. N., & Wall, M. E. (1994). Social-emotional development of students with learning disabilities. *Learning Disability Quarterly, 17*, 323–341.

Bennett, W. J. (1993). *The book of virtues.* New York: Simon & Schuster.

Betz, N., & Fitzgerald, L. (1987). *Career psychology of women.* San Diego, CA: Academic Press.

Blackhurst, A., Wright, W., & Ingram, C. (1974). *Competency specifications for directors of special education resource centers. Project SEARCH.* (Special Training Project OEG-0-72-4305 [603] Interim Report). Washington, DC: U.S. Office of Education, Bureau of the Education for the Handicapped.

Blalock, J. W. (1981). Persistent problems and concerns of young adults with learning disabilities. In W. M. Cruickshank and A. A. Silver (Eds.), *Bridges to tomorrow: The best of the ACLD, Vol. 2* (pp. 35–56). Syracuse, NY: Syracuse University Press.

Bloom, B. S. (1968). Learning for mastery. *Evaluation Comment, 1*(2). Los Angeles: University of California, Center for the Study of Evaluation of Instructional Programs.

Bloom, B. S. (1980). The new direction in educational research: Alterable patterns. *Phi Delta Kappan, 61,* 382–385.

Bloom, B. S. (1982). The role of gifts and markers in the development of talent. *Exceptional Children, 49,* 510–522.

Bloom, B. S., & Sosniak, L. A. (1981). Talent development vs. schooling. *Educational Leadership, 39,* 86–94.

Bolman, L. G., & Deal, T. E. (1991). *Reframing organizations: Artistic choice and leadership.* San Francsico, CA: Jossey-Bass.

Brand, S. (Ed.) (1984). *Whole earth software catalog.* Garden City, NJ: Quantum Press.

Brobeck, J. K. (1990). Teachers do make a difference. *Journal of Learning Disabilities, 23,* 11.

Bronfenbrenner, U. (1976). The experimental ecology of education. *Teacher's College Record, 78,* 157–178

Brown, D. S., Gerber, P. J., & Dowdy, C. (1990). *Pathways to employment for people with learning disabilities.* Washington, DC: President's Committee on the Employment of People with Disabilities.

Bruck, M. (1985). The adult functioning of children with specific learning disabilities: A follow-up study. In E. I. Siegel (Ed.), *Advances in applied developmental psychology* (Vol. 1, pp. 91–129). Norwood, NJ: Ablex Publishing Company.

Bruininks, V. (1978). Peer status and personality characteristics of learning disabled and non-disabled students. *Journal of Learning Disabilities, 11,* 484–489.

Bryan, T. (1989). Learning disabled adolescents' vulnerability to crime: Attitudes, anxieties, experiences. *Learning Disabilities Research, 5*(1), 51–60.

Burke, R. J. (1986). Occupational and life stress and the family: Occupational frameworks and research findings. *International Review of Applied Psychology, 35,* 347–369.

Caddes, C. (1986). *Portraits of success: Impressions of Silicon Valley pioneers.* Palo Alto, CA: Tioga Publishing Co.

Cammer, L. (1977). *Freedom from compulsion.* New York: Pocket Books.

Carlson, R. V. (1996). *Reframing and reform.* White Plains, NY: Longman Publishers.

Collignan, F. C. (1989). The role of reasonable accommodation in employing disabled persons in private industry. In M. Berkowitz & M. A. Hill (Eds.), *Disability and the labor market* (pp. 196–241). Ithaca, NY: ILR Press, New York State School of Industrial and Labor Relations.

Conderman, G. (1995). Social status of sixth and seventh-grade students with learning disabilities. *Learning Disability Quarterly, 18,* 13–24.

Covey, S. R. (1989). *The seven habits of highly effective people.* New York: Simon and Schuster.

Cruickshank, W. M. (1975). The psychoeducational match. In W. M. Cruickshank & D. P. Hallahan (Eds.), *Perceptual and learning disabilities in children: Vol. 1. Psychoeducational practices* (pp. 71–114). Syracuse, NY: Syracuse University Press.

Cruickshank, W., Morse, W., & Johns, J. (1980). *Learning disabilities: The struggle from adolescence toward adulthood.* Syracuse, NY: Syracuse University Press.

Dalke, C., & Schmitt, S. (1987). Meeting the transition needs of college-bound students with learning disabilities. *Journal of Learning Disabilities, 20,* 176–177.

D'Amico, R. (1991). The working world awaits: Employment experiences during and shortly after secondary school. In M. Wagner (Ed.), *Youth with disabilities: How are they doing? The first comprehensive report from the National Longitudinal Transition Study of Special Education Students.* Menlo Park, CA: SRI International.

Dane, E. (1990). *Painful passages: Working with children with learning disabilities.* Silver Spring, MD: NASW Press.

deBettencourt, L., Zigmond, N., & Thornton, H. (1989). Follow-up of post secondary-age rural learning disabled graduates and drop-outs. *Exceptional Children, 56*(1), 40–49.

Donawa, W. (1995). Growing up dyslexic: A parent's view. *Journal of Learning Disabilities, 28,* 324–328.

Dweck, C. S. (1986). Motivational processes affecting learning. *American Psychologist, 41,* 1040–1047.

Easton, J., & Ginsberg, R. (1985). Student learning process: How poorly prepared students succeed in college. *Research and Teaching in Development Education, 1,* 12–38.

Eby, J. W., & Smutny, J. F. (1989). *A thoughtful overview of gifted education.* New York: Longman.

Edgar, E., Levine, P., Levine, R., & Dubney, M. (1988). *Washington State follow-along studies 1983–1987: Students in transition* (final report). Unpublished manuscript.

Engelmann, S. E. (1977). Sequencing cognitive and academic tasks. In R. D. Kneedler & S. G. Tarver (Eds.), *Changing perspectives in special education.* Columbus, OH: Merrill.

Etzioni, A. (1969). *The semi-professions and their organization.* New York: The Free Press.

Evans, E. D., & Reiff, H. B., (1989). Undergraduate expectations and preferences toward working with students with handicaps. *The College Student Journal, 23,* 206–213.

Flanagan, J. C. (1954). The critical incident technique. *Psychological Bulletin, 51,* 327–358.

Flanagan, J. C. (1962). *Measuring human performance.* Pittsburgh, PA: American Institute for Research.

Fleming, J. (1967). The critical incident technique as an aid to inservice training. *American Journal of Mental Deficiency, 67,* 41–52.

Fournier, Y. (1992, August 4). Teacher's notes leave mom at loss. *The Carroll County Times,* p. C1.

Fourqurean, J. M. (1994). The use of follow-up studies for improving transition planning for young adults with learning disabilities. *Journal of Vocational Rehabilitation, 4*(2), 96–104.

Frederikson, N. (1984). Implications of cognitive theory for instruction in problem solving. *Review of Educational Research, 54,* 363–407.

Gardner, H. (1983). *Frames of mind.* New York: Basic Books.

Gardner, H., & Hatch, T. (1989). Multiple intelligences go to school. *Educational Researcher, 18,* 410.

Garfield, C. (1986). *Peak performers.* New York: Avon Books.

Gattiker, U., & Larwood, L. (1986). Subjective career success: A study of managers and support personnel. *Journal of Business and Psychology, 1,* 78–94.

Gay, L. R. (1981). *Educational research*. Columbus, OH: Merrill.

Gerber, P. J. (1992a). Being learning disabled and a beginning teacher and teaching a class of students with learning disabilities. *Exceptionality, 3*(4), 213–232.

Gerber, P. J. (1992b). Personal perspective—At first glance: Employment for people with learning disabilities at the beginning of the Americans with Disabilities Act era. *Learning Disability Quarterly, 15*, 4.

Gerber, P. J. (1993). Researching adults with learning disabilities from an adult development perspective. *Journal of Learning Disabilities, 27*(1), 6–9.

Gerber, P. J. (1994). TJ—Year two: Starting all over again. In D. Foucar-Szocki (Ed.), *Case studies for teacher training and educational leadership*. Harrisburg, VA: The Commonwealth Center for the Education of Teachers.

Gerber, P. J., Ginsberg, R., & Reiff, H. B. (1992). Identifying alterable patterns in employment success for highly successful adults with learning disabilities. *Journal of Learning Disabilities, 25*, 475–487.

Gerber, P. J., & Mellard, D. (1985). Rehabilitation of learning disabled adults: Recommended research priorities. *Journal of Rehabilitation, 51*(1), 62–64.

Gerber, P. J., & Reiff, H. B. (1991). *Speaking for themselves: Ethnographic interviews with adults with learning disabilities*. Ann Arbor, MI: University of Michigan Press.

Gerber, P. J., Reiff, H. B., & Ginsberg, R. (1994). Critical incidents in highly successful adults with learning disabilities. *Journal of Vocational Rehabilitation, 4*, 105–112.

Gerber, P. J., Reiff, H. B., & Ginsberg, R. (1996). Reframing the learning disabled experience. *Journal of Learning Disabilities, 29*(1), 98–101.

Gerber, P. J., Schneiders, C. A., Paradise, L. V., Reiff, H. B., Ginsberg, R., & Popp, P. A. (1990). Persisting problems of adults with learning disabilities: Self-reported comparisons from their school-age and adult years. *Journal of Learning Disabilities, 23*, 570–573.

Glesne, C., & Peshkin, A. (1992). *Becoming qualitative researchers*. White Plains, NY: Longman.

Goetz, J. P., & LeCompte, M. D. (1984). *Ethnography and qualitative design in educational research*. Orlando, FL: Academic Press.

Goldstein, A. P. (1988). *The Prepare Curriculum: Teaching prosocial competencies*. Champaign, IL: Research Press.

Goldstein, K. (1939). *The organism*. New York: American Book Co.

Gray, R. A. (1981). Services for the LD adult: A working paper. *Learning Disability Quarterly, 4*, 426–434.

Gregory, J. F., Shanahan, T., & Walberg, G. (1986). A profile of learning disabled twelfth-graders in regular classes. *Learning Disability Quarterly, 9*, 33–42.

Griessman, B. E. (1987). *The achievement factors: Candid interviews with some of the most successful people of our time*. New York: Dodd, Mead.

Guba, E. G. (1981). Criteria for assessing the trustworthiness of naturalistic inquiries. *Educational Communication and Technology Journal, 29*, 75–92.

Haager, D., & Vaughn, S. (1995). Parent, teacher, and self-reports of the social competence of students with learning disabilities. *Journal of Learning Disabilities, 28*, 205–215.

Halcomb, R. (1979). *Women making it: Patterns and profiles of success*. New York: Atheneum.

Halcrow, A. (1989). Sabbaticals in tandem with need. *Personnel Journal, 68*, 19–20.

Hallahan, D. P., & Kauffman, J. M. (1994). *Exceptional children: Introduction to special education* (6th ed.). Boston, MA: Allyn & Bacon.

Halpern, A. S. (1990). A methodological review of follow-up and follow-along studies tracking school teachers from special education. *Career Development for Exceptional Individuals, 13*(1), 13–27.

Hammill, D. D. (1990). On defining learning disabilities: An emerging consensus. *Journal of Learning Disabilities, 23*, 74–84.

Hammill, D., & Larson, S. (1978). The effectiveness of psycholinguistic training. *Exceptional Children, 44*, 403–414.

Hammill, D. D., Leigh, J. E., McNutt, G., & Larsen, S. C. (1981). A new definition of learning disabilities. *Learning Disability Quarterly, 4*, 336–342.

Haring, K. A., Lovett, D., & Smith, D. D. (1990). A follow-up study of recent special education graduates of learning disabilities programs. *Journal of Learning Disabilities, 23*(2), 108–113.

Harris, L. (1987). *Survey of employment and persons with disabilities.* Washington, DC: Louis Harris Associates.

Harvey, S. (1985). *The imposter phenomenon.* New York: St. Martin's Press.

Havighurst, R. (1972). *Developmental tasks and education* (3rd ed.). New York: D. McKay Co.

Helmreich, R., & Spence, J. (1978). The Work and Family Orientation Questionnaire: An objective instrument to assess components of achievement motivation and scientific attainment. *Personality and Social Psychology Bulletin, 4*, 222–226.

Hinshelwood, J. (1917). *Congenital word blindness.* London: H. K. Lewis.

Holland, J. L. (1985). *The self-directed search.* Odessa, FL: Psychological Assessment Resources.

Horner, M. (1972). Toward an understanding of achievement-related conflicts in women. *Journal of Social Issues, 28*, 157–176.

Huntington, D. D., & Bender, W. N. (1993). Adolescents with learning disabilities at risk? Emotional well-being, depression, suicide. *Journal of Learning Disabilities, 26*, 159–166.

Ingram, C. (1974). *An investigation of advising and instructing competencies of special education professors.* Unpublished doctoral dissertation, University of Kentucky.

Interagency Committee on Learning Disabilities. (1987). *Learning disabilities: A report to the U.S. Congress.* Bethesda, MD: National Institutes of Health.

Jasinowski, J., & Hamrin, R. (1995). *Making it in America.* New York: Simon and Schuster.

Jencks, C. (1979). *Who gets ahead? The determinants of economic success in America.* New York: Basic Books.

Johnson, D., & Blalock, J. (1987). *Adults with learning disabilities: Clinical studies.* Orlando, FL: Grune & Stratton.

Johnson, D. J., & Blalock, J. W. (1987). Summary of problems and needs. In D. J. Johnson and J. W. Blalock (Eds.), *Adults with learning disabilities: Clinical studies* (pp. 277–293). New York: Grune and Stratton.

Johnson, D. W., Johnson, R. T., & Holubec, E. J. (1987). *Structuring cooperative learning: The 1987 lesson plan handbook.* Edina, MN: Interaction Book Co.

Johnson, R. T., & Johnson, D. W. (1993). Foreword. In J. W. Putnam (Ed.), *Cooperative learning and strategies for inclusion* (pp. xiii–xiv). Baltimore, MD: Brookes.

Kimbrell, G., & Vineyard, B. S. (1992). *Succeeding in the world of work*. Mission Hills, CA: Glencoe Publishing Co.

Kirk, S. (1963). *Proceedings of the conference on exploration into the perceptually handicapped child* (pp. 1–4). Evanston, IL: Fund for Perceptually Handicapped Children, Inc.

Kirk, S. (1968). *National advisory committee on handicapped children: First annual report*. Washington, DC: U.S. Department of Health, Education, and Welfare.

Kokaska, C. J., & Skolnik, J. (1986). Employment suggestions from LD adults. *Academic Therapy, 21*, 573–577.

Korman, A. K., & Korman, R. W. (1980). *Career success and personal failure*. Englewood Cliffs, NJ: Prentice Hall.

Korman, A. K., Wittig-Berman, U., & Lang, D. (1981). Career success and personal failure: Alienation in professionals and managers. *Academy of Management Journal, 24*, 342–360.

Larsen, S. P. (1975). The influence of teacher expectations on the school performance of handicapped children. *Focus on Exceptional Children, 6*, 1–14.

Lee, C., & Jackson, R. (1992). *Faking it*. Portsmouth, NH: Boynton/Cook Publishers.

Lerner, J. W. (1993). *Learning disabilities: Theories, diagnosis, and teaching strategies* (6th ed.). Boston, MA: Houghton Mifflin.

Lewis, R. (1977). *The other child grows up*. New York: Times Books.

Lincoln, Y. S., & Guba, E. G. (1985). *Naturalistic inquiry*. Beverly Hills, CA: Sage Publications.

Lowell, E. L. (1955). A methodological study of projectively measured achievement motivation. In D. C. McClelland (Ed.), *Studies in motivation* (pp. 401–413). New York: Appleton-Century-Crofts.

Maker, J. (1978). *The self-perceptions of successful handicapped scientists*. (Grant Number G00-7701[905]). Washington, DC: The U.S. Department of Health, Education and Welfare, Office of Education, Bureau of the Education of the Handicapped.

Malcolm, C. B., Polatajko, H. J., & Simons, J. (1990). A descriptive study of adults with suspected learning disabilities. *Journal of Learning Disabilities, 23*(8), 518–520.

Margalit, M., & Levin-Alyagon, M. (1994). Learning disability subtyping, loneliness, and classroom adjustment. *Learning Disability Quarterly, 17*, 297–310.

Maslow, A. H. (1954). *Motivation and personality*. New York: Harper and Row.

McCall, G. J. (1969). Data quality control in participant observation. In G. J. McCall & J. L. Simmons (Eds.), *Issues in participant observation: A text and reader* (pp. 128–141). Reading, MA: Addison-Wesley.

McClelland, D. C., Atkinson, J. W., Clark, R. A., & Lowell, E. L. (1953). *The achievement motive*. New York: Appleton-Century-Crofts.

McClelland, D., & Pilon, D. (1983). Sources of adult motives in patterns of parent behavior in early childhood. *Journal of Personality and Social Psychology, 44*, 564–574.

McCormack, M. H. (1984). *What they don't teach you at Harvard Business School*. New York: Bantam.

McCue, M. (1993). Clinical diagnostic and functional assessment of adults with learning disabilities. In P. J. Gerber & H. B. Reiff (Eds.), *Learning disabilities in adulthood: Persisting problems and evolving issues* (pp. 55–71). Austin, TX: PRO-ED.

Mellard, D. F. (1990). The eligibility process: Identifying students with learning disabilities in California's community colleges. *Learning Disabilities Focus, 5,* 75–90.

Mercer, C. D., King-Sears, P., & Mercer, A. R. (1990). Learning disabilities definitions and criteria used by state education departments. *Learning Disability Quarterly, 13,* 141–152.

Mercer, J. R. (1973). *Labelling the mentally retarded.* Berkeley, CA: University of California Press.

Merriam, S. B. (1988). *Case study research in education: A qualitative approach.* San Francisco, CA: Jossey-Bass.

Morehead, A., & Morehead, L. (Eds.). (1972). *The new American Webster dictionary.* Chicago: Times Mirror.

Morrison, G. M. (1985). Differences in teacher perceptions and student self-perceptions for learning disabled and nonhandicapped learners in regular and special education settings. *Learning Disabilities Research, 1,* 32–41.

Myers, I. B., & McCaulley, M. H. (1985). *Manual: A guide to the development and use of the Myers-Briggs Type Indicators.* Palo Alto, CA: Consulting Psychologists Press.

National Center for Educational Statistics. (1988). *Condition of education* (p. 54). Washington, DC: U.S. Government Printing Office.

National Joint Committee on Learning Disabilities. (1981). *Learning disabilities: Issues on definition.* Washington, DC: Author.

National Joint Committee on Learning Disabilities. (1987). Adults with learning disabilities: A call to action. *Journal of Learning Disabilities, 20,* 172–175.

National Joint Committee on Learning Disabilities. (1989, September 18). *Letter from NJCLD to member organizations on modifications of the NJCLD definition of learning disabilities.* Washington, DC: Author.

Okolo, C. M., & Sitlington, P. (1988). The role of special education in LD adolescents' transition from school to work. *Learning Disability Quarterly, 11,* 292–306.

Osborne, A. F. (1963). *Applied imagination* (3rd ed.). New York: Scribners.

O'Sullivan, M., & Guilford, J. (1976). *Four Factor Tests of Social Intelligence manual of instructions and interpretations.* Orange, CA: Sheridan Psychological Services.

Palincsar, A. S., & Brown, A. L. (1984). Reciprocal teaching of comprehension fostering and comprehension monitoring activities. *Cognition and Instruction, 1,* 171–175.

Patton, M. Q. (1980). *Qualitative evaluation and research methods.* Beverly Hills, CA: Sage.

Peluchette, J. V. E. (1993). Subjective career success: The influence of individual difference, family, and organizational variables. *Journal of Vocational Behavior, 43,* 198–208.

Peraino, J. M. (1992). Post-21 follow-up studies: How do special education graduates fare? In P. Wehman (Ed.), *Life beyond the classroom: Transition strategies for young people with disabilities* (pp. 21–70). Baltimore, MD: Brookes.

Peshkin, A. (1988). In search of subjectivity—one's own. *Educational Researcher, 17,* 17–22.

Peters, T. J., & Waterman, R. H. (1982). *In search of excellence: Lessons from America's best run companies.* New York: Warner Books.

Phil, R. O., & McLarnon, L. D. (1984). Learning disabled children as adolescents. *Journal of Learning Disabilities, 17,* 96–100.

Phillips-Jones, L. (1982). *Mentors and proteges.* New York: Arbor House.

Pines, M. (1979). Superkids. *Psychology Today, 1,* 55–63.

Platt, A., & Pollock, R. (1974). Channeling lawyers: The careers of public defenders. In H. Jacobs (Ed.), *The potential of reform of criminal justice* (pp. 235–262). Beverly Hills, CA: Sage.

Preziosi, M. (1980). Organizational diagnosis questionnaire. In S. Pfeiffer & H. Jones (Eds.), *The 1980 annual handbook for group facilitators* (pp. 112–120). San Diego, CA: Random House.

Putnam, J. W. (Ed.). (1993). *Cooperative learning and strategies for inclusion.* Baltimore, MD: Brookes.

Rehabilitation Act of 1973, 29 U.S.C. § 701 *et seq.*

Rehabilitative Services Administration. (1989, August). *Evaluation of services provided for individuals with specific learning disabilities: Vol. 1. Final report.* Washington, DC: U.S. Department of Education.

Reiff, H. B. (1988). *Cognitive correlates of social perception in students with learning disabilities.* Unpublished doctoral dissertation, University of New Orleans.

Reiff, H. B. (1993, June). *Using insights and outcomes of successful adults with LD as a basis for college programming.* Paper presented at the Fifth Annual Postsecondary Training Institute Serving College Students with Learning Disabilities, Hartford, CT.

Reiff, H. B., & deFur, S. (1992). Transition for youths with learning disabilities: A focus on developing independence. *Learning Disabilities Quarterly, 15,* 237–249.

Reiff, H. B., Evans, E., & Anderson, P. L. (1989, October). *Vocational preferences of secondary students with learning disabilities.* Paper read at the International Conference of the Council for Learning Disabilities, Denver, CO.

Reiff, H. B., & Gerber, P. J. (1990). Cognitive correlates of social perception in students with learning disabilities. *Journal of Learning Disabilities, 23,* 260–262.

Reiff, H. B., & Gerber, P. J. (1991). Adults with learning disabilities. In N. N. Singh & I. L. Beale (Eds.). *Current perspectives in learning disabilities: Nature, theory, and treatment* (pp. 170–198). New York: Springer-Verlag.

Reiff, H. B., Gerber, P. J., & Ginsberg, R. (1993). Definitions of learning disabilities from adults with learning disabilities: The insiders' perspectives. *Learning Disability Quarterly, 16,* 114–125.

Reiss, H. (1961). *Duncan socioeconomic scale.* Chicago: University of Chicago Press.

Reynolds, C. R. (1986). Toward objective diagnosis of learning disabilities. *Special Services in the Schools, 22,* 161–176.

Richmond, J. B., & Beardslee, W. R. (1988). Resiliency: Research and practice implications for pediatricians. *Journal of Developmental and Behavioral Pediatrics, 9,* 157–163.

Rogan, L. L., & Hartman, L. D. (1976). *A follow-up study of learning disabled children as adults, Final Report* (Project No. 443CH600100, Grant No. OEG-0-74-7453). Washington, DC: Bureau of Education for the Handicapped, U.S. Department of Health, Education and Welfare.

Rogan, L. L., & Hartman, L. D. (1990). Adult outcomes of learning disabled students 10 years after initial follow-up. *Learning Disabilities Focus, 5,* 91–102.

Rogers, H. C. (1986). *Roger's rules for success: Tips that will take you to the top.* New York: St. Martin's Press.

Roloff, J. N. (1994). Tips and thoughts related to ADD. *The Rebus Institute Report, 3*(1), 2.

Rose, E. (1991). Project TAPE: A model of technical assistance for service providers of college students with learning disabilities. *Learning Disabilities Research and Practice, 6,* 25–33.

Rosenberg, B., & Gaier, E. (1977). The self-concept of the adolescent with learning disabilities. *Adolescence, 12,* 489–498.

Rosenberg, S. (1965) The Rosenberg self-esteem scale. In J. Paradise (Ed.), *Society and the adolescent self image.* Princeton, NJ: Princeton University Press.

Rothberg, J. (1968). Defining the tasks of teachers of the mentally retarded. *Education and Training of the Mentally Retarded, 31,* 146–149.

Rotter, J. B. (1966). Generalized expectations for internal versus external control of reinforcement. *Psychological Monographs, 80,* 1–28 (Whole No. 609).

Rourke, B. P. (1989). *Nonverbal learning disabilities: The syndrome and the model.* New York: Guilford Press.

Rutter, M. (1987). Psychosocial resilience and protective mechanisms. *American Journal of Orthopsychiatry, 57,* 316–331.

Schumaker, J., & Hazel, S. (1984). Social skills assessment and training for the learning disabled: Who's on first and what's on second? *Journal of Learning Disabilities, 17,* 422–431.

Scuccimarra, D., & Speece, D. (1990). Employment outcomes and social integration of students with mild handicaps: The quality of life two years after high school. *Journal of Learning Disabilities, 23*(4), 213–219.

Shessel, I. (1995). *Adults with learning disabilities: Profiles in survival.* Unpublished doctoral dissertation. University of Toronto, Canada.

Siegel, E. (1974). *The exceptional child grows up.* New York: Dutton.

Siegel, L. S. (1989). IQ is irrelevant to the definition of learning disabilities. *Journal of Learning Disabilities, 22,* 469–478, 486.

Silver, L. B. (1988). A review of the federal government's Interagency Committee on Learning Disabilities report to the U.S. Congress. *Learning Disabilities Focus, 3,* 73–80.

Sims, N. (1982). *All about success for the black woman.* Garden City, NY: Doubleday.

Sitlington, P. L., & Frank, A. R. (1990). Are adolescents with learning disabilities successfully crossing the bridge into adult life? *Learning Disability Quarterly, 13,* 97–11.

Smith, J. (1988). Social and vocational problems of adults with learning disabilities: A review of the literature. *Learning Disabilities Focus, 4,* 36–58.

Smith, S. (1992). Masking secret shame. In *Succeeding against the odds* (pp. 35–55). Los Angeles, CA: Tarcher.

Smith, R. W., Osborne, L. T., Crim, D., & Rhu, A. H. (1986). Labeling theory as applied to learning disabilities: Survey findings and policy suggestions. *Journal of Learning Disabilities, 19,* 195–202.

Solomon, C. M. (1991). 24 hour employee. *Personnel Journal, 70,* 56–63.

Soundview Editorial Staff. (1989). *Skills for success.* Bristol, VT: Soundview Executive Books.

Spekman, N. J., Herman, K. L., & Vogel, S. A. (1993). Risk and resilience in individuals with learning disabilities: A challenge to the field. *Learning Disabilities Research & Practice, 8*(1), 59–65.

Spradley, J. (1979). *The ethnographic interview.* New York: Holt, Rinehart, and Winston.

Steers, H., & Braunstein, H. (1976) Manifest needs questionnaire: In the role of achievement motivation in job design. *Journal of Applied Psychology, 64,* 472–479.

Sternberg, R. J. (1990). Thinking styles: Keys to understanding student performance. *Phi Delta Kappan, 71,* 366–371.

Stolowitz, M. A. (1995). How to achieve academic and creative success in spite of the inflexible, unresponsive higher education system. *Journal of Learning Disabilities, 28,* 4–6.

Strauss, A., & Werner, H. (1947). *Psychopathology and education of the brain-injured child.* New York: Grune & Stratton.

Suritsky, S. K., & Hughes, C. A. (1991). Benefits of notetaking: Implications for secondary and postsecondary students with learning disabilities. *Learning Disability Quarterly, 14,* 7–18.

Terman, L. M., & Oden, M. H. (1947). *The gifted child grows up: Twenty-five year follow-up of a superior group, genetic studies of genius.* Stanford, CA: Stanford University Press.

Thorndike, E. (1921). Intelligence and its measurement. *Journal of Educational Psychology, 12,* 124–127.

U.S. Department of Education. (1989). *Eleventh annual report to Congress on the implementation of the Education of the Handicapped Act.* Washington, DC: Division of Educational Services, Special Education Programs.

U.S. Department of Education. (1991). *To assure a free and appropriate education for all handicapped children, 1978–1990.* Washington, DC: U.S. Government Printing Office.

U.S. Equal Employment Opportunity Commission. (1991). *The Americans with Disabilities Act. Your employment rights as individual with a disability.* Washington, DC: Author.

U.S. Equal Employment Opportunity Commission. (1992). *Americans with disabilities act. A technical assistance manual on the employment provisions (title 1) of the Americans with Disabilities Act.* Washington, DC: Author.

U.S. Office of Education. (1977, December 29). Education of handicapped children. Assistance to the states: Procedures for evaluating specific learning disabilities. *Federal Register, Part 3.* Washington, DC: U.S. Department of Health, Education, and Welfare.

Valdes, K. A., Williamson, C. L., & Wagner, M. (1990). *The National Longitudinal Transition Study of Special Education Students: Statistical almanac: Vol. 2, Youth categorized as learning disabled.* Menlo Park, CA: SRI International.

Van Maanen, J., & Schein, E. (1977). Career development. In J. Hackman & J. Suttle (Eds.), *Improving life at work.* Santa Monica, CA: Goodyear.

Vidich, A. J. (1969). Participant observation and the collection and interpretation of data. In G. J. McCall & J. L. Simmons, (Eds.), *Issues in participant observation: A text and reader* (pp. 78–87). Reading, MA: Addison-Wesley.

Vogel, S. A. (1987). Issues and concerns in LD college programming. In D. J. Johnson & J. W. Blalock (Eds.). *Adults with learning disabilities* (pp. 239–275). New York: Grune & Stratton.

Vogel, S. A., Hruby, P. J., & Adelman, P. B. (1993). Educational and psychological factors in successful and unsuccessful college students with learning disabilities. *Learning Disabilities Research and Practice, 8*(1), 35–43.

Wagner, M. (1989). *The transition experiences of youth with learning disabilities: A report from the Longitudinal Transition Study* (U.S. DOE, DSEP Contract No. 300-87-0054). Menlo Park, CA: SRI International.

Wagner, M. (1993). *Trends in post school outcomes of youths with disabilities*. Menlo Park, CA: SRI International.

Wambsgans, D. T. (1990). Being successful with dyslexia. *Journal of Learning Disabilities, 23*, 9–10.

Wasserman, S. (1989). Learning to value error. *Childhood Education, 65*, 233–235.

Watzlawick, P., Weakland, J., & Fisch, R. (1974). *Change: Principles of problem formation and problem resolution*. New York: Norton.

Weiss, D. J., Davis, R. V., England, G. W., & Lofquist, L. H. (1967). *Manual for the Minnesota Satisfaction Questionnaire: Minnesota Studies in Vocational Rehabilitation*. No. 22. Minneapolis, MN: University of Minnesota.

Weiss, M. R. (1989). Youth sports: Is winning everything? *Childhood Education, 65*, 195–196.

Wehman, P. (1992). *Life beyond the classroom: Transition strategies for young people with disabilities*. Baltimore, MD: Brookes.

Werner, E. (1993). Risk and resilience in individuals with learning disabilities: Lessons from the Kauai study. *Learning Disabilities Research and Practice, 8*, 28–34.

West, M., Mast, M., Cosel, R., & Cosel, M. (1992). Applications for youth with orthopedic and other health impairments. In P. Wehman (Ed.), *Life beyond the classroom*. Baltimore, MD: Brookes.

White, W. J. (1992). The post school adjustment of persons with learning disabilities: Current status and future projections. *Journal of Learning Disabilities, 25*(7), 448–456.

White, W. J., Schumaker, J. B., Warner, M. M., Alley, G. R., & Deshler, D. D. (1980). *The current status of young adults identified as learning disabled during their school careers* (Research Report No. 21). Lawrence, KS: University of Kansas Institute for Research in Learning Disabilities.

Wiener, J. (1987). Peer status of learning disabled children and adolescents: A review of the literature. *Learning Disabilities Research, 2*, 62–79.

Wiener, J., Harris, P. J., & Shirer, C. (1990). Achievement and social–behavioral correlates of peer status in LD children. *Learning Disability Quarterly, 13*, 114–127.

Wilkens, J. (1987). *Her own business: Success secrets of entrepreneurial women*. New York: McGraw-Hill.

Will, M. (1984). *OSERS programming for the transiton of youth with disabilities: Bridges from school to working life*. Washington, DC: U.S. Department of Education, Office of Special Education and Rehabilitative Services.

Will, M. (1989). Foreword. In W. E. Kiernan & R. L. Schalock (Eds.), *Economics, industry, and disability: A look ahead* (pp. xiii–xiv). Baltimore, MD: Brookes.

Wong, B. Y. (1989). Concluding comments on the special series on the place of IQ in defining learning disabilities. *Journal of Learning Disabilities, 22*, 519–520.

Woolfolk, A. E. (1990). *Educational psychology* (4th ed.). Englewood Cliffs, NJ: Prentice Hall.

Index

Acceptance of learning disabilities, 106–107, 214–215

Accommodation, reasonable, 196–198

Accountability, personal, 173

Achievement motivation, 91

ACLD. *See* Association of Children with Learning Disabilities (ACLD)

ADA. *See* Americans with Disabilities Act (ADA)

Adaptability. *See* External manifestations

Adulthood. *See also* Adults with learning disabilities; Successful adults with learning disabilities
  critical incidents in, 154
  developmental perspectives on, 7, 61–62, 85

Adults with learning disabilities. *See also* Education; Employment; Learning disabilities; Successful adults with learning disabilities
  advice from, 201–216
  advice to, from other adults with learning disabilities, 213–216
  age and gender of participants in authors' research study, 14
  apprenticeship-like programs, 116
  authors' research on, 3–21
  childhood of, 35–50
  conferences on, 4, 62, 82–83, 119
  definitions of learning disabilities pertaining to, 60–63
  description of participants in authors' research study, 13–16
  difficulties and obstacles faced by adults, 6, 22–33, 46, 61–62, 97–98

education level of participants in authors' research study, 15

family relationships of, during youth, 43–45, 48–49, 121–122, 131, 148, 186–188

geographic location of, in authors' research study, 13

identification, screening, and selection of, for authors' research study, 11–13

income distribution of participants in authors' research study, 14

interviews used in authors' research on, 9–10

levels of educational and vocational achievement, 6–7, 63

model for success for, 99–118

occupations of participants in authors' research study, 16

peer relationships of, during youth, 40–43, 164

personal reflections on model of success, 120–141

personal satisfaction of, 45–46, 92–96

perspectives on definition of learning disabilities, 64–75

research base on, 4–5

as role models, 166–167

school experience of, during youth, 22–33, 37–40, 46, 47–48, 144–154

self-advocacy and, 193–199

spouses of, 116–117, 122

vignettes on, 21–33

Advocacy. *See also* Self-advocacy and protected experience, 193–194

Age, of participants in authors' research study, 13

Functional limitations of learning
disabilities, 67–69

Gall, Franz Joseph, 55
Gender, of participants in authors' research
study, 13
Geographic location, of participants in
authors' research study, 13
*Getting Ahead: Career Skills That Work for
Everyone* (Andersen), 90
Goal orientation
and courage to fail, 168–169
critical incidents on, 150–151
learning goals versus performance goals,
177
in model of success, 105–106, 190
personal perspectives on, by adults with
learning disabilities, 125, 127–128,
132–133, 136–137, 150–151
personal satisfaction and, 94–95
task analysis and, 169
teaching of, 167–170
Goldstein, K., 55
Goodness of fit
advice on, from adults with learning
disabilities, 212–213
in model of success, 111–113, 190
personal perspectives on, by adults with
learning disabilities, 124–125, 133,
138
self-advocacy and, 197–198
teaching of, 178–182
Grossman, Paul, 134–139

Hammer, Armand, 162
Happiness, 94–95
Helplessness, learned, 162, 173, 194,
208–209
Hinshelwood, James, 55

Iaccoca, Lee, 97
IEP, 101
In Search of Excellence (Waterman), 89
Income distribution, of participants in
authors' research study, 14
Individualized education program (IEP), 101
Individuals with Disabilities Education Act
(P.L. 101-476), 101

Information processing problems, 36, 65–67
Instruction. *See* Education
Intelligence
intrapersonal intelligence, 171, 172–173
multiple intelligences, 118, 181
Internal decisions
education for, 165–175
in model of success, 99–109
personal perspectives on, by adults with
learning disabilities, 125–126,
131–132
Interviews in research studies, 9–10, 13, 15,
17–19
Intrapersonal intelligence, 171, 172–173
IQ testing, 58

Jobs. *See* Employment; Employment success

Kirk, Samuel, 56–57, 68

LDA. *See* Learning Disabilities Association
of America (LDA)
Learned creativity
advice on, from adults with learning
disabilities, 214–215
critical incidents on, 146–147
in model of success, 113–115, 190
personal perspectives on, by adults with
learning disabilities, 123–124,
133–134, 138, 146–147
self-advocacy and, 197–198
teaching of, 182–186
Learned helplessness, 162, 173, 194,
208–209
Learning disabilities. *See also* Adults with
learning disabilities; Children with
learning disabilities
acceptance of, in reframing process,
106–107, 214–215
action concerning, in reframing process,
107, 173–174
conceptual evolution of term, 55–60
controversy over definitions of, 53–63
definitions of, 53–75, 218
definitions of, pertaining to adults,
60–63, 218
as discrepancy between ability and
achievement, 70–71

About the Authors

Henry B. Reiff received his AB in English literature from Princeton University and his MEd and PhD from the University of New Orleans. He is presently the coordinator of the Graduate Program in Special Education, director of the Academic Skills Center and 504 Services, and assistant dean of academic affairs at Western Maryland College. He has pursued his interests in adults with learning disabilities, particularly through his relationship with Dr. Paul Gerber. They have presented papers at many national and regional conferences, published numerous articles in leading educational journals, and collaborated on two books, *Speaking for Themselves: Ethnographic Interviews with Adults with Learning Disabilities* (The University of Michigan Press, 1991) and *Learning Disabilities in Adulthood: Persisting Problems and Evolving Issues* (PRO-ED, 1994). A member of organizations such as the Council for Exceptional Children, Council for Learning Disabilities, and Learning Disabilities Association, Dr. Reiff stays actively involved as an academic advisor to college students with learning difficulties.

Paul J. Gerber, PhD, is a native of Baltimore, Maryland. He received his undergraduate degree from Adelphi University and his master's and doctoral degree from the University of Michigan. Currently, he is professor of education at Virginia Commonwealth University (VCU) and has a joint appointment in the Department of Psychiatry at VCU's Medical College of Virginia. He has written extensively in the area of learning disabilities, particularly on the issues pertaining to adults with learning disabilities. In 1990, he served as the chairperson of the Pathways to Employment consensus conference for the employment of people with learning disabilities sponsored by the President's Committee for the Employment of People with Disabilities. Also, he is on the professional advisory board of the National Center for Learning Disabilities and is the vice president for Fellows of the International Academy for Research in Learning Disabilities.

Rick Ginsberg, PhD, is a professor and director of the School of Education at Colorado State University. He received his PhD in administrative, institutional, and policy studies at the University of Chicago. He has published more than 80 articles, book chapters, and technical reports, and presented numerous professional papers and workshops, most in the areas of individual and organizational change and success. He is coeditor of two books, the most recent being *Commissions, Reports, Reforms, and Educational Policy* (with David Plank, Praeger, 1995). His recent research efforts focus on educational reform issues, specifically in terms of implementing technology into schools and the impact of advances in complexity science on school operations. He currently serves on the governing board of the Colorado Partnership for Educational Renewal.